NAVY

EVAL & FITREP

WRITING

GUIDE

FOURTH EDITION
www.servicebooks.com

Visit our web site
For this and other
Professional books

NAVY EVAL & FITREP

WRITING GUIDE

FOURTH EDITION

PROFESSIONAL MANAGEMENT SPECTRUM, INC.
PO BOX 30330
PENSACOLA, FLORIDA 32503
Phone: 1-800-346-6114
Web: www.servicebooks.com

TABLE OF CONTENTS

Page

web site: www.servicebooks.com

web site: www.servicebooks.com

CHAPTER 1

EVAL & FITREP

WRITING GUIDANCE

CHAPTER 1

EVAL & FITREP WRITING GUIDANCE

Every large organization has some means to evaluate the performance of its members. Administrators call this evaluation process "performance appraisal." The U.S. Navy has two basic performance appraisal systems:

- -Fitness Reports (Fitreps) for officers and chief petty officers.

- -Enlisted Evaluations (Evals) for E-1 through E-6 personnel.

In this book the term "performance appraisal" applies equally to the Fitrep and the Eval.

PRIMARY OBJECTIVES OF GIVING PERFORMANCE APPRAISALS:

1. Identify advancement, retention and future duty potential.

2. Provide feedback to the evaluee.

OBJECTIVE AND SUBJECTIVE ANALYSIS:

OBJECTIVE ANALYSIS should be used whenever possible to document an individual's performance. Objective analysis means to quantify performance results. How much was done? What was done? Use hours, time, percentage, dollars, etc.

SUBJECTIVE ANALYSIS is the evaluator's perceptions, beliefs, or thoughts on how something was accomplished. This is an analysis of a person's "inner" qualities (or personality) and must be based on observations over a period of time. Subjective analysis is used to describe what prompted or caused an individual to do something.

PERFORMANCE APPRAISAL CHECK-LIST

1. All performance appraisals should be handled discretely. They should be worked on in private.

2. Rough working copies of past performance appraisals should be retained on file for reference for the next reporting period.

3. Insofar as practicable, reporting seniors should grade all performance appraisals of the same competitive category at one time. This will facilitate comparative grading.

4. Obtain a just and equitable spread in the marks assigned, consistent with established Navy standards.

5. Do not gravitate toward either a gratuitously high or rigidly severe policy of grading. The Navy is plagued by general over-assessment of average performers and occasional under assessment of "top performers." This serves to reduce the promotional opportunities of the "best qualified."

6. Exercise care to mark objectively, avoiding any tendency that might allow general impressions, a single incident or a particular trait, characteristic, or quality to influence other marks unduly.

7. When uncertain due to limited observation as to the appropriate mark of a graded area, mark the "Not Observed" block rather than assign a "middle-of-the-road" mark.

8. Avoid marking a new person somewhat lower than he/she deserves in order to reflect improved performance in subsequent performance appraisals. This malpractice can result in unjust advancement or duty assignment actions.

9. Before beginning to write the narrative, check over available performance data and determine the promotion category in which you intend to place the individual:

a. EARLY PROMOTE

b. MUST PROMOTE

c. PROMOTABLE

d. PROGRESSING

e. SIGNIFICANT PROBLEMS

When a decision has been reached, write a performance appraisal that will support and justify your position.

10. The "EARLY PROMOTE" and "MUST PROMOTE" performers should be immediately identified at the start of the narrative. The remaining write-up must justify and reinforce your position.

11. Ensure that due recognition is accorded when an individual demonstrates truly outstanding or exceptional professional competence and potential. In such cases accentuate the positive. State major accomplishments that have been achieved.

12. Conversely, ensure that accurate marks are assigned to individuals whose performance of duty has been manifestly unsatisfactory. Impersonal grading and concise statements of fact best serve overall interests under such circumstances.

13. If your unit has made an outstanding contribution to the Navy's mission during the reporting period, an individual's contribution to this effort should be included. Of course, the converse is true.

14. After completion of a performance appraisal, review previous worksheets on the same person, if available, to ensure that any changes in the marks on the current appraisal are intended. Any significant shift of marks in reports signed by the same reporting senior should be substantiated in the narrative.

15. When making subsequent reports on the same person, guard against repetitive phraseology, as this will reflect lack of thought.

16. When you have completed a performance appraisal, set it aside for a couple of days. Then go back and re-read it with an open, but critical, eye. Analyze the narrative to make sure that what is meant to be said is, in fact, actually being said. Give careful thought not only to what the chosen words mean to the rater and ratee, but also how a selection board may construe them.

17. When the performance appraisal is completed, review it to ensure that:
      a. All parts are consistent (marks & narrative agree).
      b. The trend in performance (increase or decrease) is intended and correctly conveyed.

18. Bear in mind that performance appraisal narratives reflect the degree and extent to which evaluators measure up to their moral obligation. Also, an evaluator's write-up may be used to judge his/her own performance.

WORD SELECTION

Words are both valuable and dangerous tools. Choose them carefully.

Some words have a meaning within a meaning. Review the following:

POTENTIAL   CAPACITY   ABILITY

To indicate that an individual has these qualities without supporting evidence will register to a selection board as "insufficient data." A person can have POTENTIAL, CAPACITY, or ABILITY and yet accomplish nothing. Write how these qualities were demonstrated.

TRIES   STRIVES

Someone can TRY or STRIVE without accomplishing anything. As above, note how these qualities were demonstrated.

ACCEPTS   ASSIGNED

Simply ACCEPTING assignments does not show initiative. Performing an ASSIGNED task does not show initiative.

NORMALLY   GENERALLY

These words mean less than always.

AVERAGE ABOVE AVERAGE EXCELLENT OUTSTANDING

These words have "canned" meanings and understandings in the Navy. ABOVE AVERAGE is generally assumed to mean less than EXCELLENT or OUTSTANDING. AVERAGE means less than ABOVE AVERAGE, etc.. If you are going to place someone's performance in a particular category, be sure to choose the correct word(s).

DO CHECK LIST:

DO start work on performance appraisals EARLY.

DO submit performance appraisals on time and in the correct format.

DO write performance appraisals directed TO selection boards.

DO write on how someone contributed above or below what is normally expected.

DO write to express, not impress. Use everyday English.

DO be fair, honest and objective.

DO write on hard, pertinent facts, not "faint praises" without substance.

DO use short, concise "bullets" or complete sentences with proper grammar.

DO BE CONCISE. Submit a short, direct, hard-hitting write-up.

DO BE SPECIFIC in terms of accomplishments & shortcomings.

DO BE FACTUAL. Quantify individual performance & achievements whenever possible.

DO BE OBJECTIVE. To the maximum extent possible, comment on quantifiable "objective" accomplishments, not on "subjective" personal notions.

DON'T CHECK LIST:

DON'T assign marks that are inconsistent with the narrative.

DON'T write performance appraisals directed TO the individual.

DON'T assign exceptionally high/low marks without comments in the narrative that clearly distinguish the performance.

DON'T include minor, isolated, or insignificant imperfections which do not impact on overall performance.

DON'T use glittering generalities which go on and on without covering anything useful.

DON'T use long words when shorter words are available.

DON'T be verbose or redundant.

DON'T restate the job description in the narrative. That space is too valuable.

DON'T write "During the period of this report" or words to that effect. It is understood, unless otherwise stated, that all actions and events in a performance appraisal occurred during the reporting period being covered. Again, narrative space is too valuable.

DON'T start too many sentences with the same noun/pronoun. Chief... He... He... His... Chief... His..., etc.. Reading becomes sluggish and boring and shows lack of attention or ability on the part of the drafter.

DON'T use a person's name without associated rank. For example, do not write "Jones is..."; instead, it should be "LT/Chief/Seaman Jones is..." A performance appraisal is an official document and an individual's rank should always accompany his/her name.

DON'T use the term "ratee." It is too impersonal and impresses no one.

CWO - LDO ENDORSEMENT
SAMPLE #22

1. Forwarded, highly recommending approval.

2. (name) displays an ideal mix of professional, military, intellectual, and leadership capabilities and abilities which mark (him/her) as an exceptional candidate for the (WO/LDO) Program in the field of ...

3. (name) has a strong desire to serve as a (WO/LDO). An extraordinary individual who relishes a demanding pace and intense workload, (name) is an inspirational leader who instills pride in (his/her) assigned personnel by setting and achieving extremely high standards of performance. Accordingly, I have the greatest possible confidence in (his/her) ability to serve admirably as a (WO/LDO).

4. (name) was initially assigned duties of ... in the ... Department. (his/her) performance in that capacity was exceptional and (he/she) was subsequently assigned duties as ... because of (his/her) dynamic leadership and overall superb performance. In this new position, (he/she) has maintained (his/her) outstanding personal performance in technical areas and has initiated positive action to improve the military and professional performance of assigned personnel. Again, (he/she) is proving that strong leadership makes the decisive difference in overcoming problems of aging equipment, personal turbulence, and marginal ... support.

5. (name) devotes the majority of (his/her) off-duty time correcting inherited problems. However, as (his/her) efforts realized improved equipment reliability and off-duty time became more (his/her) own, (he/she) became involved in conducting Sunday School classes for children. (he/she) is also an active member of the ... Club, and Secretary of the ... Association.

6. (name) is fully qualified in all respects and will perform extremely well as a (WO/LDO) in the ... area. (he/she) possesses the mental dexterity and technical competence to become an excellent (WO/LDO). (he/she) has earned my unqualified endorsement for promotion to officer status under this program.

PERFORMANCE APPRAISALS

The performance appraisal samples in this guide are constructed in various styles and contain the basic job accomplishment and potential format highly useful to selection boards. Navy-wide, however, many performance appraisals are seriously lacking in these critical areas. There are three basic reasons why a large number of performance appraisal narratives do not contain a good, hard-hitting write-up similar to the ones in this guide:

1. Often times the evaluator believes that he/she is saying something helpful in a write-up (but is not).

2. Sometimes the evaluator does not know the difference between a good and a not-so-good write-up.

3. Sometimes the drafter feels compelled, because of today's inflationary marks trend, to grade someone high and then deliberately omit a hard-hitting narrative.

Whatever the reason, a person with "high" marks and a "low" write-up has less chance of being "passed" by a selection board than does a person with "high" marks and an accompanying "high" narrative. To the trained eye of a selection board member, the distinction is easy and the judgement is final. The same work, or job accomplishment, can be committed to print in any number of ways. Some ways are better than others. The key is to remember to write for and to the selection board. All of the performance appraisal information and samples in this guide are excellent examples of how to write for/to selection boards in an impressive and manner. The style, or technique, of writing to impress selection boards is easy to grasp.

NARRATIVE STRUCTURE

Performance appraisal narratives should be structured in a manner similar to the following for maximum effect on selection boards.

FIRST, RECORD JOB ACCOMPLISHMENT PARTICULARS

For example: (use objective numbers and percentages when possible)
-Maintained high percentage of equipment reliability.
-Corrected many long-standing material discrepancies.
-Graded high at material inspections.
-Excellent appearance of "troops."
-Good organizational record-keeping abilities.
-Promotes high morale.

SECOND, LIST DESIRED "BULLETS" & "WORD PICTURE PERSONALITY" ITEMS

Search through this book and use the words or bullets that best fit the person.

THIRD, COMBINE THE FIRST TWO INFORMATION LISTS INTO DESIRED MIX

When writing the narrative, use a format similar to the below information.

(1) OVERVIEW

Summarizes the overall performance of the individual, and for top performers, provides a relative ranking. The first two or three sentences are the most important and should set the "pace" or "theme" for the entire evaluation. The first sentence is the precursor for detailed comments in subsequent sections. Supplementary comments on other achievements can be included in the next sentences. This section should also mention individual recognition received during the reporting period (awards, achievements, etc.).

(2) MISSION ACCOMPLISHMENT

This section documents individual achievements in primary and collateral duties related to mission accomplishment (i.e., what has the person done for the command?). It is an error to feel that only those in supervisory positions can contribute directly to mission accomplishment. A good watch stander who is making progress in PQS qualification is contributing to operational readiness--an important factor in supporting mission accomplishment. Of particular importance are comments in the area of directing, counseling, and leadership. With more junior personnel, it is appropriate to base comments on potential if there has been no opportunity for direct observation. As a general concept, it is proper to use both actual performance and demonstrated potential based on observed trends, in officer and enlisted performance evaluations.

(3) NAVY OBJECTIVES

This section documents performance in the "high-vis" Navy programs such as retention of subordinates and other major Navy objectives that surface from time to time.

(4) MISCELLANEOUS PERSONAL TRAITS

This section includes anything worthy or necessary of comment which has not been included in the preceding sections (military bearing, appearance, verbal expression, and the like).

(5) SUMMARY

A one-sentence 'grabber' that summarizes the personal traits and growth potential. This section includes recommendation for future duty assignments, promotion, etc.

Specific Guidance

(1) HIT THE MARK. Any "shortcoming" mentioned in the narrative should be significant, either in terms of performance or potential. People are not perfect and evaluations are written relative to the 'typically effective' person who requires an occasional reminder on personal appearance, some supervision, etc. If the comment is made that a person requires occasional supervision, it means that he/she requires supervision over and above what one normally expects. The effect, then, is that comments on minor deficiencies are automatically magnified when they are included in the write-up. Also, evaluators should recognize the negative content of phrases such as willingly accepts responsibilities; duties assigned (as opposed to volunteering); normally; and generally.

(2) BE CONCISE. A direct, hard-hitting write-up is better than an elegant one—concentrate more on content and specific accomplishments.

(3) BE FACTUAL. Quantify individual achievements when possible.

(4) BE SPECIFIC. A few phrases or sentences on individual achievements mean much more than paragraphs on billet description, command employment, etc.

(5) CONSIDERATION. Take into consideration the rate and experience level of the individual relative to the rate (and NEC) authorized for the billet assigned. If an E-4 is filling and E-5 supervisory billet, that deserves consideration and comment in the evaluation. The same is true of officers filling more senior billets.

(6) PROPER GRAMMAR. Use proper grammar. If you are not sure, check it out or do not use it in the write-up. Remember, the evaluator will, in turn, be evaluated on his or her use and command of the English language.

(7) not use continuation sheets.

(8) DO NOT restate the description of duties in the evaluation narrative section. That space is too valuable to waste.

c. Drafter's Check List. Forwarding a Fitrep or eval with all the required information will save time, help "save face," and will help get it done correctly. Remember that the report date starts day after the ending of the last report (verify leave and transit as required).

4. Each person should review the submitted draft narratives after they are returned. Note what was changed, added, or deleted and keep these in mind when drafting a narrative in the future.

5. An individual's first superior in the chain of command will initiate evaluation narratives and marks. Each subsequent superior will correct, rewrite (as necessary), and forward the evaluation, going over draft discrepancies or shortcomings with the subordinate. A copy of all evaluation drafts (unedited) will be forwarded up the chain of command along with the submitted evaluation. Remember, whether or not an intermediate senior re-works a draft, that person becomes totally responsible for the content and grammar of that draft once it is forwarded to the next superior.

DRAFTING THE NARRATIVE

Performance appraisals should be drafted with two objectives in mind.

1. To document, in SPECIFIC terms, what an individual contributed to Navy, command, and department/division mission effectiveness and accomplishment; and,

2. To document the subjective "inner" qualities demonstrated by an individual on how performance was accomplished.

Any shortcoming or deficiency mentioned in the narrative should be significant, either in terms of performance or potential. At any level in an organization some occasional, routine guidance is necessary. If the comment is made that someone requires occasional instruction or guidance, that means he/she requires more instruction or guidance than would normally be expected. In effect, comments on minor deficiencies are automatically magnified when they are included in the narrative.

NARRATIVE FORMAT STRUCTURE

The following performance appraisal structure has won general acceptance by Navy selection boards.

1. OPENING STATEMENT
2. JOB/MISSION ACCOMPLISHMENT & PERSONAL TRAITS
3. CLOSING STATEMENT

The following pages deal more specifically with this format.

1 - OPENING STATEMENT

1st   note best attributes
2nd   potential (for top performers)
3rd   awards and other special recognition received

The most closely read part of a Navy Eval or Fitrep is the opening statement.   The opening statement sets the "theme" for the remaining narrative.   The opening statement should be both POWERFUL & PERSUASIVE, an "attention getter," to immediately capture the attention of the reader.

***Examples for EARLY PROMOTE & MUST PROMOTE CANDIDATES:

...praiseworthy performance
...remarkably talented
...best ... in/at ...

...top achiever
...foremost expert
...without peer

...stellar performance
...phenomenal record
...proven top achiever

...rising star, promote now
...exceptional ...
...served with distinction

...unmatched ability
...first-rate ...
...enormously talented

...front-runner
...premier ...

...exemplary performance
...most respected
...standard-bearer

...exceptionally gifted
...highest caliber ...
...masterful ...

...absolute top performer
...outshines all others
...best overall

...stands above ...
...brilliant record
...truly exceptional

...superior ...
...most outstanding
...head & shoulders above ...

...sensational ...
...without peer

2 - JOB/MISSION ACCOMPLISHMENT & PERSONALITY TRAITS

For a good, hard-hitting write-up, this section of the performance appraisal should cover two important areas:

1. JOB/MISSION ACCOMPLISHMENT

In specific, quantifiable and objective terms, answer the questions:

-What was accomplished in meeting unit/Navy mission goals & objectives?

-Were accomplishments superior, average, or inferior to the norm?

Documenting exactly what a person accomplishes in a performance appraisal is both useful and necessary. Work accomplishment alone, however, does not give a complete description or "picture" of an individual.

2. PERSONALITY TRAITS

The careful use of a few well-chosen PERSONALITY TRAIT words can describe a person's inner qualities--what possesses a person to do something, what a person "IS."

By combining Job/Mission Accomplishment with Personality Traits, a complete "picture" of an individual is possible.
Take, for example, the following:

> "LT/Chief Jones is energetic, resourceful &
> self-reliant. (...Go on to list exactly what
> was accomplished)."

In the above example, a selection board will know what was accomplished. More importantly, the board will gain valuable insight on the individual's "inner" qualities, capabilities, and potential--"energetic, resourceful, and self-reliant."

3 - CLOSING STATEMENT

The CLOSING STATEMENT is another good place to "sell" an individual to a selection board. The CLOSING STATEMENT summarizes the theme of the write-up. You can use bullet statements similar to the ones noted above in the OPENING STATEMENT and/or comment on INDIVIDUAL GROWTH POTENTIAL.

Selection boards do not promote people simply because they do a good job in their present pay grade. The potential to successfully discharge the greater duties and responsibilities of higher pay grades must be clearly in evidence. Potential should be well documented in performance appraisals.

> *Officers are not promoted because they are
> good division officers. They are promoted
> because they have the potential to become
> good Department Heads, XOs, etc...

> *Chief Petty Officers are leaders, managers and
> administrators. CPO selection boards do not
> promote people simply because they are good at
> working with equipment. The boards promote people
> with the potential to be good leaders, managers
> and administrators.

Examples for **EARLY PROMOTE & MUST PROMOTE** CANDIDATES:

...unlimited growth potential
...virtually unlimited potential
...boundless potential
...extraordinary growth potential
...unlimited potential for increased responsibility
...selectively detail to most demanding billets

LDO/CWO RECOMMENDATIONS
...would be a welcomed addition to any wardroom, afloat or
  ashore

...I would be particularly pleased to have ... as a member
  of my wardroom

16

Sample Narrative

Chief (name) is an industrious and versatile individual who approaches any task enthusiastically and with dispatch. (he/she) is a skillful manager with the proven ability to attain a high standard of performance in any endeavor. (he/she) directs (his/her) watch team with a firm but fair hand, and provides a unified purpose and sense of direction without dulling their initiative. Readily adaptable to changes in policy, procedure, or assigned workload, (he/she) always gives a personal contribution as a special effort to ensure cohesiveness and uniformity. (name) has established a good rapport with subordinates and does not hesitate to provide personal or professional assistance, when needed, and to encourage their trust through genuine interest in their problems. Chief (name) accomplishments include:

-Qualified ESWS in 9 months, and OOD Inport in 2 months.
-Received OUTSTANDING at 2 Commanding Officer Personnel Inspections.
-Drafted and implemented 10 SOPs. Excellent in content and enhanced operational effectiveness.
-Researched, developed, and implemented comprehensive PQS standards for 5-man watch team. Standards proved so effective that all three watch teams in the department now use as guide.
-Division received grade of 97.25 during Command Inspection due, in large part, to Chief (name) organizational and technical abilities.
-Watch team operational effectiveness graded at 87.1 during Reftra-- highest grade in department.
-Received verbal and written praise from command DCA for the outstanding work and effort put into job as Repair Locker CPO.

A proponent of physical fitness, Chief (name) actively participates in various sporting events and maintains a trim physique. (his/her) conduct and appearance, on and off duty, are a model worthy of emulation by the entire CPO community. Well read; (his/her) written reports are clear and concise, and oral presentations command the complete attention of a listening audience.

Chief (name) rare and successful blend of leadership coupled with (his/her) superior management and administrative abilities assure success in virtually any assignment. (he/she) stays with a job until it is completed, regardless of the time of day or night. During the past three months (he/she) worked over 100 off-duty hours re-outfitting and organizing a repair locker. Unlimited ability and potential. Highly recommended for Warrant Officer.

Chief (name) is ready for positions of increased responsibility and trust now. Recommended for instructor duty and for a billet as Command Senior Chief Petty Officer afloat or ashore. Chief (name) is most strongly recommended for immediate selection to Senior Chief Petty Officer.

FUTURE DUTY RECOMMENDATION CRITERIA

Recommendations for special assignment should be made independent of an individual's stated preference. Evaluators should make their recommendations solely on their evaluation of an individual's potential for serving in that specific assignment.

RECRUIT COMPANY COMMANDER The recruit company commander is usually a new recruit's first encounter with a regular Navy person in a naval environment. The first impression imposed by the recruit company commander is most important. With this in mind, recommendations for this special assignment should be given to members who are authoritative leaders and who command the respect of their peers. They must be truly professional military persons. Personal appearance, military bearing, and pride in the Navy must be present in abundance.

JOINT/COMBINED STAFF, ATTACHE & NAVAL HEADQUARTERS
These are special assignments that require a great amount of administrative ability. By administrative ability is meant the capacity to cope with excessive amounts of paperwork, disseminate data, and incorporate new policies as well as changes to existing policies. Also, along with administrative abilities, the person must be a good talker as well as a good listener. Of course, a high degree of professionalism, a great amount of military bearing and immaculate personal appearance cannot be overlooked.

INSTRUCTOR
An instructor is a learned person who conveys his or her knowledge to learners. In order to accomplish this, an instructor must be an outstanding communicator who is able to express himself or herself fully and convey ideas in a clear and demonstrative manner. An instructor must be able to attain the respect of students through a combination of subject knowledge, military bearing, personal appearance, and other outward personal traits.

INDEPENDENT DUTY
The term 'independent duty' is self-explanatory. Candidates for independent duty must be conscientious, industrious, reliable, resourceful, good decision-makers, have good insight, and possess high moral character.

MAAG/MISSION

MAAG members administer United States military assistance planning and programming to military members of host foreign countries. Considerations to be taken into account when making recommendations for this type of assignment are appearance and military bearing, an ability to work directly with troops of a foreign nation, and the member's ability to speak a foreign language (bilingual).

RECRUITER

A recruiter is a salesman for the Navy—he or she 'sells' the Navy to young men and women. Therefore, a recruiter should first be an outstanding salesman. He or she should be a good talker and be able to interact with young people. Recruiters must have a clear understanding of the Naval structure and its policies and programs. Motivation, good physical shape, and pride in wearing the uniform are prerequisites for this type of assignment.

CAREER COUNSELOR

A career counselor is also a salesman. He or she not only sells a Navy career to reenlistees, but also sells the Navy's many opportunity programs to members at every level in the enlisted structure. A career counselor must be a good communicator and learned in all of the Navy's old and new policies, programs, and procedures. An interest in people and an understanding of their problems is necessary. Honesty, military bearing, and good personal appearance should also be included in considering a member for career counselor duty.

GENERAL MARKING GUIDANCE

The qualities listed on the following tables represent broad guidelines. The reporting officer should judge other qualities for specific levels of performance. Descriptions categorized as FIRST RATE are meant to build on or incorporate the descriptions listed as ABOVE EXPECTATIONS or SATISFACTORY. UNSATISFACTORY performance includes qualities listed in the BELOW EXPECTATIONS category as well as those in the UNSATISFACTORY category, and includes omissions of capabilities listed in SATISFACTORY, ABOVE EXPECTATIONS, and FIRST RATE categories.

MILITARY KNOWLEDGE/PERFORMANCE

FIRST RATE (5.0)
Works well independently; applies technical skills to job effectively; contributes extensively to command mission; has thorough understanding of complexities of job; analyses problems and readily implements best solution.

ABOVE EXPECTATIONS (4.0)
Contributes to command objectives; accepts delegated authority; proposes solutions to difficult problems; sets and pursues goals in organized manner; asks questions when in doubt.

SATISFACTORY (3.0)
Completes assigned tasks in a timely manner; requires limited supervision; evaluates information and applies problem solving; has good understanding of major duties; informs subordinates of changes.

BELOW EXPECTATIONS (2.0)
Cannot complete duties completely or on time; requires routine supervision; cannot relate technical knowledge to work.

UNSATISFACTORY (1.0)
Fails to fulfill requirements of job; requires constant assistance; misinterprets problems repeatedly.

PROFESSIONAL FACTORS

RATING KNOWLEDGE/PEFORMANCE

FIRST RATE (5.0)
Works well independently; applies technical skills to job effectively; contributes extensively to command mission; has thorough understanding of complexities of job; analyses problems and readily implements best solutions.

ABOVE EXPECTATIONS (4.0)
Contributes to command objectives; accepts delegated authority; proposes solutions to difficult problems; sets and pursues goals in organized manner; asks questions when in doubt.

SATISFACTORY (3.0)
Completes assigned tasks in a timely manner; requires limited supervision; evaluates information and applies to problem solving; has good understanding of major duties; informs subordinates of changes.

BELOW EXPECTATIONS (2.0)
Cannot complete duties completely or on time; requires routine supervision; cannot relate technical knowledge to work.

UNSATISFACTORY (1.0)
Fails to fulfill requirements of job; requires constant assistance; misinterprets problems repeatedly.

PERSONAL TRAITS

INITIATIVE

FIRST RATE (5.0)
Has well defined goals for self-improvement; makes every effort to produce only highest quality work; determines and follows most efficient plan of action; does not require supervisor's approval.

ABOVE EXPECTATIONS (4.0)
Seeks additional responsibility, exhibits drive for self-improvement in education; anticipates difficulty and works to circumvent; promotes teamwork.

SATISFACTORY (3.0)
Assumes duties in absence of supervision; accepts opportunities to learn; occasionally suggests improvements to system.

BELOW EXPECTATIONS (2.0)
Is satisfied with completing work without concern for quality; avoids added responsibility; requires guidance and supervision.

UNSATISFACTORY (1.0)
Has no desire to improve self; does not perform unless specifically directed.

PERSONAL TRAITS

MILITARY BEARING

FIRST RATE (5.0)
Wears uniform with pride; is immaculate in military and civilian dress; has impressive bearing.

ABOVE EXPECTATIONS (4.0)
Has good posture; is neat and clean; demonstrates high personal grooming standards.

SATISFACTORY (3.0)
Presents acceptable appearance routinely; keeps uniforms repaired; meets fitness criteria.

BELOW EXPECTATIONS (2.0)
Wears uniform improperly; occasionally careless of appearance.

UNSATISFACTORY (1.0)
Is sloppy, unkempt, or does not meet physical fitness standards; is a discredit to the Naval Service.

SELF EXPRESSION

SPEAKING & WRITING ABILITY

FIRST RATE (5.0)
Submits flawless written product; projects ideas in the most straightforward, comprehensive manner, keeps reference file of personal notes on important papers and matters.

ABOVE EXPECTATIONS (4.0)
Is able to translate thoughts into clear, understandable sentences; submits written work in a timely fashion.

SATISFACTORY (3.0)
Is able to prepare realistic evaluation reports; shows awareness of importance of neat, accurate correspondence; gets point across. Possesses adequate command of the English language.

BELOW EXPECTATIONS (2.0)
Cannot get meaning across in concise organized means verbally or on paper.

UNSATISFACTORY (1.0)
Demonstrates poor use of English grammar and composition. Unable to compose correspondence.

MANAGEMENT & LEADERSHIP

DIRECTING

FIRST RATE (5.0)
Promotes subordinate involvement in planning to maximize output; inspires subordinates to self-improvement; inspires complete respect and confidence of subordinates; provides challenge.

ABOVE EXPECTATIONS (4.0)
Solicits constructive criticism to improve performance; capably evaluates subordinate skills for work assignment; delegates authority for good use of personnel resources.

SATISFACTORY (3.0)
Influences subordinates to work consistently and accurately; keeps personnel informed; maintains morale while enforcing regulations; usually delegates responsibility effectively.

BELOW EXPECTATIONS (2.0)
Dictates activity of subordinates; fails to inform members of change or upcoming events; cannot maintain high morale or get job done.

UNSATISFACTORY (1.0)
Ignores suggestions of subordinates to improve performance; inhibits subordinate self-improvement; fails to delegate authority properly.

MANAGEMENT & LEADERSHIP

COUNSELING

FIRST RATE (5.0)
Maintains excellent rapport with subordinates; is always willing to assist those in and out of unit; studies personal desires and needs of each member to recommend opportunities; helps members advance in Navy or in transition to civilian life.

ABOVE EXPECTATIONS (4.0)
Discusses performance and improvement with members on a regular basis; suggests methods for professional and educational growth; shows sincere concern for subordinates.

SATISFACTORY (3.0)
Counsels members on positive and negative qualities as required; possesses good knowledge of what Navy has to offer; shows good human understanding.

BELOW EXPECTATIONS (2.0)
Counsels subordinates only if severe difficulties arise; shows little concern for welfare of subordinates.

UNSATISFACTORY (1.0)
Fails to discuss any matters with subordinates; avoids members.

PERFORMANCE APPRAISAL

BAD EXAMPLES

The following BAD EXAMPLES were actually found by an E-8/9 selection board while screening candidates' performance appraisals. You can learn from the shortcomings of others.

-Academic average of 82.25. Stood 2 in a class of 1.

-The best Personnelman I have ever seen. He is a better PNC than I ever was. Select him for E-8 now. He's better qualified than I was and you picked me. (signed by CAPT)

-His military appearance remains uncompared within the command.

-Frequently reluctant to assume responsibility or exert authority... Highly recommended for warrant officer.

-While his dress is always neat and proper, his protruding stomach detracts from his overall excellent appearance.

-Consistently reluctant to assume a new job, but once the job is started...the reluctance is gone.

-Has a high degree of self-confidence, but this should not be a stumbling block for long.

-Gets along extremely well with all classes of people from four star admirals to seaman and even the janitorial help.

-An excellent example of equal opportunity in action, he treats everyone the same rotten way.

-Her ability to associate freely with both the rank and file has contributed significantly to the morale of the legal office.

-His transfer will be sorely missed by this command.

-There is NO position within the military structure, rate or rank, which is beyond this man's ability.

-He can do 'anything better than anybody.'

-With his personality, he would make friends with the Enemy.

-Has a tendency to impress officials and superiors with knowledge and expertise in areas where his knowledge is extremely inadequate.

CHAPTER 2

INDIVIDUAL PERFORMANCE REPORTS (IPRs)

&

EVALUATION SCHEDULES

INDIVIDUAL PERFORMANCE REPORTS
(IPRs)

It is important to document subordinate superior or substandard performance AS IT OCCURS. This documentation is needed to assure accurate grading & ranking on performance appraisals. This is especially important for your "head & shoulders" performers.

As an example, assume you are in a command with 250 people. This command has 8 divisions. Each division has 3 first class petty officers, for a total of 24 within the command. When the performance appraisals on these 24 First Class reach the CO/XO it is found that the number of people recommended for the EARLY PROMOTE and MUST PROMOTE exceed command allowance.

Some of these first class petty officers, and perhaps some of the most worthy, are going to have to have their promotion recommendation lowered. The CO/XO, maybe with the assistance of the Command Master Chief, looks over all of the performance appraisals very closely and then makes the final determination. As a result, some of the First Class have had their promotion recommendation downgraded.

The performance appraisals that noted the most individual personal accomplishment retained their EARLY PROMOTE & MUST PROMOTE recommendation. The performance appraisals on individuals who had the least individual personal accomplishments listed were downgraded. This is a fairly straightforward process. Navy-wide selection boards go through the same process.

This adjustment of marks and promotion recommendations occurs in all commands all the time, and includes all pay grades, enlisted and officer.

If your people do not make this "cut," it is because of one of two factors:

*The individual did not deserve the high marks and promotion recommendation; or,

*You did not provide the proper documentation to support the marks and promotion recommendation. In this case, you let your top performer and the Navy down. There is no substitute for documenting individual superior performance AS IT OCCURS.

The following factors and possibilities make it of paramount importance that superior and substandard performance be documented while it is fresh in memory.

a. Long periods of time between performance appraisals.

b. Individuals may transfer from one job to another job, and/or from one superior to another superior one or more times during an evaluation period. Information not recorded is thus lost.

c. An individual's superior(s) may transfer during a reporting period. Again, information not recorded is lost.

Any superior in an individual's chain of command should complete an Individual Performance Report (IPR) WHENEVER superior or substandard performance is observed in a subordinate.

a. **Examples of when an IPR would be appropriate**.

(1) Official award received.

(2) OUTSTANDING or UNSAT at any type of formal inspection.

(3) Individual instances of superior or substandard job performance.

(4) Volunteering for special assignments or projects (noting the results achieved).

(5) Significant off-duty time donated to job (note if voluntary).

(6) OUTSTANDING or UNSAT appearance at quarters, or as noted during the performance of duty.

(7) Late/UA instances.

(8) On other occasions as deemed appropriate.

When an IPR has been filled out and signed, it should be routed through the chain of command up to the division officer. The division officer will determine if the IPR should be reviewed by other personnel.

Completed IPRs should be retained until the individual reported on receives the next performance appraisal. At that time, the person preparing the initial performance appraisal write-up should remove the IPRs from the file. All of the documented material should be considered, and the appropriate material included in the appraisal.

As a reminder, isolated incidents or minor infractions should not be included in a write-up. One case of being ten minutes late for quarters and one haircut reminder in a six-month period is not serious enough to be included in the narrative write-up.

ALL IPRs should be retained until the appraisal is completed and signed. After completion of the appraisal, the IPRs should be destroyed unless they are being retained for other reasons.

EXAMPLE IPR FORM

(ORGANIZATION)   INDIVIDUAL PERFORMANCE REPORT (IPR)

NAME	RATE	DIVISION/WC	DATE

PERFORMANCE

☐ MERITORIOUS   ☐ DEROGATORY   ☐ OTHER

REMARKS

SIGNATURE OF REPORTING SUPERIOR	SIGNATURE OF INDIVIDUAL BEING REPORTED ON

Routing:
Immed. Supvr_____ LPO _____ CPO _____ LCPO _____ DIV. OFFICER _____

SAMPLE EVALUATION SCHEDULE

ANNUAL EVALUATION SCHEDULE CYCLE

TIME WINDOW	EVENT/ACTIVITY
-8 weeks	Division Officer assemble key personnel, review material on file (IPRs, etc), and determine recommended marks and overall ranking.
-7/6 weeks	Division Officer: (1) Complete division marks/ranking and forward to department. (2) Assemble all information necessary to complete eval (job description, etc.). (3) Commence write-up drafts based on submitted marks/ranking.
-6/5 weeks	Department/Command approve marks/ranking & provide feedback to division officers.
-5/4 weeks	Division officers forward completed evals to department.
-4/3 weeks	Head of Department review/approve evals (forward for higher review as necessary).
-3/2 weeks	Smooth type evals, proof read, and prepare for approving official's signature.
-2/1 weeks	Approving officer sign evaluations.

END OF REPORTING PERIOD
(1) Division officer (and others if required) review evaluations with individuals.
(2) Individuals sign evals.
(3) Division retain/destroy desired material and forward official evaluation copies.

The recommended "TIME WINDOW" and the accompanying "- WEEKS" columns should be converted to actual calendar dates.

EXAMPLE:
END OF REPORTING PERIOD 30 JUNE

-1 WEEK	23 JUNE
-2 WEEKS	16 JUNE
-3 WEEKS	9 JUNE
-4 WEEKS	1 JUNE
-5 WEEKS	23 MAY
-6 WEEKS	16 MAY
-7 WEEKS	9 MAY
-8 WEEKS	1 MAY

The "LATEST" and "EARLIEST" columns on the samples on the following pages are left blank so that the pages can be reproduced locally and filled-in with the appropriate dates.

SAMPLE EVALUATION SCHEDULE

ANNUAL EVALUATION SCHEDULE CYCLE

TIME WINDOW

LATEST
EARLIEST   EVENT/ACTIVITY

.... Division Officer assemble key personnel, review material on file (IPRs, etc), and determine recommended marks and overall ranking.

.... Division Officer: (1) Complete division marks/ranking and forward to department. (2) Assemble all information necessary to complete eval (job description, etc.). (3) Commence write-up drafts based on submitted marks/ranking.

.... Department/Command approve marks/ranking & provide feedback to division officers.

.... Division officers forward completed evals to department.

.... Head of Department review/approve evals (forward for higher review as necessary).

.... Smooth type evals, proof read, and prepare for approving official's signature.

.... Approving officer sign evaluations.

.... (1) Division officer (and others if required) review evaluations with individuals.
(2) Individuals sign evals.
(3) Division retain/destroy desired material and forward official evaluation copies.

SAMPLE EVALUATION SCHEDULE

TRANSFER (& OTHER) EVALUATION SCHEDULE

TIME WINDOW

LATEST
EARLIEST   EVENT/ACTIVITY

-30 days	Division officer ensure personnel working on evaluation input.
-24 days -17 days	Division officer review/approve eval (forward for review as necessary)
-17 days -10 days	Smooth type eval, proof read, and prepare for approving official's signature
-10 days -3 days	Approving official sign evaluation
-3 days -1 day	(1) Division officer review eval with individual (2) Individual sign eval (3) Division officer retain/destroy desired material and forward official evaluation copies

SAMPLE EVALUATION SCHEDULE

TRANSFER (& OTHER) EVALUATION SCHEDULE

TIME WINDOW

LATEST EARLIEST	EVENT/ACTIVITY
....	Division officer ensure personnel working on evaluation input.
....	Division officer review/approve eval (forward for review as necessary)
....	Smooth type eval, proof read, and prepare for approving official's signature
....	Approving officer sign evaluation
....	(1) Division officer review evaluation with individual. (2) Individual sign evaluation. (3) Division officer retain/destroy desired material and forward official evaluation copies.

CHAPTER 3

BULLET INTRODUCTION

BULLETS

What is a "bullet?" A bullet is a statement that may or may not have a verb, object, or subject. Bullets are straightforward, matter-of-fact statements. Bullets serve to reduce the amount of space required to make a statement. Thus, using bullets allows more material to be covered in the same space, or the same amount of material in less space, than with formal sentence structure.

EXAMPLE OF FORMAL SENTENCE STRUCTURE:
"He is highly intelligent, possesses a stimulating imagination, and routinely provides sound advice and recommendations for anticipated problems."

EXAMPLE OF BULLET PHRASE
"Highly intelligent, stimulating imagination, provides sound advice and recommendations."

The many sample bullets in this book can be used independently or combined with other bullets. Many can be shortened more; all can be turned into complete sentences.

CHAPTER 4

WORD PICTURE PERSONALITY

FAVORABLE

WORD PICTURE PERSONALITY

INTRODUCTION
Documenting exactly what a person accomplishes in a performance appraisal is both useful and necessary. Work accomplishment alone, however, does not give a complete description or "picture" of an individual. The careful use of a few well chosen "word picture" adjectives can describe a person's inner qualities—what possesses a person to do something, what a person "IS."

By combining what a person accomplishes with what possessed him/her to do something, a complete word 'picture' of an individual is possible. Take, for example, the following:

"LT/Chief Jones is energetic, resourceful, and self-reliant. (he/she) (go on to list exactly what he accomplished)."

In this above example, a selection board would know what was accomplished. More importantly, the board would gain valuable insight to the individual's "inner" qualities, capabilities, and potential—'energetic, resourceful, and self-reliant.'

Selection boards do not promote people simply because they do a good job in their present pay grade. The potential to successfully discharge the greater duties of higher pay grades must be clearly in evidence. Potential must be documented in performance appraisals. Consider the following:

*Junior officers are not promoted because they are good division officers; they are promoted because they have the potential to become good Department Heads, XOs, etc.

*First Class Petty Officers are considered supervisors. Chief Petty Officers are considered managers. CPO selection boards do not promote good supervisors to E-7; they promote good supervisors with the potential to become good chiefs (managers).

By using the appropriate "word picture personality" characteristics listed on the following pages, selection boards can "see" and evaluate the full worth and potential (or lack thereof) of an individual.

WORD PICTURE PERSONALITY

JOB APPLICATION

The list of adjectives below express the emotional quality, the product of many factors, which manifest itself in the way the individual attacks and carries through his problems and duties.

FAVORABLE

active	deliberate	impartial	quick
adept	determined	industrious	rapid
ambitious	diligent	methodical	resourceful
aspiring	energetic	meticulous	skillful
boundless	enthusiastic	painstaking	thorough
competent	exacting	persistent	tireless
comprehensive	expeditious	precise	untiring
conscientious	flexible	punctilious	willing
zealous			

PERSONAL CHARACTER

The following list of adjectives express the inward traits of an individual and can only be learned after long and close association.

FAVORABLE

aggressive	faithful	inspiring	self-controlled
altruistic	firm	just	self-reliant
bold	forceful loyal		self-sacrificing
broad-minded	forehanded	open-minded	sincere
cautious	foresighted	persuasive	stable
courageous	friendly	prompt	tenacious
determined	impressive	prudent	thoughtful
earnest	indomitable	resolute	time-serving

MENTAL OR EMOTIONAL TRAITS

The adjectives listed below express the outward qualities of an individual, which generally denote possession of inward mental or emotional traits.

FAVORABLE

adaptable	generous	lenient	retiring
animated	good-humored	mild	serious
cheerful	good-tempered	pacific	spirited
cooperative	helpful	placid	spontaneous
cordial	humorous	quiet	tactful
courteous			

KNOWLEDGE

The following adjectives express the amount of subject matter an individual possesses, and NOT necessarily the ability to use it.

FAVORABLE

accomplished	enlightened	learned	well-read
astute	erudite	lettered	widely-read
brilliant	informed	scholarly	cultivated
Intellectual	well-grounded		

MANNER

The following adjectives express outward qualities of manner.

FAVORABLE

admirable	convincing	enterprising	pleasing
affable	cooperative	frank	polished
alert	confident	finished	quiet
amiable	courteous	friendly	receptive
animated	decisive	genial	reserved
assured	dedicated	gracious	restrained
deliberate	kindly	retiring	diplomatic
likeable	bright	discreet	magnetic
serene	calm	discerning	methodical
sociable	cheerful	dynamic	suave
commanding	earnest	moral	tactful
compelling	eloquent	observant	composed
engaging	persevering	unassuming	considerate
straight-forward			

INTELLECTUAL EQUIPMENT

The list of adjectives below express the type of, and ability to use intellectual equipment.

FAVORABLE

able	careful	thinker	normal
agile-minded	ingenious	practical	analytical
clever	judicial	profound	apt
creative	keen	proficient	astute
discerning	level-headed	quick-thinker	bright
far-sighted	logical	quick-witted	brilliant
imaginative	mature	retentive	calculating
independent	methodical	remarkable	

MENTAL FACULTY & CAPACITY
The following adjectives express intellect or intelligence.

FAVORABLE

acute	discernible	penetrating	thoughtful
alert	discreet	perceptive	witty
adept	farsighted	prudent	nimble
artful	foresighted	powerful	dexterous
bright	imaginative	quick	brilliant
ingenious	rational	clear-sighted	insightful
reasonable	clear-witted	inspirational	sane
clever	intellectual	sensible	common sense
inventive	sharp	comprehendible	judicious
sharp-witted	conceptual	keen	shrewd
conscious	knowing	skillful	crafty
learned	sly	creative	levelheaded
talented	cunning	logical	thinking
mental	deductive power		

PRESENCE OR IMPRESSION
The adjectives listed below express the mental impression that an individual's outward qualities produce on others.

FAVORABLE

attractive	distinguished	neat
dapper	immaculate	sober
dignified	impressive	spruce
tidy		

JOB RESULTS

The following adjectives express the degree, kind, or type of results obtained by an individual.

FAVORABLE

accurate	decisive	excellent	sure
achievement	dependable	good	undeniable
beneficial	desirable	meritorious	unfailing
best	effective	notable	unmistakable
capable	effectual	reliable	unquestionable
certain	efficient	successful	unqualified
commendable	enduring	superior	

Chapter 5

PHRASES,

THOUGHTS

&

IDEAS

PHRASES, THOUGHTS, & IDEAS

A

Abandoned normal path
Abbreviated schedule
Able-bodied

Abandoned traditional
Able to size up
Above and beyond

Abreast of the times
Absolutely essential
Accelerated program

Absolute dedication
Abundance of
Accelerated change

Acquainted with and understands
Across-the-board
Action not reaction

Acquainted with success
Acted in concert
Active role

Actively engaged in
Acutely aware
Added value(s)

Actively promoted
Adamant in stand
Admired character

Adversity
Aggressive agenda
Airtight case

Against backdrop of
Ahead of times
Alert to possibilities

Alive with
Always original
Amazing speed

Always gives 110 percent
Amassed abundance of
Ambitious progress

Amid changing scene of
Appease(s) others
Applaud efforts of

Analyzed various elements
Appetite for
Appreciate uniqueness of'

Appreciates hard work
Arouses
Aspiring newcomer

Around the clock
Articulate(d) new image
At crossroads

At face value
At-all-cost
Attracts followers

At pinnacle
Atmosphere conducive to
Attuned to needs

Authority figure

Award-winning

B

Back to the wall
Barely missed a beat
Bear the burden

Backbone
Beacon of hope
Beat all odds

Became focal point
Beehive of activity
Benchmark

Bedrock
Behind the scene
Bend over backwards

Benefits from understanding
Best-kept secret
Between the lines

Best foot forward
Better prepared
Beyond a doubt

Bigger than life
Blazed new trail
Blistering pace

Bit of drama arose
Blessed with
Blue-chip

Blue-ribbon
Bold new/move
Bought into focus

Body of evidence/work
Boosted spirits
Boundaries of fairness

Brazen attitude
Break-neck pace
Breakthrough

Break with tradition
Breakneck speed
Breath of fresh air

Breathed new life
Bridged the gap
Brighten the day

Breeding ground for
Bright future
Bring into line

Brings diverse background
Broad consensus
Brought about/out

Brings others together
Broader understanding
Brought to life

Build bridges
Builds commitment
Built foundation

Building blocks
Builds on
Bulldog determination

Burning desire
Business at hand
By the book

Burst of creativity
Business-like

C

Calculated risk
Came to fruition
Came up short

Called upon to
Came to terms with
Can make strong case for

Cannot accept
Captured imagination
Carefree

Capitalized on
Captured the advantage
Carefully planned

Cares deeply
Carried forward
Catalyst of/for

Cares deeply about
Carries self with
Cemented relationships

Centerpiece
Challenges status quo
Champion(s) cause(s)

Challenge of change
Challenging opportunity(ies)
Championing innovation

Change of the guard
Changed face of
Characterized by

Changed business-as-usual
Changing political landscape
Charged ahead

Charisma
Charted course
Civic responsibility

Charismatic
Choice of values
Classic example

Classic move
Clean sweep
Clear conscience

Clean and quick
Cleaned up real mess
Clear position

Cleared the path
Climate of
Close cooperation

Clearly articulated
Climbed to the top
Close(d) ranks

Coalition building
Collective influence
Come to grips with

Cohesive group
Colorful
Comfort level

Committed to
Compassionate response
Concrete support

Common enemy
Compelling reasons
Confidence restored

Confronted challenge(s)
Conquered
Conscious of image

Considerable
Conspicuous
Continued success

Continuous improvement
Conventional wisdom
Cornerstone

Coveted award
Cream rose to top
Created climate of

Crisis situation
Critical juncture
Crowning achievement

Crusader for
Culmination of
Cultural development

Cut above

Connects with others
Conscious effort
Consensus builder

Consistent pattern of
Consummate
Continuing cycle of

Conventional barrier(s)
Cooler heads prevail(ed)
Courageous act(s)

Cream of the crop
Created (new) process of
Creative masterpiece

Critical importance
Critically acclaimed
Crucial issue(s)

Crystal clear
Cultivated and nurtured
Cushion of safety

Cutting edge

D

Daily challenges of
Debt of gratitude
Decisive action(s)

Dedication extended to
Deep respect
Deeply moved

Defined character/essence
Demonstrated versatility
Determined to prevail

Devoted to
Difficult times
Disciplined passion

Dazzling performance
Deceptively simple
Dedicated efforts

Deep and lasting
Deep-seated
Defender of

Delicate balance
Despite deep cuts
Developed principles

Diehard
Difficulties encountered
Discovered

Distinctively different
Distinguished character
Do justice to

Down to earth
Dramatically illustrated
Driving force

Dynamic change

Distinguished
Disturbing conclusion(s)
Dominated field

Dramatic change/time
Dream come true
Dynamic atmosphere

Dynamic environment

E

Ear marked for
Easy to understand
Electrified

Elevated to level of
Elite
Eloquent

Embodiment of an idea
Emerging
Encourages the heart

Energy devoted to
Engaged imagination
Enjoys/Enjoyed increased

Enrich
Entertaining thought
Environment of openness

Epitome of
Equitable distribution
Established legacy/stability

Ever-present/growing
Examined all aspects
Exciting possibilities

Exercised influence
Expeditious
Exploits noteworthy

Earned place in
Eclipsed previous record
Element of risk

Eliminated all
Elite group
Embodied central idea

Embraced concept
Encourages collaboration
Enduring place in history

Enflamed the passion
Engineered path of future
Enlist emotion(s)

Enriched
Enthusiastic support
Envisions the future

Equal to task
Essential element/trait(s)
Ever-expanding obligations

Every step of the way
Excellence grew
Exciting time(s)

Exerted strong influence
Expended great energy
Explore(d) new methods

Explosive emotions
Extended range
Extraordinary challenge(s)
Exuberant
Eye-opening

Expresses conviction
Extra motivation
Extremely delicate
Eye of the storm

F

Faced many challenges
Far and away
Far-reaching

Faced tall odds
Far-reaching
Farsighted

Fast-moving
Feeling for what is right
Fertile soil for

Faultless
Fertile imagination
Feverish activity

Fierce competitor
Final decision
Firm constructive element

Filled with excitement
Finest
Firm resolve

First and foremost
Firsthand experience
Flag bearer

First stabilized, then reversed
Fitting climax
Flair for

Flawless
Flood of support
Focus on issues

Flawlessly executed
Flourishes in environment of
Focus(es) on

Focused and re-doubled efforts
For others to emulate
Force in

Foothold in
For the most part
Forever changed

Forged ahead
Formed the foundation
Forte

Formed diverse
Formula for success
Forward-looking

Foster(s) sense of
Fought diligently
Found satisfaction

Fostered improved
Fought tooth and nail
Foundation built on

Founder of
Frank assessment
Free from stigma of

Flourished
Frantic
Free-spirited

Frequent contributor
Friend and supporter
Fruitful

Fresh page in
From the onset
Fruits of labor

Fuel the imagination
Full-grown
Fundamental principal

Full of possibilities
Full-time job
Fundamentally different

Furthered cause
Future-oriented

Future begins now

G

Gained favor
Gateway to
General order of things

Gained foothold
Gave birth to
Generous assistance

Generously gave
Giant step forward
Go against the grain

Genuine act of/article
Glimmer of hope
Go along with

Go hand-in-hand
Good fortune/measure
Gracefully accepted

Golden opportunity
Got in way
Graduated to level

Grass roots
Gravity of situation
Grew in intensity

Gratifying
Great chapter in history of
Grew in wisdom and stature

Gripping reality
Growing pains
Guiding light/vision

Ground-breaking
Guided change

H

Had free rein
Hammer away
Hand-in-hand

Hallmark
Hand picked
Handicapped by

Handled delicate issue(s)
Hardy attitude
Hats off to

Hard-earned
Harnessed power
Headed in right direction

Healed wounds of
Heightened activity
Helped build

High frequency of
Historic event
Hit the books

Honest feedback
Humble beginnings

Heart and soul
Held firm
Herculean effort

Highly developed
History of
Holds on to values

Hope for future
Hunger for

I

Ideal conditions
Illuminates spirit of
Immediate turnaround

Immersed in
Impeccable taste
Implemented much needed changes

Impressive
In face of
In great measure

In mainstream
In the prime
Increased appetite for

Independent thinking
Inextricably connected
Influence on

Infuse(d) fresh ideas
Inherited unsuccessful
Inner strength

Inquisitive
Inspiration
Inspired creativity

Ignited fire in/to
Immediate impact
Immense and complex

Impassioned
Impetus to/for change
Important source of

In due course
In full stride
In high gear

In the mind's eye
In touch with
Incredible level/sense of

Indescribably
Inflicted heavy loses
Influential presence

Ingenuity
Injects life
Innovative new way/solutions

Inside information
Inspire shared vision
Instinct for

Instinctive feel
Integral part of
Intense pressure

Intimate knowledge
Intrinsically superior
Intuitive

Iron will

Instituted measures
Integrity
Intense routine

Intrinsic values
Introduce(d) new life
Invested talent/time

Irrational exuberance

J

Jolt of adrenaline
Jump-start

Judicious effort

K

Keen awareness
Key element
Keystone

Knock(ed) on the door

Kept on toes
Key to success
Kicked door open

Know-how

L

Labor of love
Ladder of success
Laid groundwork for

Landmark
Lasting impact
Launched new

Left a mark
Level playing field
Lightening quick

Long, hard road
Long-term approach
Looked up to

Loosened shackles of

Labored hard
Laid foundation
Laid to rest

Larger than life
Latent with
Learned first-hand

Level best
Lift(s) people's spirit(s)
Lively spirit

Long-lasting/-standing
Long-term relationship
Looks beyond

Lose ground

M

Made good use of
Made-to-order
Main ingredient(s)

Made the best of
Magnitude of situation
Mainstream

Major challenge(s)
Makes things work
Marked coming

Major contributor
Margin of safety
Marvelous

Massive undertaking
Mastermind(ed)
Masterwork

Master stroke
Masterpiece
Measure of success

Meet demands
Mental powers
Merits special praise

Memorable event/work
Mere words fail to
Met criteria

Meticulous
Mind-set
Mixed blessing(s)

Milestone(s)
Mired in
Mobilizes others

Monumental
Moral involvement
Most unique

Moral base
Most accomplished
Mounted major challenge

Multi-faceted
Muster up courage/strength

Multi-talented

N

Narrow(ed) the gap
Natural greatness
Needed shot in the arm

Natural enthusiasm
Near perfection
Nerves of steel

Never before
New way of thinking
Newfound

New and exciting
New wrinkle surfaced
Noble undertaking

Nose to the grindstone
Notable exception
Nourishes spirits

Not to be forgotten
Nourished
Nurtured

O

Of first rank importance
On guard for
Onward and upward

Opened door for/to
Opportunity to create
Orchestrated

Outward calm
Over the top
Overall strategy

Overnight success
Overwhelming

On business end of
On hot seat
Open-handed and above board

Opened new horizon
Optimistic appraisal/outlook
Outcome never in doubt

Over and above
Overabundance of
Overestimate(d)

Overtaken by events
Overwhelmingly positive

P

Pace of change
Part and parcel
Passed the torch

Passionate advocate
Paved the way
Perfect blend/choice

Persona
Personal test of courage
Pick up the pieces

Pinnacle
Pivotal situation
Plain and simple facts

Played out on giant scale
Poised for
Political landscape

Popular belief
Positive thinking
Potential crisis

Painstakingly work
Particularly productive
Passing of the guard

Pat on the back
Peacemaker
Perfect opportunity

Personal crusade
Phenomenal change
Pillar of strength

Pioneer spirit
Places high premium
Played full part

Pleasantly surprised
Policy maker
Pomp and circumstances

Positive movement
Potent
Potentially dangerous

Power base
Pragmatic
Precious source of

Presence of mind
Priceless
Prime reason

Problem solver
Productive pursuit
Professional grace

Profound influence
Progressive new
Proper balance

Proved mettle
Provided outlet for
Public trust

Pursue all avenues
Pushed forward
Put an end to

Powers of observation
Precious little/few
Precision

Press(ing) ahead
Prime mover
Prized position

Process of discovery
Productivity increased
Professional triumph

Profoundly affected
Promise of things to come
Properly prepared

Provided chemistry necessary
Prudent
Pulled out all stops

Pursued with tenacity
Pushing the limit(s)
Put lid on

Q

Quantum leap
Quick to

Quest for
Quickly soared to top

R

Radiates
Raised spirit(s) of
Rare insight

Real change
Realized full potential
Rebounded from

Record shattering
Redefined
Reform oriented

Radically different
Range of performance extends to
Reached new heights/summit

Real division in
Reasonable solution
Recipe for success

Redeeming qualities
Reenergized efforts
Refreshing thought(s)

Reinforced actions
Rejuvenated
Relentless pursuit

Remarkable achievement
Renowned for
Reservoir of experience

Resilient
Respected figure
Revered for

Revolutionary new
Rich in vitality
Rigorous testing/evaluation

Rock hard
Rose from depths of

Reinvigorated sagging
Rekindled flame
Relish with zest

Rendered obsolete
Reputation
Reshaped

Resounding success
Responded in full measure
Revitalized

Revolutionized
Rich past experience(s)
Risk taker

Rooted in history
Rush of adrenaline

S

Safeguard
Search of excellence
Second nature

Selective field
Sense of commitment
Sensitive to

Serious crisis
Served to
Set the stage

Shaped events
Sharply focused
Shot in the arm

Sight set on
Significant gains
Significant milestone

Safely weathered
Searches for opportunities
Seed(s) of success

Self-styled
Sense of direction
Sent clear message/signal

Served the purpose
Set new precedent
Set up and take notice

Sharp increase
Sheer energy
Shouldered responsibility

Sign of hope
Significant influence on/in
Simple and straight-forward

Simply the best
Single-minded
Situation of extreme(s)

Sincere honor
Singular purpose
Snatched victory

Solely responsible
Solidified
Sought after by

Solid contributor
Sorely needed
Soul of organization

Sounding board
Sparking
Special feel for

Source of knowledge/light
Spearhead
Special gift

Special quality(ies)
Spell of good luck
Spirit of comradeship

Speedy recovery
Spelled success
Split-second

Spotless
Staggering range of talent
Stalemate avoided

Squeaky clean
Stainless record
Stand on own two feet

Stand tall
Started from scratch
Stately appearance

Stands alone
State of the art
Status symbol

Stay(ed) in background
Stem rising tide
Straight as an arrow

Steady stream of
Step ahead of
Straight shooter

Straightforward response
Strengthened resolve
Strenuous schedule

Strategy aimed at
Strengthens others
Stretched boundaries

Stretched to limits
Strike a blow
Strong advocate

Strident support
Striking results
Strong background

Struggled to stay afloat
Substantially improved
Successful strategy

Studied works of
Successes mounted rapidly
Successfully challenged

Summon(ed) up the courage
Surpassed
Survival of the fittest

Sunny disposition
Surpassed all expectations
Sustained commitment

Sweeping reform
Symbol of
Systematic

Sweet victory
Sympathetic ear

T

Tackle(s) any
Task at hand
Tense time(s)

Takes pleasure in
Tenacious
Testimony to

Tests new ideas
Threshold of
Tight knit group

Thirst for
Thrives in/on
Time to take stock in

Time-tested
Tireless efforts
Took special interest in

Timeless
Took inventory of facilities
Top to bottom

Top-notch
Total focus
Track record

Tore down barrier(s)
Tough nut to crack
Traditional concept

Transcends
Trial and error
Tried and true

Transformed
Tricky business
Triumph

True to form
True visionary
Trusted advisor

True transformation
Trusted
Turbulent

Turbulent times
Turnaround

Turn(ed) the tide
Turning point in

U

Ultimate test
Unbearable
Uncluttered thought

Unassailable performance
Unbeatable combination
Undaunted

Under any circumstances
Underdog
Underscore(d) the importance

Under pressure
Underlines importance
Underwent process of

Unencumbered
Unequaled admiration
Unforeseen events

Unenviable position
Unexplored avenues
Unglamorous task(s)

Unification of
Uninhabited
Unique sophistication

Unifying force
Unique insight
Uniquely suited

Unleashed
Unmistakable
Unpredictable

Unlocked door of opportunity
Unprecedented
Unrelenting

Untapped resource(s)
Up and coming
Uplifting experience

Unusual circumstances
Up to the task
Urgent business

Ushered in era of

V

Valid option
Vigilant
Virtue of hard work

Valuable insight
Vintage
Virtuoso

Visionary
Vitality
Voyage of discovery

Vital role
Volatile

W

Wages relentless
Watershed
Weight of responsibility

Warmly received
Weathered the storm
Well versed

Well-founded
Whole-hearted
Widely accepted

Whatever it takes
Wide-spread support
Widely embraced

Willpower
Winning game plan
Wipe the slate clean

Window of opportunity
Winning ways
With particular clarity

Work under adversity
Workhorse
World of good

Workaholic
World class
Worthy of remark

CHAPTER 6

TOP PERFORMERS
(5.0-4.0)

TOP PERFORMERS
(5.0-4.0)

WORD BANK

ACTIVE, DESCRIPTIVE, POSITIVE

ABSOLUTELY	ABUNDANT	ACCLAIM
ACCOMPLISHED	ACCOMPLISHES	ACCURATE
ACE	ACHIEVES	ADEPT
ADMIRABLE	ADMIRED	ADROIT
ADVANCED	ADVANTAGE	ALL-AROUND
ALL-OUT	ALL-STAR	ALWAYS
AMAZING	AMBITION	AMBITIOUS
AMIABLE	ANALYTICAL	A-ONE
APPLAUDED	ARDUOUS	AROUSES
ARTFUL	ARTICULATE	ARTISTIC
ASPIRING	ASSET	ASTONISHING
ASTOUNDING	ASTUTE	AUDACITY
AVID	AWE-INSPIRING	AWESOME
BANNER	BEST	BLOCKBUSTER
BOLD	BOUNDLESS	BRAINCHILD
BRAVE	BREATHTAKING	BRIGHT
BRILLIANT	BROAD-BASED	CELEBRATED
CENTERPIECE	CHALLENGES	CHAMPION
CHANCE-TAKER	CLEAR-CUT	CLEAR-HEADED
CLEAR-SIGHTED	COMEBACK	COMMENDABLE
COMPELLING	COMPETITIVE	COMPLEX
COMPREHENSIVE	CONQUERED	CONSCIENTIOUS
CONSIDERABLE	CONSIDERATE	CONSUMMATE
CONTRIBUTES	CONTRIBUTION	CORNERSTONE
COUNTLESS	COURAGE	COURAGEOUS
CRAFTED	CRAFTSMANSHIP	CREATED
CREATES	CREATIVE	CREATIVITY
CRUCIAL	CRYSTALLIZED	CULTURED

DECISIVE	DEDICATED	DEMANDING
DEMONSTRATES	DETERMINED	DEVELOPS
DEVELOPS	DEVOTED	DEVOTION
DEXTERITY	DISCOVERED	DISCOVERY
DISMANTELED	DISTINCTION	DISTINGUISHED
DOMINANT	DOMINATED	DOMINATES
DOMINATING	DOMINEERS	DRAMATIC
DRIVE	DYNAMIC	EAGER
EARNEST	EDUCATED	ELABORATE
ELEGANT	ELEVATED	ELITE
ELOQUENT	EMBODIMENT	EMBRACED
EMINENT	ENCOURAGED	ENDEARING
ENDLESS	ENERGETIC	ENERGIZE
ENERGIZED	ENERGIZES	ENERGY
ENHANCED	ENLIGHTENED	ENORMOUS
ENORMOUSLY	ENRICH	ENRICHED
ENRICHES	ENRICHMENT	ENTERPRISING
ENTHUSIASM	ENTHUSIASTIC	ENVIABLE
EPITOME	ESCALATED	ESSENTIAL
ESTEEM	EVERLASTING	EXACT
EXACTING	EXCEEDS	EXCELLENCE
EXCELLENT	EXCELS	EXCEPTIONAL
EXCEPTIONALLY	EXEMPLARY	EXPANDS
EXPEDIENT	EXPEDITES	EXPEDITIOUS
EXPERIENCED	EXPERT	EXPERTISE
EXPIDITES	EXPLOITED	EXPLOITS
EXTENSIVE	EXTRAORDINARY	EXTREMELY
EXUBERANCE	EXUBERANT	EYE-OPENING
FABULOUS	FANTASTIC	FARSIGHTED
FAULTLESS	FINEST	FIRST
FIRST-CLASS	FIRST-RATE	FLAWLESS
FLEXIBLE	FOREMOST	FORERUNNER
FORESIGHT	FORMIDABLE	FORMULATES

FRESH FRONT-RUNNER FRUITFUL
FUELED FULL-FLEDGED FULL-SCALE
FURTHERED GALLANT GALVANIZED

GARNERED GENERATED GENERATES
GENIUS GENUINE GIFT
GIFTED GLORIOUS GO-GETTER

GRAND GRANDIOSE GREAT
GREATER GREATEST GREATNESS
GROUND-BREAKING GUNG HO HARD-HITTING

HIGH HIGHEST HISTORIC
HONOR HONORABLE HONORED
ICON IDEAL ILLUSTRIOUS

IMAGINATIVE IMMEASURABLE IMMENSE
IMPECCABLE IMPETUS IMPORTANT
IMPRESSIVE IMPROVED IMPROVES

INCALCULABLE INCOMPARABLE INCREDIBLE
INDEPENDENT INESTIMABLE INEXHAUSTIBLE
INFECTS INFINITE INFLUENTIAL

INFORMED INGENIOUS INGENUITY
INITIATIVE INNOVATION INNOVATIVE
INQUISITIVE INSATIABLE INSIGHT

INSPIRATION INSPIRED INTELLECT
INTELLECTUAL INTELLIGENT INTENSE
INTENSIVE INVALUABLE INVENTED

INVENTIVE INVIGORATES INVINCIBLE
JOURNEYMAN KEEN KNOWLEDGEABLE
LANDMARK LARGE LARGE-SCALE

LAUDABLE LAUDATORY LAUNCHED
LEADING LEARNED LETTERED
LIFELINE LIMITLESS LOFTY

LYNCHPIN MAGNETISM MAGNIFICENT
MAINSTREAM MAINTAINS MAJESTIC
MAMMOTH MANDATE MANDATED

MARVELOUS	MASSIVE	MASTER
MASTERFUL	MASTERLY	MASTERPIECE
MASTERY	MATCHLESS	MATURITY
MAXIMUM	MEANINGFUL	MEMORABLE
MERIT	MERITABLE	MERITORIOUS
METICULOUS	MIRACULOUS	MODEL
MODERNIZED	MOLDED	MONUMENTAL
MOTIVATED	MOTIVATES	MOTIVATOR
MUCH-NEEDED	MULTI-TALENTED	NATURAL
NERVE-RACKING	NO-NONSENSE	NON-STOP
NOTEWORTHY	NUTURED	OPTIMUM
ORGANIZES	OUTCLASS	OUTDO
OUTGREW	OUTMATCHED	OUTSHINE
OUTSTANDING	OVERABUNDANCE	OVERABUNDANT
OVERCAME	OVERCOMES	OVERSHADOWES
OVERWHELMING	PAINSTAKING	PARAGON
PARAMOUNT	PEERLESS	PERFECT
PERFECTION	PERSONIFICATION	PERSONIFIES
PHENOMENAL	PINNACLE	PIONEERED
PIVOTAL	POISED	POLISHED
POSITIVE	POSITIVELY	POTENT
POWERFUL	PRAGMATIC	PRAISEWORTHY
PRECIOUS	PRECISE	PRECISELY
PRECISION	PREDOMINANT	PREEMINENT
PREMIER	PRESTIGE	PRESTIGIOUS
PREVAILED	PRICELESS	PRIDE
PRINCIPLED	PRIZED	PROFESSIONAL
PROFESSIONALISM	PROFICIENT	PROFOUND
PROGRESSIVE	PROLIFIC	PROMINENT
PROMOTE	PROMOTED	PROMOTES
PROTOTYPE	PROUD	PROVED
PROWESS	QUICK	QUINTESSENTIAL
RADIATES	RAPID	RARE
REBOUNDED	REBUILT	RECORD-BREAKING

RECORD-SETTING   REFORMED   REFRESHING
REGAL   REHABILITATED   REJUVENATED
RELENTLESS   REMARKABLE   RENOWN

RENOWNED   RESCUED   RESILIENT
RESOLUTE   RESOLVES   RESOURCEFUL
RESTORED   RESTRUCTURED   REVITALIZED

REVIVED   REVOLUTIONARY   REVOLUTIONIZED
SACRIFICE   SACRIFICED   SACRIFICIES
SALVAGED   SAVVY   SCHOLAR

SCHOLARLY   SEASONED   SELF-MOTIVATED
SENSATIONAL   SEVERE   SHARP
SHOWCASE   SIGNIFICANCE   SIGNIFICANT

SINGLE-MINDED   SIZABLE   SKILLED
SKILLFUL   SOPHISTICATED   SPARKED
SPARKS   SPEARHEADED   SPECIAL

SPECTACULAR   SPIRIT   SPIRITED
SPLENDID   SPONTANEOUS   SPOTLESS
STABILIZED   STAGGERING   STANDARD-BEARER

STANDOUT   STAR   STELLAR
STERLING   STRENGTHENED   STRENUOUS
STRESSFUL   STRIKING   STRONG

STRONG-WILLED   SUBSTANTIAL   SUCCESSFUL
SUPER   SUPERB   SUPERFINE
SUPERIOR   SUPERLATIVE   SUPPORTS
SUPREMACY   SUPREME   SURPASS

SURPASSED   SURPASSES   SYMBOLIZES
TALENTED   TENACIOUS   TERRIFIC
THRIVES   THRIVING   TIGHT-KNIT

TIME-HONORED   TIMELESS   TIRELESS
TOP   TOP-DRAWER   TOPFLIGHT
TOP-GRADE   TOP-LEVEL   TOPMOST

TOPNOTCH   TOP-QUALITY   TOP-RANKED
TOP-RANKING   TRAILBLAZER   TRANDSCENDS
TRANSCENDS   TRANSFORMED   TRANSFORMS

TREASURE	TREMENDOUS	TREND-SETTER
TRIUMPH	TRIUMPHANT	TRIUMPHED
TRUSTED	ULTIMATE	UNBEATABLE
UNBELIEVABLE	UNBLEMISHED	UNCANNY
UNDOUBTEDLY	UNEQUALED	UNEQUIVOCALLY
UNERRING	UNFAILING	UNIQUE
UNLIMITED	UNMATCHED	UNMISTAKABLE
UNPARALLELED	UNPRECEDENTED	UNQUESTIONABLY
UNRIVALED	UNSURPASSED	UNTIRING
UNWAVERING	UPBEAT	UPGRADED
UPPERMOST	UPSCALE	UPSTANDING
UTMOST	VALUED	VAST
VIABLE	VIGOR	VIGOROUS
VIM	VIRTUE	VIRTUOSO
VISIONARY	VITAL	VITALITY
VITALIZE	VULNERABLE	WATCHDOG
WELL-DESERVED	WELL-EARNED	WELL-READ
WELL-ROUNDED	WELL-TIMED	WELL-TUTORED
WELL-VERSED	WHIZ	WIDE-RANGING
WIDE-REACHING	WIDE-SCALE	WIDESPREAD
WILLPOWER	WINNER	WISDOM
WISE	WONDERFUL	WONDERWORK
WORKHORSE	WORTHWHILE	WORTHY
ZEAL	ZEALOT	ZEALOUS
ZENITH		

TOP PERFORMERS

BULLETS

track record	...multi-talented individual
timely fashion	...new territory
launched new ...	...profound impact
mental focus	...superior quality ...
united front	...energetic spirit
dramatic rebound	...real visionary
champion of ...	...acted swiftly
turned ... around	...moral courage
impact performance	...nearly impossible
powerful combination	...best possible ...
internal courage	...take-charge person
founder of ...	...clearly better
exceptionally proficient	...adopted philosophy
frantic pace	...dramatic increase
incredible challenge	...landmark decision
really good ...	...earned confidence
challenged the ...	...exceptionally fine
meritorious service	...advanced education
progressed beyond ...	...fragile foothold
best ever ...	...supported by ...
rebounded from ...	...emotional intensity
unlimited future	...challenging environment
agile mind	...agonizing problem(s)
critical component	...earned gratitude
balanced attack	...mustered strength
thrust into ...	...ambitious plan
no-nonsense approach	...an original
astounding success	...at crossroads
towering performance	...back-breaking pace
clearly decisive	...grueling schedule

badly needed ...	...launched full-scale ...
balanced approach	...notable contribution
enduring legacy	...unqualified success
mental sharpness	...superior talent
bailed out	...all-star performance
supreme confidence	...difficult situation
prominent aspect	...psychological value
bitter-sweet	...crunch time
unflinching dedication	...lasting impression
grueling task	...bold plan
uniquely successful	...realistic assessment
alarmed by	...great asset
unblemished personal ...	...guiding beacon
recognized as ...	...mental toughness
character builder	...refined talent
charismatic leader	...opportunities abounded
chartered course	...large degree
driving force	...mutual benefit
thrives on ...	...classic example
advanced skills	...unlimited possibilities
remarkable will	...high voltage
orchestrated new ...	...difficult undertaking
at forefront	...pulled together
meteoric rise	...tireless efforts
team effort	...originated incomparable
out performed	...notable increase
refreshing new ...	...class act
dynamic leadership	...solid increase
uniquely resourceful	...all-time high
broadened scope	...talent for ...
emotional leader	...demanding standards
nimble mind	...polished talent
unprecedented increase	...growing reputation

renewed dedication	...growing trend
driving desire	...mentality of ...
oversaw growing ...	...helped start ...
cornerstone of ...	...unlimited potential
correct decision	...monumental undertaking
negotiated difficult ...	...endowed with ...
landmark event	...crafted unique ...
tireless individual	...aspired to ...
totally impressive	...gratifying work
fast mind	...created new ...
initiated revolutionary ...	...employed new ...
unparalleled success	...creative atmosphere
eager beaver	...punishing schedule
eager to ...	...mentor for ...
far reaching	...almost immediately
technological breakthrough	...bold advance
reduced overall ...	...genuine article
personal integrity	...none better
no peers	...devoted to ...
did homework	...pressure-cooker environment
higher standard	...unique challenge
vital link	...vocal proponent
meticulous attention	...perfect timing
significant change	...commands attention
ultimate test	...commended for ...
vital in/to ...	...actively pursued
substantial gain	...spent hours ...
master at ...	...single handedly
much appreciated	...net gain
incredibly efficient	...without precedent
high octane	...unique insight
strong performance	...withstood adversity
difficult challenge	...great opportunity

unmatched personal ...	...supremely gifted
competitive nature	...brought stability
difficult to ...	...superior organizer
on-going success	...many challenges
symbol of ...	...great mind
diplomatic approach	...adopted position
concrete assurance	...guiding light
stood ground	...broke barrier(s)
polished image	...helping hand
best overall	...clearly superior
engaged in ...	...alarming rate
gamely tackled	...creative energy
beyond question	...dramatic impact
found solution	...swept away
dramatic results	...total quality
earned respect	...easily exceeded
can-do person	...aggressive posture
tireless undertaking	...grass-roots support
established new ...	...significant headway
crucial decision	...finely crafted
promising career	...critical period
acute problem(s)	...emotional anchor
intellectually superior	...bleakest hour
performance parallels ...	...endless possibilities
bankable asset	...watched over ...
enormous sophistication	...mental agility
enterprising individual	...creative excellence
fast lane	...advocate for ...
aggressive approach	...outclassed the/all ...
technological achievement	...grand vision
established superb	...acquired skills
critical responsibilities	...re-doubled efforts
unmatched ability	...exemplary performance

watchful eye	...grand master
expanded horizon	...constant attention
amazingly complex	...brutal tasking
totally mastered...	...solid foundation
noble undertaking	...great desire
extremely difficult	...wholehearted support
burning ambition	...dramatic change
exuberant curiosity	...creative force
brilliant career	...far better
gigantic task	...rare gem
restored pride	...initiated new ...
embodiment of ...	...proper action
highest expectations	...deserving of ...
highest level	...measurably improved
top innovator	...far superior
fashioned ... into	...articulated successful
crucial time/period	...builds character
restructured complex ...	...fast rising
defensive posture	...gained respect
joined together	...iron will
natural competitiveness	...thoroughly enjoys ...
maximum effort	...shining moment
provided continuity	...fast track
testament to ...	...favorable climax
immediate impact	...inspires others
provided spark	...key role
jump started ...	...well above ...
poised for ...	...heroic effort(s)
finest work	...people oriented
beyond doubt	...perfectly balanced
cooperative effort	...perfectly clear
significant improvement	...successful resolution
successfully adapted	...pioneering spirit

highly regarded	...most critical
level above	...extraordinary ability
monument to ...	...especially desirable
first successful	...hot talent
restored confidence	...major player
first-hand experience	...boosted morale
grand design	...flourished in/as ...
proven top ...	...wealth of ...
self confident	...extremely helpful
top priority	...budding talent
redoubled efforts	...gift for ...
advanced approach	...towered over ...
huge achievement	...became prominent
reached climax	...remarkable feat
proven abilities	...totally original
enthusiastic approach	...natural talent
capitalized on ...	...forthright manner
increasingly difficult	...incredible resourcefulness
growing involvement	...bitter struggle
serious work	...winning attitude
thorough understanding	...force in ...
leading role	...fresh new ...
number one	...leading player
fresh start	...prototype for ...
fulfilled all	...blossomed into ...
back-breaking work	...full force
collective decision	...organized successful
confined in/by ...	...ever-ready to ...
driving influence	...high principles
respected for ...	...without question
clearly defined	...blessed with ...
well crafted	...immediate concern(s)
shaped future	...shouldered responsibility

generous effort(s)	...rededicated effort
strongly endorsed ...	...critical timing
went beyond ...	...inspired tutoring
elite group	...highest possible
gifted individual	...standard-bearer in ...
given opportunity	...good faith
shining example	...total commitment
pressed advantage	...standout in/as ...
scholar of...	...great success
greater challenge	...moral integrity
builds on ...	...focused on ...
sound principles	...increasing pressure(s)
without equal	...presided over ...
wide-spread recognition	...scrambled to ...
captured imagination	...careful balance
self starter	...fierce determination
combination of ...	...hands down
commanding presence	...spectacular results
hard pressed	...confronted by/with ...
ever-present optimism	...inspired leadership
seemingly inexhaustible	...committed to ...
strongly defends ...	...spectacular increase
most outstanding	...instant success
won support	...heavy load
rare commodity	...heavy sacrifice
premium on ...	...held together
seized opportunity	...well documented
helped achieve	...even-handed
instinct for ...	...achieved milestone
presented opportunity	...crown jewel
researched new ...	...strenuous task
caters to ...	...helped create ...
pivotal role	...intrigued by ...

crucial turn	...eloquent analysis
boosted efficiency	...high risk
propensity for ...	...unflagging support
shaped destiny	...gained confidence
inspired camaraderie	...elevated position
proof positive	...enthusiastic support
highest respect	...break through
aggressive procedures	...demands more
historic achievement	...honed skills
conservative approach	...ever-more challenging
honed to ...	...instrumental to ...
acute awareness	...icon of ...
ideal situation	...premier performer
most prominent	...carefully cultivated ...
secure in ...	...diffused situation
clearly reflects	...formidable task/mission
identifies with ...	...brilliant insight
eye-catching talent	...ignites excitement
seeks opportunities	...bright future
first-rate performance	...ignores obstacles
unique solution	...seasoned veteran
efforts won	...absolute loyalty
immediately recognized ...	...cut above
strengthens understanding	...immense help
breathtaking pace	...developed new ...
immense undertaking	...greatest in/at ...
tremendous effort	...above reproach
efforts rewarded	...important lesson
pivotal event	...unparalleled record
sparked serious ...	...hands-on person
comfort zone	...incorporated diverse
sophisticated approach	...proper decision(s)
turning point	...triggered reaction

pressure-filled situation	...new dimension
fast becoming ...	...indestructible will
highly acclaimed	...gained foothold
inexhaustible energy	...truly a ...
focused attention	...bright side
promising future	...aroused enthusiasm
infectious optimism	...clearly talented
inherent problem(s)	...strong foundation
cutting edge	...determined to ...
became reality	...inherited poorly ...
highly accomplished ...	...considerable energy
precious few	...unceasing devotion
immense talent	...despite odds
free spirited	...dramatic turnaround
immediate success	...gained ground
warmly received	...spotless reputation
well prepared	...driven to ...
galvanized forces	...exhaustive research
dynamic situation	...matchless talent
unmatched enthusiasm	...clear signal
first time	...professional triumph
profound changes	...super motivator
fully developed	...undervalued as ...
contributions exceeded	...essential element(s)
actively sought	...rigors of ...
without doubt	...special treat
put together ...	...quickly adapted
exceptional ability	...radiates enthusiasm
quickly mastered	...big help
enormous odds	...almost impossible
overwhelming choice	...blazing success
shining hour	...premier ... in ...
specialist in/on ...	...vision transcended .

intangible quality	...personal involvement
significant impact	...constructed new
intense devotion	...prefect chemistry
achieved highest ...	...uncharted territory
highest ranking	...worthy of ...
downward spiral	...unbreakable spirit
vigorous pursuit	...clear cut
sheer willpower	...forerunner in/of ...
shifted attention	...unfailing optimism
raw talent	...wonderful talent
shines brightly	...developed hard-hitting
invaluable ability	...overcame serious ...
nurtured new ...	...pure dynamite
invincible determination	...far more ...
intense dedication	...fiercely proud
pushed for ...	...in spotlight
very pleased	...enhanced overall ...
crucial role	...new philosophy
dogged determination	...added advantage
shaped the ...	...gallant effort
top achiever	...consistently outstanding
banner performance	...guiding hand
ambitious goals	...obvious choice
prominent in ...	...nurturing atmosphere
iron fist	...jumped headlong
keenly aware	...cares about ...
strong values	...exceptional talent
formidable accomplishment	...added dimension
important new ...	...key issue(s)
inner drive	...aggressive schedule
expanding success	...highly competitive
clear picture	...innovative ideas
precedent-setting work	...hungry for ...

dominant force
creates own ...
demanding schedule

important assignment
crowning achievement
hard charger

crystal clear
impressed everyone
leading edge

noteworthy accomplishments
novel approach
close relationship

impressive record
limited resources
force behind ...

demanding job
limitless talent
lofty goal(s)

credited with ...
logic suggests ...
full implications

focal point
constantly searching
mainstay of ...

fierce spirit
hand-picked to/for ...
exuberant personality

made headway
made possible ...
unusually talented

crafted new ...
something special
copes with ...

...innovative solution(s)
...key to ...
...knows first-hand

...uncanny ability
...admired for ...
...greatest possible ...

...nucleus of ...
...leader in ...
...rock solid

...unequalled skill
...level best
...life-long advocate

...lighting fast
...infinite possibilities
...unending perseverance

...endless opportunities
...loaded with ...
...lofty goals

...stunning achievement(s)
...brilliantly executed
...embarked on ...

...long-term benefits
...amazing accomplishments
...praiseworthy performance

...creative imagination
...low profile
...eye catching

...bolstered morale
...high profile
...longtime star

...vaulted into ...
...new direction
...unbreakable will

magnetic personality	...broad stroke
fundamental issue(s)	...courageous effort
highly successful	...inner strength
maintains poise	...clear thinking
major breakthrough	...provided inspiration
endured severe ...	...full plate
eye for ...	...correctly addressed ...
showcased talents	...major transition
success story	...countless hours/times
forged ahead	...highest principles
grew into ...	...important asset
unencumbered by ...	...contagious enthusiasm
foremost expert	...best trained
lasting impact	...flair for ...
sweeping changes	...viable option(s)
exceeded expectations	...vigorous approach
unending energy	...over achiever
important ramification	...closely monitored
critical factor(s)	...boundless energy
eminent authority	...fixture in ...
flawless performance	...powerhouse in ...
learning experience	...model for ...
bold move	...fierce competitor
ingrained respect	...striking performance
monumental effort	...truly exceptional
hard choices	...close-knit organization
monumental task	...bounced back
innumerable opportunities	...widely celebrated
truly rewarding	...powerful element
highly focused	...most extraordinary
intense measure(s)	...trusted advisor
most impressive	...consistent work
inspiration to ...	...infectious enthusiasm

many firsts	...forever changed
motivational speaker	...intensive effort(s)
ardent supporter	...untapped potential
passionate intensity	...grew professionally
highest order	...major development
exceeded all ...	...overcame major ...
very special ...	...never ending
unparalleled growth	...calculated risk-taker
sparkplug for ...	...fearless commitment
never wavered	...powerful personality
someone special	...something more
new frontier	...better off
impeccable appearance	...strict standards
proving ground	...firm purpose
invested in ...	...above all
critical situation	...guiding principles
fought for/to ...	...added bonus
remarkable success	...burning desire
winning combination	...unfazed by ...
team player	...wise move
fostered unparalleled	...matured as ...
grueling schedule	...provided much-needed
firm belief	...continues to ...
favorable environment	...mental alertness
impetus for ...	...rising star
emerging talent	...impressive response
stunning performance	...daunting challenge
valuable commodity	...firmly embraced
tremendous boost	...main mission
evolved into ...	...trademark efficiency
substantial progress	...achieved all ...
intense pressure	...richly deserved
finest example	...painstaking efforts

unique qualities	...high powered ...
tremendous support	...moral responsibility
experienced severe ...	...passionate commitment
unsung hero	...exacting standards
undying faith	...finest hour
peerless performer	...monumental challenge
positioned to ...	...consummate job
possesses great ...	...prime condition
strong move	...principal architect
ever watchful	...principal issue(s)
prized for ...	...deep commitment
always exceeds	...superbly executed
problem solver	...magnificent job
problematic solution(s)	...most amazing ...
won respect	...productive beyond ...
changed ... forever	...demanding experience
strong bond	...upstanding individual
quiet demeanor	...razor sharp
quite good	...cultivates understanding
host of ...	...true gem
delicate balance	...rallied support
moved forward	...architect of ...
trademark determination	...versatile & ...
solidified position	...rapid increase
improved conditions	...hard ball
life-long commitment	...excellence in ...
abundantly clear	...on-going demand
bar none	...carries clout
imposing enthusiasm	...enormous influence
discovered new ...	...reached zenith
solid reputation	...record setting
great pride	...diverse talent
record speed	...positive action

rekindled spirit(s)	...made transition
magic touch	...catalyst for ...
unstoppable will	...efforts gained
fertile mind	...never quit(s)
high energy	...distinctive presence
personal obligation	...relentless energy
successfully weathered	...catapulted into ...
unstoppable desire	...very competitive
deep respect	...relieved tension
more than ...	...passion for ...
especially difficult	...remained loyal
perfect chemistry	...virtually overnight
reputation for ...	...standard bearer
essential ingredient	...resolved crisis
professional success	...improved outlook
lightening speed	...exceptionally talented
boosted the ...	...resurrected faltering .
hard-earned experience	...retentive mind
meticulously organized	...revolutionary new ...
delicate balance	...prevailed over ...
revolutionized concept	...rich diversity
meticulous uniforms	...valuable addition
expert in/at ...	...sterling performance
bottom line	...rigorous tasking
positive expectations	...roll model
get-tough attitude	...maximum capacity
considerable improvement	...top class
defining moment	...basic superiority
immediate improvement	...gained reputation
properly focused	...self sacrificing
capacity for ...	...introduced new ...
works magic	...hot, new ...
first to ...	...Herculean task

exemplary in ...
explicit agenda
rushed forward

always there
most active
extensive research

highly specialized
rapidly changing ...
complicated task(s)

growing confidence
rarely seen
absolutely finest

professional landscape
worked double-time
widely acknowledged

significant contribution(s)
rational approach
meticulous approach

sizable contribution
abundance of ...
tremendous asset

beyond reproach
critical acclaim
personal sacrifice

smart move
positive influence
record time

soared above
solemn duty
unparalleled ability

defining time
deeper issues
anchored team

...rose above
...upward spiral
...valuable asset

...impressive progress
...set standards
...rapid rise

...vanguard of ...
...rose to ...
...essence of ...

...deflected criticism
...moved ahead
...sheer fortitude

...renowned for ...
...exemplary character
...perfect combination

...volunteered to/for ...
...transformed workplace
...massive scale

...hardworking, limitless .
...skyrocketed to ...
...personal sacrifice

...valuable research
...highly organized
...regal manor

...centerpiece of ...
...unusual dedication
...smooth transition

...soft landing
...admirable talent
...complex problem(s)

...enthusiastic about ...
...spearheaded move
...special talent

fully prepared	…profound effect
spurred progress	…stable foundation
staged comeback	…fully understands
stands above …	…analytical mind
utmost importance	…heavy hitter
stark courage	…fundamental change
personally supervised …	…steadying influence
potential for …	…equally successful
legacy of …	…flawless planner
potential gain	…stands alone
bell weather	…unwavering support
stark reality	…upper hand
power of/to …	…truly cares
solved complex …	…powerful force
motivates others	…clear-cut best
rapid development(s)	…vast improvement
major achievement	…highly resilient
dedicated professionalism	…priceless contribution(s)
steel determination	…valiant efforts …
sterling reputation	…stickler for …
stirs imagination	…recovered from …
sensitive position	…serious agenda
deepest respect	…impressive record
abundant energy/talent	…sharp contrast
ushered in …	…cemented reputation
sharp increase	…positive motivator
excels at …	…positive results
shattered the …	…reached pinnacle
enormous challenge	…strengthened the …
overcomes difficulties	…finest … in …
changing dynamics	…high level
rich tradition	…completely revolutionized
major event(s)	…right direction

especially successful

further developed

meticulous ... skills

undying devotion

future oriented

heavy commitment

shattered records

positive solutions

compelling presence

completely new

most enduring

real professional

perfect match

picture perfect

unbeatable in ...

decisive action

masterful stroke

reconfigured complex ...

uncompromising professionalism

mastery of ...

heavily influenced

under pressure

underlying strength

underscored by ...

undiminished enthusiasm

undisputed leader

significant increase

commands respect

tireless dedication

solid effort

unrestrained vigor

pillar of ...

unshakable commitment

...defining role

...rigorous schedule

...calming influence

...tailor made

...campaigned for/against ..

...personification of ...

...esprit de corps

...strengthened resolve

...ever resourceful

...significant commitment

...physically challenging

...ultimate challenge

...unbeatable combination

...steadfast support

...headline performance

...significantly enhanced ...

...evolved concept

...major impact

...undaunted by ...

...competitive spirit

...single-most important

...matchless enthusiasm

...daunting task

...strong support

...every aspect

...undying determination

...positive steps

...active management

...uniforms always ...

...decided advantage

...unrivaled success

...massive undertaking

...unshakable determination

strategic agenda
actively supports
comparable to ...

very first ...
substantial increase
substantial improvement

intelligent, dynamic leader
rare talent for ...
bell weather performance

found way to ...

accomplishes more than ...
overwhelming support in/as ...

took active stand
always inspection ready
resident expert in ...

stands alone in ...
among select few
most impressive in/as ...

bright future ahead
exemplary performance in ...
active interest in ...

great things happen
grew in importance
closely tied to ...

excited & energized
well spent energy
acutely sensitive to ...

strong force in/as ...
enormous capacity for
commendable faculty for ...

put pressure on ...
genuine affection for ...
burst of energy

...pioneer in ...
...single-minded purpose
...straight-forward approach

...fiercely dedicated
...overcomes obstacles
...virtually all ...

...enormous ability in/as ...
...successful stroke of ...
...long, hard work

...followed through on ...
...acute sense of ...
...passed huge hurdle

...did everything possible
...begins each day
...consistently outstanding at...

...direct influence on ...
...defied conventional logic
...admirable ability to ...

...seized the opportunity
...constantly exploring new ...
...fullest use of ...

...came to forefront
...best interest of ...
...looked very good

...found time to ...
...exceptional managerial skills
...brimming with energy

...commands fullest respect
...rare quality of ...
...exceeded all expectations

...quality work in/on ...
...earned distinction in/as ...
...marked the beginning

well suited to/for ...
exceptional example of ...
profound effect on ...

shaped the future
turning point in ...
absolute superb performance

provided needed spark
very magnitude of ...
channeled energy into ...

buried in work
strong management acumen
admired for achieving...

changed the way ...
became known (for/as) ...
provided much needed ...

among the first
always responds with ...
runs tight ship

insatiable appetite for ...
earned gratitude of ...
consummate ability to ...

groundbreaking work in/as ...
continues to grow
very vocal about ...

exceptional performance in/as ...
strong proponent of ...
contributed immensely to ...

acute sensitivity to/for ...
wholehearted pursuit of ...
important first step

cool under pressure
always there for/to ...
provided key link

...always alert to/for ...
...by sheer will
...unique opportunity to/for ...

...good deal of ...
...exemplary personal conduct
...margin for error

...important part of ...
...enormous talent for ...
...always ready for/to ...

...won hearts of ...
...career filled with ...
...took center stage

...source of unending ...
...important step forward
...uninterrupted record of ...

...personally involved in ...
...much more than ...
...productive member of ...

...consummate standards of ...
...advanced art of ...
...most outstanding at ...

...set the tone/pace
...good eye for ...
...mapped a strategy

...continued superior ... skills
...on solid ground
...resounding success in/as ...

...contributed significantly to...
...wide array of ...
...expertise led to ...

...best organizer in ...
...mover & shaker
...gained upper hand

crisis management situation
uniformly outstanding results
earned high marks

primarily responsible for ...
very symbol of ...
addressed serious issue(s)

giant leap forward
invested in future
radiates ... to subordinates

placed focus on ...
unequaled skills in/as ...
attained new level

major turning point
laid groundwork for ...
over the top

inspires unequaled loyalty
solid, proven leadership
creates climate of ...

fruits of labor
brave new direction
growing sense of ...

poured energy into ...
faced crisis with ...
renewed sense of ...

heavily influenced by ...
played major role
unequaled success in ...

fine line between ...
undying support for ...
secured place in ...

thrives on competition
impressive array of ...
explored ways to ...

...shot of adrenaline
...inner desire to ...
...critical need of ...

...most impressive performance
...phenomenal record in/as ...
...exceptionally strong in

...brimming with confidence
...quantum gain in ..
...constant source of ...

...at forefront of ...
...managed to keep ...
...in top form

...provided impetus for/to ...
...raised the level
...perfect example of ...

...lived up to ...
...highest quality work
...loaded with talent

...loads of talent
...ran headlong into ...
...window of opportunity

...reached new heights
...plain hard work
...at peak of ...

...without help completed ...
...go the distance
...new heights of ...

...bold, imaginative leader
...made due with ...
...unmatched appearance & ...

...impeccable standards of ...
...reflects proudly on ...
...maturity beyond years

refused to accept ...
excellent contributions in ...
took control of ...

overcame serious obstacles
paved the way
breathed new life

all eyes on ...
up & coming
full speed ahead

highest expertise in/as ...
regardless of circumstances ...
wide range of ...

unsurpassed ability to ...
worked harder than ...
bold & imaginative ...

followed in footsteps
spearheaded effort to ...
special gift for ...

valuable source of ...
great ability to ...
faced ... head-on

provided badly needed ...
right person for/to ...
impeccable performance in/as ...

across broad spectrum
pressed into service
filled with determination

recipe for success
unquenchable thirst for ...
stellar track record

invaluable organizer & ...
highest moral courage
positively the best ...

...exceeded bounds of ...
...certain quality to ...
...excels wherever assigned

...did precisely what ...
...rejuvenated team spirit
...invests in long-term

...well known for/as ...
...step ahead of ...
...dramatic change in ...

...inspiration to others
...genuine care of/for ...
...more than ready

...superior performance as/at
...confidence to succeed
...gravity of situation

...pushed forward despite ...
...on frontline of ...
...great personal initiative

...face of adversity
...concentrated efforts on ...
...defining moment in ...

...represents best in ...
...mustered the courage
...called on to ...

...gets job done
...courage of conviction
...ambitious goals always ...

...carried through on ...
...personal contributions led .
...completed grueling task

...great contributor to ...
...among elite group
...difficult first step

especially adept at ...   ...filled with enthusiasm
rare ability to ...   ...big part of ...
finest values of ...   ...well developed understanding

gave birth to ...   ...firm grasp of ...
changed face of ...   ...pressed forward on ...
immaculate personal appearance   ...creates & maintains ...

overcame drawback of ...   ...full plate of ...
makes things happen   ...fit perfectly in ...
perfect balance between ...   ...did very best

actively engaged in ...   ...ready for challenges
reaped big payoff   ...most important role
dramatic improvement in ...   ...first-rate results in/as ...

achieved lofty goals   ...widely admired for/as ...
fit in with ...   ...great knowledge in/of ...
perfect blend of ...   ...all but impossible

very bright at ...   ...gave meaning to ...
worked overtime to ...   ...degree of difficulty
careful not to ...   ...generated interest in ...

came through when ...   ...faced crisis situation
adapted to meet ...   ...opened door for/to ...
considerable talent for ...   ...go-getter who can ...

potentially explosive situation ...set out to ...
expert in field   ...keeps priorities straight
commendable job in/as ...   ...spent countless hours

intuitive instinct for   ...on top of ...
reached full stride   ...ignited spark in ...
caught attention of ...   ...dramatic increase in ...

impressive uniforms & ...   ...set foundation for ...
bold first step   ...healthy appetite for ...
worked hard to/at ...   ...lit spark under

high point in ...   ...ice in veins
came to appreciate   ...active involvement in ...
solid work ethic(s)   ...shed light on ...

delivered first rate ...
faced major task(s)
added life to ...

recognized importance of ...
goes forward despite ...
raised position of ...

on the move
established strong bonds
reached the top

improved quality of ...
in full stride
winning attitude transformed ..

solid gain(s) in ...
intense self discipline
won the day

added new dimension
kept up spirits
reached full potential

served with distinction
set best example
hit full stride

spent long hours ...
healed the wounds
delivered full measure

infused others with ...
fully paid dues
pursued with vigor

made a difference
especially proud of ...
razor-thin margin of ...

power of persuasion
cast the dye
bridged the gap

...generated idea of/to ...
...hit pay dirt
...ideal balance between ...

...fully recovered from ...
...nourishes spirit of teamwork
...hours on end

...in driver's seat
...carried on despite ...
...down to earth

...bold new approach
...praiseworthy work as/on ...
...advanced skills in ...

...knows value of ...
...extraordinary array of ...
...increase in stature

...brings excitement to ...
...goes all out
...in face of ...

...power of insight
...faced serious hurdles
...increasingly driven by ...

...had crucial role
...inexhaustible source of ...
...geared up to/for ...

...recognized need to/for ...
...initiated programs that ...
...number one ... in/at ...

...initiative responsible for ...
...remarkable work in/as ...
...faced staggering odds

...judge of talent
...championed cause of ...
...actively involved in ...

knows no limits	...full measure of ...
created something special	...bold new ideas
power to shape ...	...just the beginning
facilitates competitive spirit	...keeps getting better
solid across-the-board performance	...stepped in & ...
determined passion for ...	...in tandem with ...
gave top priority	...key participant in ...
key to success	...exploits opportunities to ...
against staggering odds	...stands above others
doubled number of ...	...driving force behind ...
reflects credit upon ...	...essential element of/in ...
kindles spirit of ...	...reached bounds of ...
knows how to ...	...brought to fruition
remarkable leadership talent	...obvious passion for ...
infused (organization) with ...	...prepared to take ...
won approval of ...	...labor of love
laid foundation to/for ...	...rapidly evolving situation
carried out demanding ...	...acute management acumen
fueled the growth	...head held high
knows no bounds	...worked hard at/to ...
brutally demanding task	...full-time crusader for ...
lion's share of ...	...broad range of ...
made a difference	...sent clear signal
lit fire under ...	...pursued variety of ...
firmly in control	...made mark in/as ...
developed method to ...	...gave stability to ...
made measurable improvement	...lifted the spirits
fully engaged in ...	...ahead of schedule
fantastic sense of ...	...far & away
spread like wildfire	...keen understanding of ...
essential part of ...	...marshaled the troops
extremely well organized	...winning combination of ...
most difficult tasking	...sheer weight of ...

in position to ...	...distinguished self by/in ...
mastered way(s) to ...	...established ... system that ...
navigated troubled waters	...gained attention of ...
substantial number of ...	...brings out best
hand picked to ...	...hardworking with limitless ...
developed roadmap to/for ...	...gave rise to ...
carried the day	...none better at ...
pursued new course	...shining example of ...
played crucial role	...brought life to ...
plunged headlong into...	...obvious talent for ...
In rapid succession	...masterful accomplishment of
of particular importance	...at height of ...
made presence felt	...lifted heavy weight
with great clarity	...devotion to duty
only one who ...	...opened new door(s)
worth more than ...	...has eye on ...
distinguished record as/in ...	...called into play
set standard(s) for ...	...good reflection on ...
well schooled in ...	...exceptional work in/as ...
took advantage of ...	...beehive of activity
consistently high standards	...valued member of ...
dominates field of ...	...highly proficient as/in ...
skilled technical specialist	...keen knowledge of ...
stood up against	...better than ever
great eye for ...	...beyond the ordinary
big impact on ...	...on way up
driving force in ...	...won confidence of ...
valuable asset to ...	...stronger than expected ...
dynamic leader who ...	...inspired bold new ...
positive mental attitude	...earned absolute confidence
took a stand	...earned deepest respect
much needed progress	...adds new dimension
brightens spirits of ...	...total winning attitude

...overcomes all obstacles
...passionate belief in ...
...more versatile than ...

...superior conduct & ..
...rescued a slumping/faltering ...
...frenzy of activity

stands far above ...
...variety of ways
...earned enviable record

...succession of accomplishments
...motivating force in ...
...overwhelming support of

...highly regarded for/as ...
...particularly strong in/at ...
...very model of ...

...single-handedly accomplished ...
...logical & direct
changed dynamics of ...

...loyal & devoted
...great sense of ...
...restored trust in ...

...contributed much to ...
...embodies concept of ...
...earned respect of ...

...defied all expectations
...strong, dependable leadership
...educated others in ...

...strong sense of ...
...accomplishments far exceed ...
...the heart of ...

...emerged from ... with
...keen appreciation for ...
...always highest demeanor

...more to come
...earned chance to ...
...always willing to ...

...earned place in ...
...long term solution
...earned reputation for ...

...character without question...
...instant decision-making ability
...chipped away at ...

...protective measures included
...deeply involved in ...
...great source of ...

...keen eye for ...
...clear vision of ...
...clearly the best

...on brink of ...
...great proving ground
...especially good in/at ...

...connects with people
...rose to challenge
...situation compounded by ...

...accepted the challenge
...positive impact on ...
...very heart of ...

...earned special trust
...measure of success
...cleared major hurdle

...changed future of ...
...considerable amount of ...
...embodiment of personal ...

...highly sought after
...tireless crusader for ...
...equal to any ...

played pivotal roll

achieved complete success

ever more challenging

very active in ...

rich knowledge in/of

great instinct for ...

fresh new talent

ever-increasing reputation to/for ...

amazing accomplishments include

so valuable that ...

outstanding accomplishment in

close to impossible

without a doubt

brings people together

gained new prominence

carried the torch

closely involved in/with ...

efforts contributed to ...

world of knowledge

without equal as/in ...

keen desire for/to ...

enthusiasm never falters

proved to be ...

stood out from ...

has feel for ...

tested the water(s)

in the trenches

level playing field

extraordinary contributions to ...

proven top performer

without peer in ...

singled out as/for ...

prudent use of ...

...opened way to/for ...

...can do spirit

...stood up for ...

...represents essence of ...

...out front in ...

...long term increase

...on threshold of ...

...set sights on ...

...good sense of ...

...first person to ...

...masterful use of ...

...made good on ...

...outshines others in ...

...in spite of ...

...new page in ...

...personal hand in ....

...opportunity to shine

...strong bond established

...matchless talent for ...

...thirst for knowledge

...rarely observed talent

...personally improved the

...matchless ability to ...

...air tight plan

...at heart of ...

...simply has fun

...major step forward

...alert, farsighted leader

...extremely adept at ...

...total quality performance

...firmly established as ...

...matter of principal

...natural ability to ...

has skills to ...
gained reputation for ...
pushed limits of ...

brought ... to life
work ethic(s) above ...
has power of/to ...

leads way in ...
at ease in/with ...
leaned over backward

articulate in all ...
never ceases to ...
battled number of ...

terrific progress in/on ...
risked everything to ...
saved the day

astounding degree of ...
covered in detail
sensational ability to ...

sense of accomplishment
meaningful contribution to/in ...
shouldered heavy responsibility

.extensive expertise in ...
.sense of purpose
.tried everything to ...

.two thumbs up
.signaled beginning of ...
.cut teeth on ...

.stirs the spirit
.unflagging support of ...
.soared to new ...

.leads others to ...
.sterling performance as/in ...
.stirred imagination of ...

...rekindled teamwork spirit
...new level of ...
...conscious effort to ...

...repaired damage to ...
...pushed the envelope
...natural aptitude for ...

...relentless drive inspirationa
...brought ... to forefront
...endured demands of ...

...first time ever ...
...garnered attention of ...
...understands value of ...

...scratched the surface
...ascended to top
...led the way

...energized & led ...
...relentless pursuit of ...
...work centered on ...

...carried weight of ...
...high octane performance
...showcased skills by/in ...

...personal agenda included .
...showed the way
...larger than life

...unbeatable ability to ...
...never gave up
...battery of tests

...remarkable ability to ...
...laudable conduct &
...natural gift for ...

...attention turned to ...
...extensive knowledge of ...
...heavily involved in ...

strength to conquer ...
cream of crop
learned valuable lesson

tackled ... head on
carved out new ...
talent to lead

surprising show of ...
unflappable in backing ...
created atmosphere of ...

high energy style
won support of/for ...
meticulously accurate in ....

.engenders trust & ...
.heavy dose of ...
.topnotch results in/as ...

.level above peers
.worthy of respect
.transformed structure of ...

.sense of urgency
.performance underscored by ...
.tried & true

.unblemished record as/in ...
.more productive than ...
.totally impressive as ...

.uncanny sense of ...
.won right to ...
.backed effort(s) to

.took lead in ...
.secured loyalty of ...
.left mark on ...

..urgent demand for ...
..shining moment in ...
..culmination of efforts

...left legacy of ...
...never-ending desire to ...
...succeeded in building ...

...meticulous military appearance
...performed admirably in/as ...
...model of today's ...

...based on trust
...enjoys excitement in/of ...
...take charge person

...thoroughly meticulous at/as ...
...natural knack for ...
...lead role in ...

...enjoyed responsibilities of ...
...top shelf organizer
...string of successes

...total inspiration to ...
...new generation of ...
...tremendous amount of ...

...tremendous effort & ...
...at center of ...
...high degree of ...

...top-rate planner & ...
...surpassed all expectations
...critical turning point

...understands art of ...
...zoomed past contemporaries
...banner performance in/as ...

...cutting edge of ...
...at apex of ...
...upstanding individual with

...ushered in new ...
...veracious appetite for ...
...more than expected

superior talent for ...

new breed of ...

crucial role in/as ...

waged winning battle

weathered the storm

triggered move to ...

new concept of ...

tight line between ...

achieved great success

gets excited about ...

very essence of ...

set record for ...

focused considerable talent

raised level of ...

nothing short of ...

bright beacon of ...

fought way though ...

real problem solver

spends free time ...

front runner in ...

across the board

course of action

real professional, always ...

common sense approach

great deal of ...

recognized as most/best ...

possesses skills to/that ...

fundamental principles of ...

especially effective as ...

tremendous individual drive

appearance above reproach

truly great at ...

well-earned reputation as/for ...

...took decisive action

...laudable efforts in/as ...

...true love for ...

...wave of praise

...welcomed the challenge

...stroke of genius

...attributes needed to ...

...special talent for ...

...flawless execution of ...

...flurry of activity

...focused attention on ...

...good things happen

...forged an impressive ...

...pushed bounds of ...

...experienced & dedicated

...on fast track

...great idea person

...long history of ...

...fresh, invigorating ideas

...came to fruition

...big step forward

...stayed the course

...forged link between ...

...absolute top performer

...highest moral integrity

...splendid performance as

...ray of hope

...will not tolerate ...

...overcame all obstacles

...performance regularly exceeds

...captured essence of ...

...vote of confidence

...pointed the way

solves complex problems	...addressed concerns of ...
valiant effort to ...	...innovative & progressive
went the distance	...took the initiative
deep commitment to ...	...started from scratch
mounted an aggressive ...	...deepest respect for ...
answered the call	...captured spirit of ...
back on track	...appearance level above ..
turned adversity into ...	...innate leadership capacity
broke new ground	...integral part of ...
took full advantage	...build up of ...
vital role in/as ...	...applauded for actions
position of authority	...ardent supporter of ...
excites imagination of ...	...source of inspiration
around the clock	...exciting new talent
superb facility for ...	...turned bleak situation
deeply cares for/about ...	...strong moral principles
captured attention of ...	...beat the odds
vast experience enhanced by ...	...became basis for ...
particularly strong expertise	...moved quickly to ...
profound improvement in ...	...superior ability to ...
decided to tackle	...benchmark of excellence
whirlwind of activity	...sharp eye for ...
good chance of/to ...	...well thought out
exemplary record as ...	...stands for something
acutely aware of ...	...strong moral fiber
captured the imagination	...daily work ethics
turned the tide	...vital part of/in ...
built organization that ...	...much more complex
superb contributions in ...	...deeply committed to ...
exceptionally skilled in/at ...	...became a standard
above & beyond	...built a winning ...
loves the work	...found new energy
valiant individual effort	...built strong foundation

universally acknowledged as/for ...   ...well versed in
ground-breaking performance in/as ...

discovered new way to ...
impeccable performance in/as ...
work habits valuable asset to ...

spirit of cooperation is/has ...
does more with less
pulled out all the stops

thorough & meticulous in detail
does things better than ...
more than able to ...

tested the limits of ...
attacks problems head on
set the stage for ...

charismatic & decisive leader
expert in field of ...
met challenge(s) head on

exceptionally talented as a ...
ahead of the times
creativity virtually inexhaustible

rose to the occasion
superior ability to inspire others
impressively managed & led ...

far exceeds peers in ...
solved the puzzle of ...
addressed challenges head on

took on heavy responsibilities
made most of opportunities
quality of work outshines ...

burst of creative energy
lasting measure of success
across the board increase

takes the time to ...
immediate turn around
mentally alert with gift for ...

...command mission always first
...took ... in full stride
...drew on vast experience

...restless for a challenge
...comes to work each day with .
...for years to come

...body of work exceeds
...air of self confidence
...driven by desire to ...

...high profile approach to ...
...extremely well versed in ...
...faced problems head on

...faced the challenge head-on
...achieved level of excellence
...plans for the future

...pulled the plug on ...
...rarely observed ability to ...
...made easy work of ...

...continues to soar above ...
...top of the heap
...stands alone in field of ...

...made a statement by ...
...personal sacrifice led to ...
...passed on tradition of ...

...brings added dimension to ...
...worked way up to become ...
...never-ending desire to ...

...capable of performing above .
...took full advantage of ...
...need for personal challenge

...praised for work in/as ...
...never-ending capacity to/for
...added new dimension to ...

new point of view

went the extra mile to ...

came a long way

far ahead of peer group in ...

direction of team effort led to ...

breath of fresh air

moved with due caution

solid move in right direction

made name for self

active in development of ...

decisive leadership led to ...

one of the first to ...

did not yield in face of ...

came up very big

made lasting mark on ...

strong ... during entire tour

improvements in ... due to...

highly respected for ability to ...

skilled eye, trained hand

did the right thing

breathed new life into ...

superb watch team leader

mastered number of skills

sign of things to come

highly energetic person who ...

expedient in discharging ...

left ... a better place

broad range of successes

devotion to duty & ...

first order of business

no one does better job of ...

on front line of/for ...

proper course of action

...struck at heart of ...

...likes to be challenged

...nipped ... in the bud

...stood tall in face of ...

...opened door to a new

...great source of knowledge

...pays close attention to ...

...peerless in areas of ...

...shot in the arm

...rapid, intense worker

...mastered wide array of ...

...strong moral character/fiber

...every vital aspect of ...

...tested as never before

...went to work on ...

...made quick work of ...

...possesses great deal of energy

...put great energy into ...

...unbound initiative & ability to ...

...always treats others with ...

...put to the test

...demands nothing short of ...

...quick to take lead in/when ...

...rose to the top

...brings ... to the table

...quality of work far exceeds ...

...fired up imagination of ...

...unusually thorough & accurate

...commands respect for best ...

...thrives in atmosphere of ...

...sheer weight of presence

...fine tuned process of ...

...set excellence standards for...

earned high praise for ...

a plus to morale

most productive person in/at ...

had to deal with ...

picked up the pace

works twice as hard

hard work paid off

stepped in and filled ...

erased any trace of ...

achieved superb results in/on ...

took ... to next level

far and away better than ...

fairness & respect cornerstone of ...

idea person of some persuasion

stellar performance resulted in ...

prolific worker with unbound ...

for the first time

got ... off the ground

astute use of resources led to ...

led technical team in ...

always a top priority

took active part in ...

individual spark of creativity

much needed shot in the arm

presence of mind to ...

never lost sight of ...

set standards for ... qualification

personal commitment led to ...

in touch with reality

brought out the best

inexhaustible drive & initiative

sets standards of excellence in ...

got off on right foot

...first-rate, always gives ...

...works extremely well with ...

...set the pattern for ...

...first person to qualify for ...

...had to fight for ...

...changed the face of ...

...matches individual talent to job

...brought new sophistication to

...has great advantage of ...

...leaves nothing to chance

...cream of crop in area of ...

...step in right direction

...decision maker, plans always ...

...qualified ... in less than (...time)

...reversed the tide of ...

...contributes full measure to ...

...sound initiatives led to ...

...most impressive record of ...

...exceptionally well versed in ...

...ignited the spirits of ...

...hard charger with ability to ...

...played major role in ...

...brings ... to the job ...

...in face of adversity

...tremendous effort & results

...filled a void in ...

...heart & soul of ...

...shifted into high gear

...could not be stopped

...equal to the task

...always a step ahead of ...

...elicits very best from others

...most effective at promoting ...

at core of the action
creative leadership resulted in ...
elevated ... to new level

rare treat to see ...
head of the class
took the lead in ...

on the bright side ...
worked around the clock
worked in partnership with ...

truly cares for all shipmates
right place, right time
likes to be first

meaningful contribution to/in ...
energetic, never fails to ...
brings out the best in ...

jumped at the opportunity
positive motivator of others
extended period of time

knew exactly what to do
in the thick of the action
rose to the challenge

creative talent led to ...
stands in upper tier
on way to the top

inspires mutual respect of ...
gets most out of ...
always on top of ...

knows ... forward & backward
personal initiative without equal
worked very hard for/to ...

held in high esteem
challenged to step up and ...
quality of work truly impressive

...exceptionally skilled in/at ...
...day in & day out
...quick to praise others for ...

...trained at every level
...right tools for the job
...no detail too small

...a ray of sunshine
...gets down to business
...from the ground up

...never takes eye off ...
...steadfast in requirement to ..
...insight in ... led to ...

...quick mind & tireless energy
...conducted in-depth research
...kept sharp eye on ...

...knack for directing team ...
...builds on team spirit
...ensures highest degree of ...

...held door open for/to ...
...got the ball rolling
...more than made up for ...

...no challenge too difficult
...lived up to expectations
...took every measure to ...

...fantastic sense of planning ..
...kept attention focused on ...
...exceptional initiative & drive

...played serious role in ...
...laid the groundwork for ...
...across a broad spectrum

...knowledge of ... resulted in ..
...launched one of the ...
...immediate & decisive action

threw caution to the wind	...never runs out of ...
committed to principles of ...	...serious effort in area of ...
set standards of excellence in ...	...came to the rescue
expertise rarely observed in...	...searches for new ways to ...
put into place a ...	...wide range of innovative ideas
deserves more credit for ...	...shined in face of ...
gifted with ability to ...	...makes special point to ...
unrivaled in ability to ...	...surged to the front
thrives on new challenges	...stands above peers in ...
up to the task	...wasted no time in ...
respected for ability to ...	...turns ideas into reality
forever changed face of ...	...giant step forward
wide repertoire of talents	...inspiring leader/supervisor
unfailing devotion to duty	...served as a model
willing to work hard	...forever on lookout for ...
.responded in kind with ...	...always counted on to ...
.nothing short of astounding	...on a grand scale
.up to the challenge	...places high value on ...
.force to be reckoned with	...sets & reaches highest goals
.makes good things happen	...tough nut to crack
.real talent to succeed	...forged an iron spirit
.a breath of fresh air	...with back to the wall
.without equal in ability to ...	...unending desire & ability to ...
.time & time again	...top of the line
.more talent, more results	...articulate in ability to ...
.places great emphasis on ...	...frequently works extra hours
.sets outstanding example for ...	...sheer force of will
.places high premium on ...	...no question about it
.on cutting edge of ...	...a new wave of ...
.works long, hard days	...set to work on ...
.disciplined mind with ability to ...	...places mission ahead of ...
.brought a full measure of ...	...installed ... program that ...
.disciplined mind, expert in ...	...wave of the future

leads by example--a pace setter
made significant contribution to ...
highest achiever in field/area of ...

admired for staunch support of ...
maintained perfect balance of ...
gift for getting along with others

remarkable talent for leading ...
leads with uncommon expertise
ace technician with rare ability to ...

high respected for ability to ...
superior knowledge of specialty
particularly strong expertise in ...

innovative plan led to increased ...
places highest emphasis on team ...
always achieves command goals

knowledge of specialty impressive
self starter, with desire for challenge
instituted many procedures that ...

developed new procedures in ...
knowledge ... led to/resulted in ...
self-starter, works extremely in/as ...

innovative approach to ... led to ...
fact-gathering process led to ...
in top professional form when ...

person of action, dynamic leader
personifies leadership by example
.admirable talent for completing ...

.instills sense of unity & pride in ...
.solves most difficult problems with ...
.winning attitude transformed ...

.highest standards of excellence
.fosters high team effort & unity
.innovative, attuned to changes in ...

completed major upgrade in ...
model of performance in/at ...
found new prescription for ...

beyond reproach demeanor & ...
standard-bearer for ability to ...
highly motivated & involved in ...

courageous leader evidenced in/by ...
faultless planning & execution of ...
rare ability to create & maintain ...

made measurable improvement in ...
asks for & completes toughest jobs
superb working knowledge of/in ...

devised technical system to/on ...
performance regularly exceeds ...
unparalleled appearance & bearing

astonishing work record includes ...
superb technical background in ...
courageous effort resulted in ...

impressive leader & organizer
quality of work far superior to ...
provides innovative solutions to ...

accomplished specialist in/as ...
meets or exceeds all deadlines
brought excitement back into ...

attained remarkable results in/on ...
bold leadership responsible for ...
loyal & dedicated to all members of ...

performs tasks with accuracy & dispatch
high standards for own work & that of others
excellent contributions to command...

always finds time to help shipmates
completed (rating/specialty) requirements in (time)
best knowledge of (rating/specialty) in recent memory

highly talented with excellent working knowledge of/in ...
maintained equipment reliability at amazing ...
personally increased operational readiness by ...

dynamic leader, thrives on new challenges
attains quality results at any tasking level
commands, receives highest standards from ...

best trained & most knowledgeable ...
consistently above expected norm in ...
able to accommodate & correlate large number of details

dynamic leadership/supervision inspires ...
economy of effort & vision of future evidenced on daily basis
hard charger with faultless planning in/of ...

consistent top performer in/as (rating/specialty)
personally immersed in programs that promote ...
established superb ... PQS package for ...

completes all work successfully & ahead of time
earned abiding loyalty of others through full enforcement of ...
dedicated professionalism highlights ...

attentive to detail in completing most difficult tasking
maximum economy of funds, optimum use of materials
demands & receives full day's work, morale never higher

absolutely no tolerance for violations of ...
.performance underscored by pride & ...
.exceptionally skilled & motivated to ...

.completes ambitious work schedule day in, day out
.able to research & plan ... because of in-depth knowledge in/of
.each work day productive, with quality ...

.dedicated many off-duty hours to ...
.completes large volume of work each day
.maximizes strengths of subordinates by ...

accomplished ... in superior fashion
led watch team to (score) during (event)
excellent problem-solving facilities

limitless ability to complete most difficult tasking
developed up-to-date operating procedures in area of ...
cornerstone of technical knowledge

inspection-ready uniforms worn on daily basis
juniors frequently seek advise on personal & professional matters
subordinates, best trained, most productive in ...

experience & technical knowledge highly valued by superiors
leadership highlighted by compassionate, intelligent treatment
more thorough in use of resources than peers

proven ability to attain high standards of performance
demonstrated expertise completing ...
fantastic job of setting & achieving goals

superior knowledge of ... led to ...
outstanding success as group leader
fits each subordinate with challenging assignments

developed up-to-date technical standards for ...
embodies qualities most sought in leaders
all-around superior technical knowledge led to ...

fosters exceptionally high morale within ...
generates enthusiasm in juniors to do top notch work
excellent working relationship with ...

puts in extra hours assisting shipmates
most proficient & knowledgeable ... in (organization)
never loses enthusiasm or desire to help others

organized extensive update of ... in/for ...
noteworthy ability to interact with persons of all backgrounds
demonstrated professional excellence by/in ...

encourages trust through genuine interest in subordinates
gets results regardless of complexity of effort required
continually seeks toughest jobs, enjoys challenge

organized monumental task of ...
proponent of leadership by example
more successful with each challenge

unusually perceptive troubleshooting skills in ...
volunteers for most complex tasks, outstanding results
takes personal satisfaction completing tasks/projects early

character & appearance without equal in ...
superior knowledge & performance in ...
superior technical knowledge allowed ...

watch team effectiveness graded (...) at ...
exceptional personal example of ...
surpasses high standards of...

tackled aggressive agenda with ...
sincere interest in professional development of shipmates
always quick to respond to emergencies with ...

tackles most demanding tasks with great success
unblemished safety record despite ...
selectively assigned most demanding tasks

stands alone in sheer technical excellence in/on ...
tact & compassion cornerstones of ...
proven leader capable of inspiring & motivating juniors

remarkable ability to plan & manage diverse projects
strongest personal commitment enforcing equal opportunity
proven top performer for quality of work

inspirational leadership, superb counselor
master at achieving results with limited resources
highly cooperative, always lends helping hand

sets high goals, expects no less from subordinates
personally sees each person receives ...
only person onboard to qualify .. in (time)

consistently outstanding results in ...
exemplifies Navy spirit, pride & commitment
fair & equitable treatment cornerstone to/of ...

actively encourages average performers to new heights
excellent record-keeping abilities
unique ability to overcome obstacles in/as ...

great personal contribution to team effort
performance regularly exceeds all requirements
repeatedly earned highest praise for knowledge in/of ...

gets along extremely well with others
enforces strict compliance with/in
overcomes problems of all complexity & magnitude

recruit poster quality appearance
personal involvement guarantees success
actively encourages others to assume additional tasks

personal knowledge led to planned & coordinated ...
contributes measurably to overall performance of ...
cornerstone of expertise in (rating/specialty)

highly competent in all technical aspects of specialty
excellent use of available resources
polished manner sets outstanding example of a leader

inspires fullest cooperation & support of subordinates
most experienced & talented ...
positive attitude generates enthusiasm among ...

exemplary conduct & military appearance
master at providing direction & leadership
knowledge & industrious with knack for getting job done correctly

possesses great initiative & imagination
unequaled record of safety & accomplishment
implemented operational phase of technical ...

great personal commitment to dignity & worth of each individual
ready wit & pleasing personality enhances ...
advice in/on ... actively sought by peers

engenders spirit of cooperation throughout ...
unique ability to facilitate cooperative effort of others
juniors give their all in crisis situations

fully understands complex problems associated with ...
most efficient & effective ... at/in ...
promotes highest level of human equality

strong leadership & management acumen
master at use of available resources
strong leadership abilities resulted in ...

approaches major & menial tasks with enthusiasm
facilitates understanding among ...
strong sense of dedication, moral obligation

knowledge of ... increased operational readiness of...
highly accomplished leader & counselor
upgraded operational capability of ...

consistently superior performer in/as ...
quality & quantity of work without peer
fosters increased professionalism throughout ranks

actively seeks out & eliminates bias of any kind
imparts high level of pride & motivation to ...
great personal initiative results in ...

aggressively follows through on/in ...
executed particularly demanding task(s) of ...
readiness to accept added responsibility without equal

possesses more knowledge of/in (rating/specialty) than ...
well earned reputation for openly enforcing human equality
quick to commend others for effort, personal accomplishment

knowledge to analyze all facts & solve problems
constantly contributes to unit effectiveness by ...
quickly gets to crux of any problem

radiates team spirit & cooperation
masterful ability to lead & develop ...
rallied individuals together to form superb watch team

unending willingness to assist others in any capacity
rare blend of personal candor & professional judgment
knowledgeable in ... with great foresight

rare creative spark of leadership
ability to elicit best work from subordinates
enjoys complete confidence of ...

widely read with retentive memory especially in ...
quick to take lead solving technical problems in ...
continually volunteers to assume additional responsibility

excels without direct supervision in ...
respected by peers for knowledge of/in ...
gives maximum effort, achieves maximum results

grasps facts & situations quickly
hand-picked for ... due to superior knowledge in/of ...
merits complete trust & confidence of ...

dignified & diplomatic approach to ...
exhibits superior initiative & resourcefulness
real knack for getting job done ahead of time
expertise far beyond peer group

managerial & leadership skills of highest caliber
always ahead of peers when it comes to ...
genial, cooperative, real morale booster

always alert for ways to improve procedures & raise efficiency
highly respected by subordinates & superiors for ...
personally rejuvenated ... program that ...

markedly improved ... because of strong technical background
led (organization) to superb grade of ... on ...
highly respected (rating/specialty) because of ability to ...

personally reviewed & rewrote ... qualifications/standards
individual drive motivating & refreshing
determined & tireless worker with top quality results

focuses effort & energy on team performance
possesses tremendous initiative & resourcefulness
quality of work always exceeds ...

ground-breaking performance in/as ...
completes work to perfection in/as ...
excellent leader & manager of personnel time & equipment

commitment to ... unequaled demonstrated by ...
attains high standards of performance in/as ...
originated incomparable technical standards for ...

earned respect for courage & demeanor in/by ...
morale & esprit de corps especially high
decisions & efforts contributed markedly to team ...

earned respect for strict enforcement of ...
highest personal honor, integrity
outstanding accomplishment(s) in ...

matchless thirst for knowledge in ...
exceptionally qualified in area of ...
great contribution to unit morale in/by ...

tireless worker, completes tasks ahead of time
highest caliber performance & work quality
strengthens morale by cultivating sense of pride in work

exceptionally performance in/as ...
strong commitment to developing subordinates, gets results
technical expertise measurably improved effectiveness of ...

always focused on command objectives, results ...
strong leader, instills ... in subordinates
charming personality, impeccable appearance

exceptionally well developed ability to fix ...
always one step ahead of potential problems
strong advocate of individual & human rights

knowledge of/in ... led to noted improvements in/on ...
enjoys my complete trust & confidence as ...
asks for most demanding assignments no matter how difficult

take-charge individual, not content until all tasks completed
streamlined operational effectiveness of ...
ensures each individual afforded full dignity & rights

volunteers for any & all assignments with great success
attacks & completes toughest jobs with zeal & determination
mission accomplishment always first

possesses unlimited knowledge in/on ...
ground-breaking results by completing ...
qualified ... in (time), mostly off-duty hours

accomplished most demanding tasks
highly accurate, enthusiastically completes ...
upholds highest traditions of courage & honor

transfers goals & objectives into concrete, workable plans
conscientious with excellent understanding of ...
developed & executed extensive program to/that ...

earned my complete confidence as technical ...
improved morale dramatically in/by ...
great foresight & ability to use resources wisely

excellent leadership principles led to ...
improves attitude & performance of all hands by ...
promotes high morale & team spirit

confident of abilities, works exceptionally well in/on ...
thoroughly familiar with all phases of ...
especially adept at technical aspects of/in ...

ingrained respect for shipmates helps ...
always contributes to team effort in/by ...
thrives on pressures of immediacy & responds resourcefully

team person, highly cooperative with others
continuing source of innovative ideas
runs taut watch team, highest morale

stimulates enthusiasm & positive action of others
infuses juniors with own enthusiasm & dedication
produces top quality results in hectic work environment

works does not require correction
infectious enthusiasm quickly spreads to others
knowledge of immense significance in ...

standards of integrity of highest quality
uncompromising principles for quality of work
enjoys fast-paced environment, excels in ...

stays ahead of peers in (rating/specialty) by ...
contributed significantly to (organization) ...
stays on top of ..., reads professional books in spare time

extremely helpful & attentive to needs of ...
great honor & courage of conviction
technical know-how to plan & complete ambitious workload

initiated growth & development of ...
provides leadership to realize full subordinate potential
initiated operational procedures that ...

team player, places great emphasis on ...
masterful use of personnel & equipment
real, rare talent for directing & counseling juniors

informed & well read in all areas of ...
professional manager & leader, understands delegation
totally dedicated to mission accomplishment

leadership, tact inspires respect & devotion
great initiative & keen logic in seeking solutions to ...
calm & composed, correct decisions in most demanding ...

best experienced & most knowledgeable ...
provided expert technical advise to ...
creative thinking & innovative problem solving abilities

thrives on completing difficult tasks
original thinker, never caught short
person to see when faced with difficult problems

uses authority to accomplish tasks in most successful manner
diplomatic approach to ... results in ...
great pride in maintaining high standards of personal ...

outstanding technical knowledge in ...
patient, understanding nature helps ...
suggestions on ... incorporated at ... level

received outstanding in/at (rating/specialty) inspection/drill
secured immediate support of ...
demands & receives only the best of subordinates

flawless, dignified in appearance
key person to see in technical matters of ...
intelligent, compassionate treatment of others

outshines others in sheer ability to ...
executed ... with high degree of skill
selected & served with distinction in/as ...

personable, highly respected leader
thirst for knowledge, desire for challenge
outstanding support & cooperation

secures cooperation of others easily
thinks through problems & acts decisively
puts forth maximum effort on daily basis

masterful accomplishment of ...
knowledgeable, original thinker, offers innovative ideas in/on .
elicits maximum effort from juniors

successfully draws on abilities & strengths of others
leadership effectiveness set new standards in/for ...
directly responsible for superior ...

flawless knowledge of/in ... led to ...
leadership skill to superbly organize forces & plan events
real motivator, highly respected leader

accomplishments as ... especially noteworthy
routinely works extra hours to ...
wears uniform with great pride

ambitious & energetic, dislikes idle hands or mind
selected as ... because of superior knowledge of/in ...
updated technical aspects of ...

attacks each task with zeal & enthusiasm
technical knowledge & competence rarely observed in/within
working knowledge in (rating/specialty) far superior to peers

shining example of proper dress & grooming
singularly outstanding performance
high state of operational & material readiness due to ...

sought by others when problems arise in/with ...
maintained errorless records for/on ...
always seeks additional responsibility

exceptional planner & organizer
unending urge & ability to succeed
extremely well organized, mission oriented

significant improvement in ... due to ...
always has innovative solutions to ...
highest caliber performance in ... demonstrated by/in ...

.unparalleled reputation for knowledge in/of (rating/specialty)
.especially efficient & effective in/as ...
.untiring, thrives on tough challenges

.skillful leader with proven ability to ...
.measurably improved quality & performance of ...
.at top of peer group in (rating/specialty)

.highest degree of loyalty & cooperation from ...
.unusually knowledgeable & effective as/in (rating/specialty)
.exceptional results in all tasks

.work quality significantly contributed to ...
.sets the standard in (organization) for technical expertise
.thinks through complex problems

maintained extraordinary high morale during ...
working knowledge of/in (rating/specialty) simply outstanding
vast experience enhanced by ...

measurably improved reliability of ...
unusually accurate & effective in ...
very talented & knowledgeable in area of (rating/specialty)

exceptional soundness of judgment
highest level of personal conduct
virtually unlimited potential as a/an ...

skillful leader, inspires others to ...
successful in correlating various jobs into overall ...
maintained ... percent reliability in/on ...

consistently instills high performance in ...
outstanding at ... personnel inspections
maintains superior rapport at all levels

fosters cooperation & harmony among all ethnic groups
generates spirit of teamwork throughout ...
very knowledgeable & efficient in ...

unusual insight in ... responsible for ...
excellent in execution of command objectives
made significant technical contributions in/to ...

adds more to job than expected, completed(s) ...
generates superb spirit of harmony & cooperation
provides unified purpose & sense of direction

makes quality independent decisions
makes special effort to ensure (organization) cohesiveness
markedly improved operation of ...

spiritual force & moral fiber necessary of quality Naval leader
volunteered for demanding job of/as ...
always plans ahead, never caught short

establishes climate that makes juniors want to give best effort
thinks of new ways to improve team effectiveness
unswerving devotion to principles of human dignity

maintains high degree of readiness in ...

applies innovative solutions to difficult problems in ...
clear cut goals, acts with initiative & purpose

most effective at getting all subordinates can give
every operational commitment met or exceeded
maximum effort & results in directing efforts of ...

volunteers to tackle any assignment, meets with great success
highest personal commitment to ...demonstrated by ...

exceptionally strong knowledge in/of ... resulted in ...

special talent for developing team ...

appointed to ... qualification board because of expertise in...
maximum efficiency, minimum waste of time

technical knowledge in .. far exceeds ...
maintains highly accurate, up-to-date records in ...
excellent combination of tact & direct supervision

TOP PERFORMERS
(5.0.4.0)

BULLETS

PERSONAL TRAITS

...Fully capable of meeting new situations head-on and applying (himself/herself) in a highly resourceful manner.

...Highly cooperative, always willing to help, invariably a leader in conference or group discussion.

...Physically fit, possesses stamina to carry on in demanding situations.

...Possesses every basic attribute to excel.   Capable and dedicated, achieves uniformly outstanding results.

...A continuing source of innovative ideas and positive contributions.

...Meticulously accurate with high sense of personal responsibility for quality of work.

...Capable, competent, and well versed in the mechanics of duties.

...Erect in posture, wears uniform with great pride.

...Wins acceptance of ideas through understanding and good two-way communications.

...Completes tasks on time and successfully, does not sacrifice quality for quantity.

...Drive, professionalism, and personal integrity have repeatedly earned highest praise from all quarters.

...Takes exceptional pride in personal image, wears immaculate, inspection-ready uniform on daily basis.

...Patience, understanding nature, and ability to delve into the heart of a problem have earned great respect and rapport among subordinates.

...Analytical, decision-making ability, and adaptability to changing situations make (him/her) competent in any situation.

...Contributes full measure to any task, willingly accepts added responsibility.

...Work habits merit trust and confidence of others.

...An active listener, gets involved, grasps facts, feelings, and attitudes of others.

...Thoughts and actions spur results.

...Possessed with an unending urge—and ability—to achieve.

...Relentless and energetic drive is inspirational.

...Exhibits initiative and resourcefulness in solving problems. Does not rely on outside advice or guidance.

...Employs personalized approach in dealing with subordinates.

...Understands worth and dignity of each individual, successfully pursues a "follow me" leadership role.

...Mission effectiveness is enhanced by state of training and material readiness of organization.

...Thoroughly familiar with all phases of work and makes good use of this knowledge and experience whenever presented with problem or task.

...Motivated, concerned, and involved. Eager and interested in every facet of job.

...Demonstrates boldness, couples with grasp of practicality, in attacking all responsibilities.

...Has total commitment to Navy and support of seniors and command objectives.

...Sound in judgement, eager, willing to accept added duties and authority.

...Positive, constructive, and creative in outlook. Plans ahead with great foresight.

...Adds more to job than expected, put duties, responsibilities, and desires of others ahead of own interests.

...Has stamina to tackle most difficult assignments, and the judgement and ability to obtain quality results.

...Devoted to duty and willing to perform above what is expected.

...Unswerving devotion to principles of equal opportunity.

...Highest personal honor, integrity, and intellectual capacity.

...Continually alert for ways and means to increase personal knowledge and professional growth.

...Dedicated, knowledgeable, and reliable in execution of all responsibilities.

...Works full day on assigned duties and then puts in extra hours assisting shipmates.

...Unflappable in backing chain of command goals and objectives, routinely gives shot in the arm to new projects.

...Response in stress situations always favorable and demonstrates potential for high operational visibility jobs.

...Calm and affable nature are valuable assets in daily activities.

...Displays a relentless and energetic drive that has inspired and won plaudits of many.

...Highly innovative, attuned to changes, takes "crash projects" in stride.

...Successfully stepped into increasingly more difficult jobs with equally continuing success.

...Performance characterized by positive actions taken to meet growing responsibilities.

...Always contributes full measure to any task.

...Enjoys Navy lifestyle and is quick to offer positive advice to subordinates on ways to increase their worth and contribution to a team effort.

...Duties, across the board, have been skillfully performed.

...Physically fit, erect in carriage, squared-away uniforms.

...Technical competence and dependability have gained complete confidence of subordinates and superiors.

...A self-starter who can plan ahead, usually has most of a project laid out before formal tasking.

...Motivates personnel through personal and positive involvement.

...Readily offers constructive suggestions regarding matters outside chosen technical field.

...Possesses inexhaustible drive and initiative.

...An ingrained respect for fellow shipmates, secures high degree of loyalty and cooperation from subordinates, instills rare sense of personal responsibility for the quality of their work.

...Exemplary character, exercises mature judgement.

...Has meticulous military appearance, congenial personality, and positive attitude and outlook.

...Enjoys fast-paced operational environment, and is quick to lend helping hand to ensure cohesiveness and accomplishment.

...Aggressive in seeking out answers to developing problems and applying innovative solutions.

...A top achiever in any task assigned or assumed.

...Possessed of friendly, cooperative spirit and "can do" attitude.

...Deep concern for well being of others, total dedication and support to the Navy and the command.

...Decisions and efforts have contributed markedly to continued operational and administrative success of organization.

...Enjoys my complete trust and confidence in discharging all duties.

...Literally becomes personally immersed in programs and projects that promote high morale and camaraderie.

...Readily offers sound, constructive advice and suggestions on matters within and outside normal job with success.

...Possesses stamina, intelligence, and judgement to tackle any assignment and produce quality results.

...Daily and inspection appearance above reproach, highly professional military bearing.

...Applies excellent blend of common sense and logic when unforeseen problems arise.

...Attacks each assignment with maturity, zeal, and determination.

...Follows through with action and enthusiasm.

...Not satisfied with any performance short of perfection.

...Quick and innovative mind, always alert for new action.

...Sincere, easy-going, uncommonly likeable individual.

...Continually volunteers to shoulder additional responsibility.

...Ability to create and maintain confidence, respect, and professionalism in any organization.

...Excellent in attitude and capability.

...Timely and correct completion of primary and collateral duties has been exemplary.

...Personal involvement in management of training efforts stimulated professionalism and facilitated learning.

...Studious by nature, meticulously accurate as to facts, and thorough in work.

...Takes personal pride in appearance; shoes highly polished, uniforms pressed, and hair well groomed and short.

...Work is complete, thorough, and accurate; leaves no loose ends for others.

...Highly reliable and dependable in any situation, thrives on problems and situations which one of lesser ability and confidence would shun.

...Uncompromisingly committed to the principles of equal opportunity and fair treatment to all service members.

...Displays continued excellence and enthusiasm in the performance of duty.

...Unique ability to perform under pressure.

...Has the energy, initiative, and mental qualifications to tackle any assignment.

...Continually puts forth maximum effort in all areas of responsibility with consistently outstanding results.

...Knowledge of profession and job is impressive and desire to use experience in assisting others is commendable.

...Thoroughly meticulous in work and thought.

...Honest, sincere with unquestionable integrity.

...Widely read with retentive memory, continually seeks to broaden experience and increase professional knowledge.

...Gets satisfaction from doing rather than contemplating a completed project.

...Can be relied upon to take the initiative in implementing changes in policy or procedure.

...Ready wit and pleasing personality enhances morale.

...Dedication to duty in conjunction with desire to excel in any endeavor results in unusually high standard of performance.

...Repeatedly proven readiness to meet increasingly more responsible positions and challenges.

...Logical and direct in approach, factual in argument, tactful by nature.

...Confident of abilities, always one step ahead of the action.

...Personally aware of individual worth and dignity of subordinates and demonstrates awareness in daily interactions.

...Conscientious individual with excellent understanding and working knowledge of specialty.

...Maintains impeccable personal appearance and commands similar high standards of subordinates, encouraging respect for Navy tradition and regulations.

...Alert, dynamic, highly intelligent with a creative mind.

...Encourages peers and subordinates to assume additional responsibility and authority.

...Continually seeks personal growth and development.

...Adapts quickly to changing operational situations and provides innovative solutions to stay on top of unfolding developments.

...Ability to express thoughts clearly and courage to stand on principle.

...A cornerstone of technical knowledge, management skill, and military tradition.

...Rapid, intense worker, produces accurate and timely results.

...Sense of fair plan and intense advocacy of individual and human rights.

...Devotion to duty, uncompromising professionalism and unflagging support of command and Navy goals.

...Vast experience enhanced by intelligence, sincerity, and ability to communicate with others.

...Intense dedication to duty, personal sacrifice, and uncompromising standards of conduct.

...Cultivates understanding, harmony, and esprit de corps.

...Confident of abilities, will take action when necessary without waiting for guidance or orders.

...Particularly effective in creating environment that makes subordinates want to seek career in the Navy.

...Stands above peers in terms of character, ability to get things done, and in demonstrated professional competence.

...Self starter, work is marked by integrity and initiative.

...Sobriety, punctuality, and strong sense of duty highlight daily performance.

...Enjoys fast-paced environment of job.

...Sincere counseling techniques secures complete trust and loyalty of subordinates.

...Attentive to detail, thorough and meticulous in manner.

...Has a good deal of drive and persistence and directs energy in attacking all tasks and projects.

...Positive "can do" attitude is infectious and enhances operational effectiveness.

...Performs duties with vision, judgement, and superior intellectual capacity.

...Well liked by subordinates, contemporaries, and seniors.

...Deep sense of pride and respect for Navy regulations and traditions.

...Readily adaptable to changing situations and demands.

...Has the courage of conviction without being contentious.

...Imaginative, inquisitive, and creative, not content with old procedures and continuously explores new ideas with a view to improved effectiveness.

...Mentally alert, foresighted, thinks quickly on feet.

...Displays patience in training inexperienced subordinates.

...Energetic self-starter with a warm, helpful, and alert manner.

...Actions and manners reflect creditably on Navy.

...Conceives and develops new concepts and procedures that result in significant improvements in ...

...Resourceful in complicated or unusual situations.

...Exemplifies highest standards of moral integrity (deportment, or personal habits).

...Independent and perceptive thinker, recommendations have contributed appreciably to command's effectiveness.

...Poised and confident, maintains composure under pressure.

...Remarkable ability to adapt to requirements of superiors.

...Displays ingenuity in solving complex problems, or in devising temporary "fix."

...Superb facilities for effective personal interaction and leadership.

...Team player, places high emphasis on cooperation and team work.

...Frequently gives freely of off-duty time to work with subordinates to bring them up to own high standards of efficiency and performance.

...A strong sense of duty and a desire to do a good job under any conditions or circumstances.

...Thinks clearly and logically and is able to accommodate and correlate a large amount of details in day-to-day duties.

...Facilitates communications and understanding between people with different points of view.

...Capacity to exercise high degree of imagination, ingenuity, and creativity is virtually inexhaustible.

...Attuned to work environment, always one step ahead of the action.

...Strong personal belief in Navy traditions and customs.

...Instills pride in accomplishment, patriotism, and a sense of adventure.

...Strong desire and ability to be helpful outside normal area of responsibility.

...A student of human nature, displays social poise and tact (and: courteous, respectful, gracious, pleasant, frank, open-minded, even-tempered).

...Very diligent and invariably continues to work on a problem until every significant detail has been covered.

...Impartial, just, and ethical.

...Appearance is "recruit poster" quality.

...Quiet individual with pleasing and poised personality.

...Enjoys fast-paced operational environment, quick to lend a helping hand.

...Demonstrates unsurpassed professionalism.

...Generates a spirit of harmony and cooperation.

...Proven performer under pressure and stress.

...Displays innate ability to coordinate myriad of details simultaneously.

...Has a polished manner, a keen sense of humor, and a personality that radiates enthusiasm even under adverse conditions.

...Self-motivated and resourceful, can be relied upon to complete difficult assignments without direction or guidance.

...Enjoys discussing the rewards and adventures of Navy life.

...Provided essential mission-ready support throughout the past year under most demanding and adverse situations.

...Highly proficient in all aspects of job, frequently used to train new managers and supervisors.

...Poised, can meet unusual and taxing situations without becoming rattled or confused.

...Has initiative, ideas, and aggressively follows through.

...Displays continued excellence and enthusiasm in performance of duties.

...Uncompromisingly committed to the principles of equal opportunity and fair treatment to all service members.

...An intense desire and ability to be helpful and cooperative.

...Thinks through problem areas and acts decisively on own.

...Takes the initiative in seeking additional duties.

...Tactful, courteous, and well mannered.

...Meticulously accurate, with great sense of personal responsibility for every task, regardless of complexity or effort required.

...Fosters increased professionalism throughout ranks.

...Strong sense of dedication, moral obligation, and pride of rank.

...Inspects spaces frequently, knows what to look for, and results invariably bring about improvements.

...Even temperament and steadying influence instills sense of unity and pride of accomplishment.

...Approaches menial tasks with same enthusiasm and attention afforded major projects.

...Despite a high demand environment, remains calm and can be depended upon to render solid, logical judgements.

...Works quickly and efficiently, yielding results of the highest order.

...Energetic and logical with analytical thought process.

...Saved thousands of dollars through acute awareness, perseverance and personal diligence.

...A rare blend of personal candor, professional judgement, and self-starting motivation.

...Demonstrates a strong sense of dedication, wins support of subordinates and always achieves command objectives.

...Demonstrates remarkable ability to adapt to requirements of superiors, always putting the job ahead of personal desires, often at inconvenience to self.

...Work efficiently planned, completed, and carefully inspected.

...Ability to complete independent studies which can be used as guide for action by others.

...Knowledgeable and mature, uses communications as tool to arouse interest and enthusiasm of others.

...Exhibits personal and professional qualities that are prerequisite for personnel seeking greater responsibility.

...Shining example of proper dress and grooming.

...Ambitious and energetic, dislikes idle hands or mind.

...Demeanor promotes trust, efficiency, and high state of morale.

...Achieves high state of training and maintains high degree of readiness, and at same time attends to welfare and well being of subordinates.

...Alert, earnest, and capable, and attitude toward job ensure it is done correctly the first time.

...Has totally mastered each and every professional, managerial, and leadership function within peer group.

...Actively solicits additional tasks and duties.

...Conduct and appearance always of highest caliber, demonstrates pride in self and service.

...Takes advantage of slack periods to pursue professional and personal goals.

...Maintains positive attitude and works well under pressure.

...Completes all tasks with alacrity and zeal.

...Meticulous in manner and attentive to detail.

...Very quick, but thorough, completing large volume of work each day.

...Frank, sincere, and honest in interpersonal dealings.

...Appearance is impeccable in either dress or work uniform, sets outstanding example for subordinates and peers.

...Maintains smooth flow of information up and down the chain of command.

...Hand picked for present job. Superior results support that decision.

...A high level of drive and energy, sharply focused to task at hand.

...Possesses well-rounded knowledge of Navy's latest career programs. Ideally suited to work today's young sailors.

...Maintains high standards for own performance and that of others.

...Energetic and dedicated, leads by example.

...Original thinker, ability to devise and organize procedures with maximum efficiency and minimum waste.

...Unafraid of accepting new and added duties, and has ability to produce quality results.

...Never loses capacity for enthusiasm and desire to help.

...Constantly learning, reads professional books and completes correspondence courses during off-duty and spare time.

...Sincere and outgoing personality is highly conducive to morale and fosters team effort and unity.

...Performs all duties with ease and confidence of a professional, attending to every detail.

...Dedicated, with an obvious willingness to serve with pride in any endeavor.

...A decision maker, develops plans and policies to attain goals.

...Consistently superior performer, totally dedicated to mission accomplishment.

...Ability to overcome obstacles and to secure cooperation from others is indicative of ability to work independently and get the job done.

...Presents a neat, highly acceptable appearance in uniform and civilian attire.

...Exemplary character, exercises mature judgement.

...Uses available personnel and material resources with imagination and ingenuity.

...Straightforward in discussion, factual in presentation, persuasive and tactful in action.

...Readily tackles any job with intention and desire of mastering it--with unqualified success.

...Positive, constructive, and creative outlook.

...Grasps pertinent details rapidly.

...Not afraid of changing ways of doing business to eliminate those practices which drive good people out of the Navy, and to make a Naval career as attractive and satisfying an experience as possible.

...Development has been marked by meticulous precision in action and mature judgement in thought.

...A fantastic sense of humor and genuine interest in welfare and morale of others.

...Work produces results quickly and efficiently without organizational friction.

...Strikes effective balance between needs of service and needs of individuals.

...A self-starter with a natural ability and aptitude for technically oriented tasks.

...Sharp appearance evidenced daily, is immaculate.   Uniforms reflect neatness in dress and attention to detail.

...Has sincere interest in welfare and self-development of subordinates and openly encourages—and expects—professional and personal development.

...Rapid, thorough, and highly accurate in administrative and staff work.

...Completely competent in all technical and procedural aspects of chosen specialty.

...Positive, constructive, and creative in outlook.

...Displays aggressive work habits and an unending willingness to assist others in any capacity.

...Dedicated manager, positive and confident leader, maintains superior rapport at all levels of command.

...Possesses exceptionally valuable characteristics of soundness of judgement and eagerness and capacity to learn independently.

...Exemplifies the spirit and pride and professionalism that is keynote of today's Navy: Industrious, reliable, adaptable to changing situations, and cooperative.

...Fit and trim in posture, takes great pride in maintaining high standards of personal appearance and demeanor.

...A disciplined mind with the ability to grasp and retain pertinent detail and information.

...Conscientious, punctilious, with a keen appreciation of responsibilities.

...Impeccable dresser, maintains very sharp appearance through personal physical fitness programs.

...Rare ability to create and maintain confidence, respect, and professionalism.

...Dedication, drive, and desire to put forth best effort in any capacity has increased operational effectiveness of this command.

...Thrives on pressures of immediacy and responds resourcefully with sound, innovative suggestions.

...Not content with idle time, seeks out solutions to any variety of problems during slack periods.

...Motivated, enjoys challenge, seeks personal responsibility, and is a high achiever.

...Places high priority on human goals. Generates spirit of equality, teamwork, and high morale throughout organization.

...Pleasant, pleasing personality allows (him/her) to both give and receive cooperation.

...Intelligent, stable, and possessed of an orderly mind.

...Dedicated with an obvious willingness to serve with pride in any endeavor.

...Attentive to responsibility, reacts decisively and positively to changing requirements.

...Concerned and humane, ensures each individual is treated with fairness and equality.

...Continuing source of new, innovative, and workable ideas.

...Possessed of a wide education and strong moral fiber.

...Charismatic and decisive, with good touch of common sense.

...Confident of abilities, will take positive and correct action when necessary without waiting for guidance or orders.

...Highly intelligent, possesses stimulating imagination, and routinely provides sound advice and recommendations for anticipated problems.

...Places high values on human goals and has adeptly integrated this feeling into dealings with others.

...Demonstrates persistence and conscientiousness in attacking any assignment.

...Remains calm when faced with situations aggravated by personnel shortages and new, untrained personnel.

...Steady and deliberate, compiled impressive maintenance record.

...Individual drive is motivating and refreshing.

...Possesses the mental dexterity and intellectual capacity to comprehend and tackle any assignment with unusual success.

...Pleasant in personality and reasoned in action.

...Smart, neat, and scrupulous in personal grooming.

...Deep degree of trust and respect accorded by co-workers.

...Cheerfully devotes numerous extra hours to ensure all problems and projects are being taken care of by following each through to successful completion.

...Amicable personality, spiced with good wit and humor.

...A "team player," places great emphasis on cooperation and coordination.

...Works methodically and carefully, highly accurate results.

...Meticulous military appearance, congenial personality, and positive attitude which is demonstrated in daily contact with seniors and subordinates.

TOP PERFORMERS
(5.0-4.0)

BULLETS

MANAGEMENT & LEADERSHIP

...Fits each subordinate with challenging assignments, encourages self-esteem.

...Possesses professional competence to know what to do, fortitude to decide how to do it, and dynamic leadership to inspire others to accomplish it.

...Maintains highly accurate and easily understood methods of tracking and monitoring organizational work and accomplishment. Always knows what's planned and what's happening.

...Skillful manager of time, can quickly and efficiently diagnose problems and failures and supply effective remedies without delay.

...An informed leader who genuinely cares about the professional development and well-being of subordinates.

...A professional manager—understands principle of delegation.

...Mentally alert, with gift for devising organizational instructions and administrative procedure.

...Delegates authority effectively, does not run a one-person show. Delegation based on trust and mutual understanding.

...Morale never higher; yet, demands and receives full day's work from each individual.

...Goal oriented, demonstrates strong sense of duty and remarkable ability to plan, manage, and administer.

...Draws on abilities and strengths of subordinates.

...Is aggressive and initiates workable ideas for improvement of doing things more accurately, more quickly, and more thoroughly with the same means and resources as contemporaries.

...Alert, with creative mind, able to develop effective and efficient procedural methods and prepare excellently written and easily understood instructions covering them.

...A student of human nature with superior ability to inspire cooperation from subordinates.

...Provides meaningful work assignments, with which subordinates can identify and become personally involved.

...Has spiritual force and moral fiber necessary in a Naval leader.

...Possesses the spark of leadership, creative ability, and self-confidence to excel in any assignment.

...Highly flexible, adjusts management techniques to meet requirements of task at hand.

...Does not act before all facts have been properly evaluated.

...Executes excellent management practices by blending concern for others with job accomplishment.

...Thinks clearly and logically, able to accommodate and correlate large number of details in efficient and effective use of available manpower and material.

...Possessed of the vision, courage of conviction, moral integrity, and the capacity to inspire others to strive for excellence.

...Displays firm grasp and use of effective leadership principles.

...An original thinker, offers many new, innovative and well thought out ideas, many of which have been turned into policy and are proving highly beneficial.

...Made (himself/herself) the "person to see" when subordinates need guidance of either personal or professional manner.

...Manages and controls use of maintenance equipment, including the more complicated and sophisticated, with unusual definition and precision.

...Ability to recognize potential of subordinates and provide the leadership to realize that potential.

...Genial, cooperative, with the courage of conviction.

...Possesses those special qualities it takes to be successful: Communicates easily; instills pride; encourages average performers to strive for excellence; and, commends people for effort, commitment, dedication, and personal accomplishment.

...Exerts personal influence over subordinates while allowing sufficient latitude for growth and creativity.

...Has capacity to make spontaneous and intuitive judgements of considerable value.

...Expresses self with force and confidence. A real leader with a knack for getting the job done.

...Discusses strong and weak points with subordinates and takes sincere interest in improving their performance.

...Exceptional manager and organizer, ensures upward mobility of subordinates through carefully planning job enhancement and job enrichment programs.

...Strengthens morale by cultivating sense of well being and pride in belonging.

...A good listener, but will draw own final conclusions.

...Directs subordinates without dulling their initiative or deadening their interest or enthusiasm.

...Actively solicits junior personnel for their thoughts and ideas in variety of administrative and operational matters. Stimulates thought and action of others.

...Pleasant personality blends well in any work group, yet never loses sight of responsibilities as leader and supervisor.

...Consistently demands and receives only best from juniors.

...Organization functions smoothly, effectively, and reliably. Regularly meets commitments.

...Uses past experience, common sense, and excellent direct supervision to elicit most from subordinates.

...Balances schedule and workload according to priorities and produces quality results.

...A loyal, energetic, and conscientious leader.

...Introduces new ideas and encourages development of juniors.

...Encourages subordinates to put forth best effort, carefully explains advantages and rewards of self-improvement and a successful Navy career.

...Personified leadership by example.

...Straightforward but empathetic approach to subordinates with difficulties have resulted in quick resolution of many personal and professional problems.

...Masterful supervision and imaginative utilization of onboard personnel and equipment assets demonstrated on daily basis.

...Fair, impartial leader, respects rights of others.

...Inspires fullest cooperation and support of subordinates.

...Efficient organizer with sense of duty and desire to do a good job.

...Maintains awareness of changing situation, provides preventive rather than remedial management.

...Tactful, positive manner quickly gains respect and loyalty of subordinates.

...Grasps essentials of problem quickly, can think through a complex problem with rapid logic, aware of, but not distracted by, inconsequential details.

...Quick thinker who makes positive, supportable independent decisions.

...Motivates subordinates instead of driving them. They are eager to follow.

...Demonstrated outstanding success as negotiator, arbitrator and group leader.

...Extremely quick to adapt to changing situations and never at a loss to find solutions.

...Individual of remarkable leadership talent and directional motivation.

...Impressively managed equipment assets and a maintenance work force and achieved high degree of combat readiness.

...Takes positive, decisive action in knotty situations.

...Every goal and objective met timely and correctly the first time around.

...A master at providing direction and leadership to junior personnel.
...Rare ability to apply corrective counseling and have it accepted in positive manner.

...Directs subordinates with firm but fair hand, providing unified purpose and sense of direction without dulling initiative.

...Backs juniors and allows to develop at rapid pace.

...Anticipates future tasks and through prior planning is never placed in position of pushing a deadline.

...Gets along extremely well, securing cooperation of contemporaries, and loyalty of subordinates. Guides and directs with understanding and tact.

...Exceptionally well qualified to examine existing organization and procedure to determine economy and efficiency.

...Directs subordinates by giving vision and purpose.

...Strong leadership, management acumen, technical knowledge, and personal diligence.

...Subordinates are best trained and most productive in the department.

...Excellent problem-solving facilities. Frequently emerges as chairman or spokesman in group activities.

...A dynamic leader, aggressive in job accomplishment.

...Ability to adjust to day-to-day workload variations while remaining attuned to overall priorities.

...Possesses constructive imagination necessary for unsupervised problem solving.

...Sells ideas and influences others with great success.

...Highly competent manager and administrator, with knack for passing own knowledge and experience to others.

...Has personal and professional interest in each subordinate. They respond by giving their "all" in tough and crisis situations.

...A knowledgeable individual of great foresight-well prepared for any contingency.

...Ability to facilitate cooperative effort of others.

...Proven leader, capable of inspiring and motivating subordinates by demonstrating professional competence and by intelligent and compassionate treatment of subordinates.

...Proficiently exercises broad directive control over various tasks and projects simultaneously.

...Quick to take the lead in coordinating activity and providing guidance and supervision.

...Establishes climate that makes people receptive to ideas and suggestions.

...Integrates mission requirements with individual needs and capabilities of subordinates.

...Clarifies and enforces unified action, challenges juniors.

...Works within well developed and defined long-range sense of direction and purpose.

...Initiated programs are designed to achieve maximum economy of funds and optimum utilization of materials.

...Has infectious enthusiasm that enlists cooperation and support of others.

...Never too busy to take time to teach and guide juniors, either upon request or when it is observed that additional instruction may be necessary.

...Ability to create enthusiasm for a given task.

...Demonstrates creative thinking and innovative problem solving techniques.

...An excellent administrator, will handle any job in highly creditable manner.

...Always busy, yet patient, sympathetic and understanding with subordinates who have problem.

...Definitely leader-type, has clearly demonstrated capacity for effectively and efficiently directing and controlling activities of others and for assuring high quality results.

...Ability to cut through confusion and conflicting information and get to crux of any problem.

...Has ability to succeed in multiple and diverse responsibilities with uncommon success.

...Ability to communicate effectively up and down the chain of command gained respect and admiration of juniors and seniors.

...Positive Navy attitude and personal application of distinctive leadership consistently inspired higher achievements from peers and subordinates.

...Fair and exacting, led by example and was always available to discuss better ways to accomplish a job.

...A master at achieving maximum use of limited resources.

...Astute on-scene leadership produced exceptionally positive results and maintained extremely high morale and a strong sense of purpose throughout (organization).

...A person of action who dynamically leads the way in setting and implementing command policy.

...Superbly carried out responsibilities to the distinct benefit of the command.

...Innate ability to anticipate problems and plan for their resolution contributed significantly to the enviable cohesiveness enjoyed by organization.

...Always has time for subordinates despite heavily taxed work schedule.

...Initiative, drive and readiness to accept responsibility are proven to be without limit.

...Unique understanding of people, knowledge of equipment, and emphasis on training were key factors in (organization) ability to react positively to any situation.

...Managerial skills are of the highest caliber.

...A role model for subordinates.

...Sound professional recommendations, base on experience and technical knowledge, are highly valued by superiors.

...Technical expertise, tenacity of purpose and enthusiasm are indicative of
...

...Rallied together divided factions within (organization) and focused their efforts, attention and energies on a common goal.

...Always provides superb performance under stressful situations.

...Rare individual who possesses maturity, intelligence, and technical know-how to plan ambitious workload for (himself/herself) and others, and leadership and dedication to successfully complete those assignments.

...Organization consistently maintained in high state of operational and material readiness.

...Maintains good work organization and disciplines subordinates competently and impartially.

...Has capacity to analyze facts, correctly understand and solve problems.

...Seizes every opportunity to promote the Navy and explain career opportunities and benefits. Open, friendly personality instrumental in gaining necessary respect to present Navy's career programs, with conviction, at formal and informal gatherings.

...Cheerful and cooperative, unassuming, fair and unbiased in exercising authority.

...Exerts personal influence with tact.

...Industrious manner and ability to get job done inspires trust and confidence.

...Maintains excellent blend between short-and long-term command objectives and accomplishment.

...Strengthens subordinate's feeling of belonging through personal commitment and involvement.

...Industrious and willing worker, extremely accurate, placing great emphasis on detail.

...Engaging, good humored, and tactful and promotes good will.

...Stable and confident of abilities, readily and quickly adapts to changing situations.

...Intense individual whose paramount interest is in efficiency of own organization.

...Uses authority to assign and accomplish tasks in firm but fair manner.

...Great foresight, prepared for any eventuality.

...Recognizes potential of subordinates and provides necessary guidance to reach that potential.

...Consistently successful in obtaining complete and willing cooperation of others.

...Designed clear cut set of goals and moves toward them with initiative and purpose.

...Policies are prudent, in consonance with directives from higher authority, and implemented uniformly.

...Established a managerial and planning and control system that fully supported and enforced command objectives.

...Actively sought by subordinates for innate ability to get to the crux of a personal problem and help any concerned individual.

...Possesses direction of vision and economy of effort.

...Exercises high degree of imagination, ingenuity, and creativity in problem solving.

...Has progressive viewpoint with sound judgement; analysis of problems and choice of methods of accomplishing desired results are exceptionally good.

...Takes personal interest in supporting and developing professional attitude in subordinates.

...Instills self-confidence, uses incentives and reinforcement.

...Ability to achieve agreement among individuals and groups in furtherance of their common interests.

...Excellent planner and organizer, does not wait for instruction.

...Invariably submits timely and perceptive solutions to staff problems.

...Forceful without being overbearing and strict without generating resentment.

...Tactful and diplomatic, has ability to express and strongly support views on controversial subjects without arousing antagonism or resentment.

...Promotes harmony and fosters high morale.

...Exercises initiative, responds well to unusual situations or procedures.

...Displays superior administrative ability and managerial skill in organizing forces and planning events.

...Reinforces good behavior and corrects substandard behavior.

...Wit, charm, and vitality quickly wins acceptance in group efforts and puts (him/her) in driver's seat at gatherings.

...Observes chain of command principles, effectively delegates administrative and managerial responsibilities.

...Uses subordinates to best advantage, operates an efficient and productive organization.

...Fostered development from an embryonic state to a highly effective and responsive organization.

...An excellent manager and organizer who is willing to accept any assignment no matter how difficult.

...Especially adept at fitting people to jobs and training them quickly.

...Radiates confidence, composure, and competence.

...Ability to organize personal time and that of others.

...Style of leadership designed to improve proficiency and morale of organization.

...Not naive or abrupt--uses tact and diplomacy.

...Strengthens morale by cultivating sense of belonging.

...Maintenance program is well organized and effectively executed.

...Competent and capable, leads by doing and showing.

...Discipline enforced on fair and consistent basis.

...Exudes spirit of well being and friendliness and improves attitude of all hands.

...Always open to inspiration and intuition, translates thought into action.

...Guidance to subordinates is clear and comprehensive. They always know what is expected of them.

...Ability to develop correct and logical conclusions.

...Takes sincere and persuasive interest in encouraging subordinates to improve their technical skill (or professional competence, resourcefulness, reliability).

...Commends superior performance and takes prompt corrective action in cases of substandard performance.

...Operates organization in climate that permits swift resolution of unforeseen circumstances.

...Skilled in concentration and evaluation, has capacity to make spontaneous and intuitive judgement.

...Professional, accomplished administrator and manager who understands and effectively uses principle of delegation.

...Knowledgeable of Navy's career-oriented programs, especially school and duty station opportunities, provides good, sound advice on how to best take advantage of these options.

...Masterful supervisor with creative and imaginative use of on-board assets.

...Demonstrates skill in science of sound reasoning, valid deduction, and wise decision.

...Skillful manager, proven ability to attain high standards of performance.

...Establishes challenging yet attainable goals.

...A quick wit, good sense of humor, and easy going nature ensures amenable working relationships up and down the chain of command.

...Infectious enthusiasm enlists cooperation and support from others.

...Fosters prudent business management principles.

...Quiet in demeanor, tactful and thorough in positive handling of subordinates, quickly gains their respect and loyalty.

...Leads by doing and showing—a pacesetter.

...Transfers goals and objective into concrete, workable plans.
...Intelligent, dynamic leader, thrives on new challenge.

...An excellent manager of personnel and equipment entrusted to personal care.

...Day to day performance elicits positive and productive response from subordinates.

...Anticipates upcoming requirements and stays well ahead of rapidly unfolding situations.

...Has earned both abiding loyalty of subordinates and deepest respect of seniors.

...Professional attitude radiates to subordinates, causing them to respond with full effort.

...Establishes dialogue process with subordinates that enhances understanding and mutual respect.

...Ability to assimilate information and data and apply it to task at hand.

...Directs efforts of junior personnel toward quality work while promoting high morale and team spirit.

...Energetic and persevering by nature, anticipates future requirements and takes necessary steps to assure proper action ahead of impending deadlines.

...Concerned with well-being of subordinates. Maintains positive control and minimizes internal friction.

...An invaluable manager, counselor, and source of knowledge in every area of responsibility.

...Tact, concern for others, the "follow me" style of leadership elicits maximum effort and support from juniors.

...Always prepared for emergency procedures, ready for contingencies.

...Aggressive, but not overbearing, most effective in getting everything subordinates can give.

...Possesses decision-making facility that focuses on high issues and is action oriented.

...Displays excellent combination of tact and direct supervision, ideally suited to work with today's young, inquisitive sailors.

...Management effectiveness has set new standards of excellence in technical and maintenance performance.

...Manages team of personnel with uncommon expertise, reliably providing scheduled services despite critical manpower shortages.

...Aware of changing situations, operates on preventive rather than remedial management.

...Has good judgement, common sense, and a sense of reality.

...An efficient organizer with a sense of duty and a desire to do a good job.

...Thinks clearly and logically and is able to accommodate and correlate a large number of details in the day-to-day management and leadership of available manpower and equipment.

...Decisions are always based on best available information.

...Possesses commendable faculty for getting projects started, keeping them moving, and accomplishing objectives.

...Thoroughly familiar with all phases of job and makes good use of this knowledge and experience whenever presented with a problem or task.

...Unwilling to be content to sit back and relax during slower periods of operation. Involves (himself/herself) directly with training and furthering readiness, morale, and esprit de corps.

...Has good working relationship with subordinates and takes advantage of situations to inform them of Navy's continued need for knowledgeable and proficient career-oriented individuals.

...Ability to apply corrective counseling and have it accepted in positive manner.

...Possesses good judgement, common sense, and a grasp of reality.

...Ability to elicit the best of men.

...Balances schedule and workload according to required priorities.

...Engenders spirit in subordinates to do their best.

...Personable, well liked and highly respected—continually exhibits outstanding leadership qualities.

...Has ability to create and maintain confidence, teamwork, and respect.

...Assumptions are logically derived from facts at hand.

...Bold, tempered with a grasp of practicality.

...Clearly demonstrated capacity for effectively and efficiently directing activities of others while ensuring high quality results.

...Good judgement, quick, decisive, and correct in action.

...Continually searches for ways to improve procedures and raise efficiency. Many suggestions incorporated at supervisory and management level.

...Outstanding manager, performs all duties without prompting.

...Gets subordinates involved in change and new ideas.

...Understands worth and dignity of each individual, successfully pursues "follow me" leadership style.

...Handles subordinates firmly and positively, but with such dexterity and tact to inspire a feeling of respect and devotion which assures a well done job in any assignment.

...Cheerful and cooperative, firm but unbiased in exercising authority.

...Quickly grasps essential elements of a problem, uses great initiative and keen logic in seeking solutions.

...Superior manager and leader, can distinguish between motivating and non-motivating forces. Takes maximum advantage of this rare quality.

...Highly qualified to teach subordinates the art and science of managerial and organizational techniques.

...A dedicated proponent of leadership by example, continuing education and training. Upward mobility in Navy is particularly evident.

...Ability to generate enthusiasm in subordinates and to instill in them a desire to do top notch work.

...Forceful and factual. Contributes to informal and formal group gatherings and meetings.

...Possesses ability to devise operational procedures that get job done properly and economically.

...Enjoys complete trust and confidence of subordinates while simultaneously practicing and enforcing strict adherence to established policy.

...Maintains high standard for own performance and instills, with success, this trait in subordinates.

...Organization enjoys high level of morale and a low infraction rate.

...Thinks out new ways and means to improve effectiveness with which a job can be done.

...Understands needs and knows capabilities of subordinates.

...Conducts frequent one-on-one informal discussions on future career opportunities of a Navy career.

...Established and strictly enforced highly effective controls on organizational materials. Reduced operating budget by ...%.

...Accepts responsibility and challenge in stride. Demonstrates versatility and exceptional managerial skills.

...Unique ability to solicit and receive full incentive and effort of subordinates.

...Realizes that people are most important and precious Navy resource and own leadership is highlighted by intelligent and compassionate treatment.

...Assertive yet considerate, leads by example.

...Personal leadership characteristics and tactful and understanding manner secures complete loyalty of subordinates and causes them to exert every effort to earn a personal "well done."

...Carefully evaluates views of subordinates before making final decision.

...Informed leader with genuine concern for well being and development of subordinates.

...A "team player," highly cooperative with others.

...Firm believer in chain of command, keeps superiors and subordinates aware of changing situations.

...Highly talented with a good sense of organization, a spontaneous propensity to leadership, and a reputation for dependable and accurate work.

...Unwilling to sit back and relax during slow periods. Involves (himself/herself) directly with training and furthering readiness, morale, and esprit de corps.

...Excellent working relationship with subordinates. Informs them of career opportunities and encourages self-development.

...Ability to devise operational procedures, and to write-up instructions thereafter in an intelligent and sensible manner so that they can be readily understood.

...Actively encourages individual growth and development of personnel, provides subordinates with definite, positive guidance.

...Extremely well organized, mission-oriented, and empathic with subordinates, has infused in subordinates own enthusiasm and dedication.

...Strict, yet fair disciplinarian.

...Tactful and considerate of others, inspires mutual respect and self-confidence.

...Designs clear-cut goals and moves toward them with initiative and purpose.

...Mature thought process and sound logic used to arrive at valid conclusions.

...Places high importance on value of teamwork, fully realizing that without collective effort within and outside the department the command cannot fully succeed in mission.

...Uses authority to assign and accomplish tasks in firm yet fair manner.

...Strong leader, instills in subordinates same desire to excel.

...A "doer," a take-charge individual who is not content until all tasks have been completed correctly.

...Has ability to organize group work effectively, to properly divide tasks and allocate responsibilities, and to successfully correlate the various fractions of a job into one overall complete job.

...Personable, highly respected, exhibits outstanding qualities as a leader.

...Adapts quickly to changing operational situations and provides innovative solutions.

...Individual drive is motivating and refreshing. Masterful supervision and imaginative use of onboard assets demonstrated on daily basis.

...Does not hesitate to provide assistance to those in need and to encourage trust through genuine interest in personal and professional problems.

...Sets high goals and expects no less of subordinates.

...Original thinker, offers new, innovative ideas.

...Organizational practices stimulate sense of identification, belonging, and esprit de corps.

...Sincere, concerned, and honest leader, juniors frequently seek out advice on personal and professional matters.

...Outstanding manager and leader, performs all duties without prompting.

...Encourages independent action, adds to productivity and efficiency.

TOP PERFORMERS
(5.0-4.0)

BULLETS

SELF EXPRESSION

...Drafts correspondence correctly. Reports and replies always prompt, thorough, and accurate.

...Well read and educated, correspondence always precise and descriptive, conveying thoughts and concepts succinctly.

...Excellent speaker, can discuss wide variety of subjects with confidence and conviction.

...Commands large vocabulary, very skillfully and effectively in oral and written communications.

...Excellent writer whose reports, letters, and memos well constructed and comprehensive.

...interesting and convincing conversationalist—people listen.

...Highly capable speaker, interesting and convincing.

...Authoritative manner of speaking commands complete attention.

...Use of the English language is articulate, correct, coherent, and easily understood.

...interesting speaker, more importantly, a good listener.

...Meticulous and methodical in staff work.

...Articulate and persuasive, excellent writer and orator.

...Communicates ideas in vivid, descriptive terms.

...Speaks in clear, concise terms easily understood by others.

...Continually demonstrates talent to communicate effectively with others. Written reports concise and coherent.

...Expresses (himself/herself) excellently both in writing and speech. Logical and direct in approach, factual in discussion, making points clearly.

...Written products clear and cogent, require minimum editing. Staff work on time and complete.

...Poised and ready, presents ideas in clear, easily understood manner.

...Written material always to the point, well researched and documented.

...Exceptionally good speaker, presents ideas clearly and effectively, inspires confidence in soundness of personal views.

...Speaks and writes with great clarity.

...An excellent communicator with ready and pleasing wit.

...Use of English language articulate and easily understood. Interesting conversationalist.

...Ability to express views clearly and concisely of great value in group work.

...Uses correct grammar, spells and punctuates correctly.

...Interesting conversationalist, with ability to clearly and logically state views.

...Compositions orderly and coherent. Sentences not lengthy or choppy.

...Exceptionally valuable in conference or group work. Expresses elf clearly and logically, views are respected by others.

...Articulate and persuasive writer and orator.

...Staff work skillfully prepared and submitted in timely manner.

...Clear in thought, direct in manner without being blunt in speech.

...Skilled communicator, able to express ideas accurately and precisely.

...Oral commands and written directives are concise, firm, and clear. They are readily understood and promptly executed.

...Reports are clear, concise, and convey desired meanings.

...Prepares skillful and timely reports, always prepared and up to date. Completes large volume of staff work each day.

...Excellent understanding of English language.

Verbal expressions reflect self-assurance and poise, and writing is clear and concise.

...Has good and varied command of the English language. Written work reflects style characteristic of substance and content. Widely read.

...Authoritative manner of speaking commands complete attention of listening audience. Speaks in terms understood, but not shallow in content.

...Possesses varied command of the English language; particularly adept at expressing ideas and thoughts in concise written form.

...Excellent in writing and speech, logical, direct, clear and concise.

...Good versatility in use of English language, enunciates well with excellent diction, and brief and concise in written communications.

...An excellent vocabulary and with clear, terse method of speaking and writing.

...Presents ideas in easily understood manner and written material requires virtually no editing.

...Highly accurate and professionally written reports contributed in large measure to high level of efficiency enjoyed by (organization).

...Innate ability to communicate clearly with subordinates, enabling organization to function without confusion of purpose. Reports forwarded up the chain of command equally succinct, exact, and graphic.

...Excellent ability to put thoughts into words, conveying both views and feelings with clarity and conviction.

...Expresses self clearly and concisely. Speaks easily and straight-forwardly without undue repetition.

...Excellent vocabulary, uses correct grammar, good diction and enunciation.

...Speaks with good tone and inflection, voice reflects confidence.

...Persuasive in argument, sincere in expression, can gain and hold attention of others. Excellent teacher and instructor.

...Accomplished public speaker, either on scheduled or impromptu basis.

...Exhibits noteworthy talent for drafting smooth correspondence.

...Possesses good command of English language, vivid and descriptive in oral and written communications.

...Excellent ability to communicate clearly with others.

TOP PERFORMERS
(5.0.4.0)

SAMPLE WRITE-UP PARAGRAPHS

(name) performance continues to be underscored by pride, self-improvement, and accomplishment. Excellent potential. Awarded Navy Achievement Medal for superior performance as ......Working with others in unified and cohesive manner a particularly strong asset. Has ability to immediately establish and maintain excellent rapport with others on all levels. Much of this is due to the fair, open, and unbiased manner in dealing with people. High achiever possessed with imagination and initiative.

(name) appearance and personal behavior are on par with other exceptional qualities of performance. Records and correspondence always correct and up to date and among the best in (organization). Proven leader and accomplished specialist in professional field.

(Name) is a top performer. Unlimited potential. Totally professional, poised, mature, and dedicated. Significant achievements include: Awarded Navy Achievement Medal for ... Awarded Letter of Commendation from ... for sustained superior performance during (period). Awarded Letter of Appreciation for......

Neat, trim, and fit. Immaculate "recruit poster" quality appearance. Articulate in speech, polite in manner. Submits timely, accurate paperwork. Enjoys loyalty, cooperation, and support of subordinates. Intelligent and dedicated, always volunteers for additional work to help shipmates and increase own knowledge, skill, and worth. Rising star of unlimited potential. Highly qualified and recommended for any demanding and challenging billet within or two pay grades above (present rate/rank).

Unequaled ability to obtain maximum results of available material and manpower resources. Unyielding dedication and loyalty. Analytical in thought, reasoned in mind. Humane and compassionate. Works full day on operational matters and then dedicates off-duty hours to catch up on administrative matters. Immaculate personal appearance. Cheerful, witty, and friendly, asset to high morale. "Head and shoulders" above contemporaries.

Self-starter and inspirational leader. Seasoned counselor. Demanding yet fair. Impressive leader and organizer. Strong moral fiber, respected by subordinates and superiors. Top achiever of boundless potential and ability.

Industrious, meticulous, and accurate, (name) aggressively tackles any job. Unparalleled potential. Intolerant of mediocre performance, yet aware of personal limitations. Unhesitatingly offers constructive criticism when warranted. Subordinates tactfully led. Accomplishments and strengths include........

Achieves high quality results regardless of tasking level. Stimulates pride and professionalism. Excels in self and subordinate development. Unusually accurate, thorough, and effective in oral and written communications. Drafts smooth correspondence and instructions. (name) optimizes available manpower and material resources. Flawless planning and execution efforts virtually guarantee success of any job. Highly respected throughout chain of command for professional knowledge and personal professionalism. Unbounded potential. (name) is a proven leader, manager, and organizer

(name) most productive and versatile (peer group) at this command. Proven top quality organizer, administrator, and manager. Unlimited potential for increased responsibility and authority. I awarded him a Navy Achievement Medal for sustained superior performance. Possesses great deal of energy, highly industrious, doesn't believe in idle time. Friendly personality, quick wit, establishes and maintains atmosphere of pride and professionalism. Partial listing of accomplishments include......

Capable of making independent judgment and decision. (name) fully enjoys Navy life, is quick to point out career benefits, will not tolerate open dissent toward Navy or command policies or procedures. "Recruit Poster Quality" image. Poised and mature with thirst for knowledge and desire for challenge. Positive motivator, intelligent, and articulate. Self-starter with great personal initiative and leadership skills. Head and shoulders above contemporaries. Commanding presence, decisive, and determined. (name) has earned my strongest endorsement for immediate promotion to .... Unlimited potential, of immense value to Navy--promote now.

(name) sets standards by which excellence is measured. Proven manager and leader of unbound ability. Superb working knowledge of systems and equipment has increased operational excellence and capability of (organization) and was basis for being awarded a Navy Achievement Medal.

Displays character, initiative, resourcefulness to accept & accomplish most demanding tasks. Energetic, conscientious, dedicated. Ideas and suggestions greatly assisted in developing new procedures to improve upon ...

Self-starter. Bold and imaginative leadership and management style. Especially adept dealing with people. "Follow me" leadership. Demeanor, confidence, and spirit of cooperation highly commendable in many crisis management situations. Dedicated professional who thrives on new challenges. (Name) is a dynamic leader and superb manager. Ideally suited for top ......positions.

(name) is a dedicated, cheerful, and hard-working individual who performs all duties in an accurate and enthusiastic manner. Boundless potential. Ability to adapt to change and perform in a superior manner became quite evident during periods when......Displays positive attitude. Dress & grooming impeccable. Dignified appearance, reflecting obvious pride in self and service.

Calm, affable manner prime assets. Potential for positions of higher authority. Quick to take the lead in coordinating activity and providing necessary guidance and supervision.

Completely self-reliant, strives for perfection and sees all projects through to successful conclusion. Fully exploits information and tools available to produce the most effective response. Excellent in writing and speech. Logical and direct in approach, factual in argument, making points clearly and concisely.

(name) is motivated toward a career in the Navy. Devotion to duty. Willing to perform above and beyond what is normally expected. Excellent candidate for increased and more demanding duties.

Consistent top performer within peer group, constantly seeking new and more effective methods in performing (organization) duties. Knowledgeable of all methods and procedures within area of responsibility Individual drive is motivating and refreshing. Believes in Navy and its purpose, always upholding the highest tradition of the Naval Service. Unbound potential.

Exceptional manager and organizer whose demonstrated expertise as a leader has measurably improved overall performance and readiness of this command. Commands fullest respect and support of others. Willing to accept any assignment regardless of scope.

Original thinker who has demonstrated ability to devise and organize operational and administrative procedures that weigh time, personnel, and money while ensuring the most efficient and economic methods are applied to any task. Superb administrative and managerial skills. Work marked by integrity and initiative.

Meticulously accurate with great sense of responsibility for quality of work. A tireless worker, cheerfully devotes numerous extra hours to ensure all projects and problems are being taken care of and are followed through to successful conclusion. Courage of conviction and strong moral character exhibited foster high morale, esprit de corps, and a total winning attitude.

(name) sterling performance noted in previous report continued through this reporting period. Excellent potential. Consistently executed weighty responsibilities of the (billet) with fervor, determination, and overall superb success. Very talented. Good sense of organization. Spontaneous propensity to leadership. Reputation for dependable and timely work. Strong and able in all areas. Most significant quality is ability to impart extensive operational experience and knowledge in subordinates. Specifically, (name) was responsible for the following list of accomplishments:.....

Astute management of personnel and equipment assets and close attention to the material condition of work spaces have markedly improved...... Tactful, strong leader. (Name) is truly an exceptional (peer group). Ready for increased responsibility now. "Front runner" within peer group.

(name) is an outstanding (peer group).   Unlimited potential for future growth and increased value to the Navy. Discharges all responsibilities with complete professionalism and tireless dedication. Ready, willing, and able are by bywords. Conscientious, tireless, and persevering. Sound leadership techniques and effective management acumen.

(name) does not believe in idle time or unfinished projects. Manages own time and that of others to best possible advantage. Possesses managerial and organizational expertise rarely observed in contemporaries. Completes large volume of work each day, frequently working extra hours.

(name) performance, both militarily and professionally, nothing short of outstanding. Displays keen interest in work. Potential to fill positions of greater trust and responsibility not normally available within ...structure.

Sets and maintains high standard of performance. Continually maintains high state of operational and material readiness despite antiquated equipment and non-availability of spare parts and material support.

Methodical and extremely conscientious, (name) actions well planned, smoothly executed, and in the best interest of a job well done. In addition to his primary duties, qualified ...

Regardless of complexity or magnitude of the task at hand, (name) can be relied upon to see that it is completed expeditiously and efficiently. High level of expertise is particularly exemplified by..... Dedicated leader whose standards of integrity and military bearing are of finest quality.

Accomplished counselor, (name) readily shares experience with personnel in both military and personal matters and they seek out advice with regularity. Personally encourages every subordinate to set highest possible goals for themselves and then counsels them on means available to realize those goals, both professional and personal.

(name) is one of the finest (peer group) in the United States Navy. Potential is unlimited. Dedicated service to this command. Played vital role in achievement of this command's mission. A cornerstone of technical knowledge, management skill, and military tradition. I awarded a Navy Achievement Medal for work as (billet). Vast experience is enhanced by intelligence, sincerity, and ability to communicate effectively with all levels of command. Intense dedication to duty, personal sacrifice, and uncompromising standards of conduct have provided the impetus for the organizational growth and development of the department.

Possesses the spark of leadership, creative ability, and self-confidence to excel in any task. Received a grade of "outstanding" at..... Morale and esprit de corps high. Initiative, accuracy, drive, and ability highlight daily performance.

(Name) is industrious & versatile. Approaches any task enthusiastically and with dispatch. Skillful manager with proven ability to attain a high standard of performance. Directs watch team with firm, fair hand. Provides unified purpose and sense of direction without dulling initiative. Readily adaptable to changes. Established good rapport with subordinates. Accomplishments include ....

Rare and successful blend of leadership coupled with superior management and administrative abilities assure success in any assignment.. Proponent of physical fitness. Conduct and appearance, on and off duty, are a model worthy of emulation. Written reports clear and concise. Oral presentations command complete attention of listening audience. Unlimited ability and potential. Ready for positions of increased responsibility and trust now.

Superior leader, manager, and organizer. Virtually unlimited potential. Continually supports and enforces command goals and policy. Mature, articulate, and dedicated. Meets or exceeds all deadlines. Runs taut watch team and enjoys my complete confidence and support. -Excels in self-directing and self-pacing.

(Name) strong leadership, management acumen, technical knowledge, and personal diligence have resulted in the following specific achievements...... Total commitment to the Navy, support of seniors, and leadership significantly enhanced readiness, retention, and morale. Most strongly recommended for promotion to .....

(name) sets an exceptional example as a leader and manager. Virtually unlimited potential. Works a full day in assigned job and consistently puts in many extra hours assisting in areas outside normal area of responsibility. Exceptional orator. Staff work always timely and correct. Neat, trim and physically fit, a model of military bearing and Navy tradition.

Attained professional and technical knowledge and competence rarely observed within peer group. Ability to obtain quality results in any environment cornerstone of (name) success as a leader. Emphatic demeanor and timely responsiveness inspired and maintained high morale and team spirit throughout (organization).

(name) contributions to mission effectiveness include:... Consistently performed all duties in outstanding manner and has exhibited traits that are highly desirous of a Naval (peer group)--strong leadership abilities; an excellent manager of material and equipment; tact and compassion; and, an innovative and intelligent view of the future.

Intelligent, energetic manager and organizer. Enjoys fast-paced work environment. Head and shoulders above contemporaries with virtually unlimited potential. Quick thinker, makes positive decisions that are easily supported. Completely dependable, performs all tasks with accuracy and dispatch. Professional attitude radiates to subordinates, causing them to respond in kind with full effort and cooperation. A sampling of (name) accomplishments include:.

(name) excels wherever assigned. Invaluable manager and counselor, and a source of knowledge and inspiration in every area of responsibility. Capacity for higher responsibility. Strong managerial and leadership traits.

(name) has knack for getting job done where others fail. Established routines which strengthened chain of command, facilitated smoother flow of correspondence, and created highly professional working atmosphere. Always a contributor to group effort. Works easily with seniors and subordinates. Sobriety, punctuality, and strong sense of duty highlight daily performance. Trim, physically fit, always "inspection ready." (name) overall outstanding performance contributed significantly to high level of success achieved by this command.

Outstanding (peer group). Top notch manager and organizer. Well versed in all facets of technical specialty. Energetic and resourceful, plans ahead. Impressively managed (organization) Devised highly effective management control system to track and identify.... Accomplishments and achievements include:...... Excellent staff and paperwork--well researched, timely, and accurate. Ambitious career counseling and training program: Fit, trim, and erect in carriage.

(name) is a star performer with desire for challenge. Has great deal of energy, doesn't believe in idle time. Firm, fair unbiased leader. Demands high standards of performance from self and subordinates. Effectively capitalizes on subordinate strengths and improves weaknesses. Enjoys fast-paced work environment. Should be selectively detailed to demanding and responsible billets. Highly talented, a front runner.

Tact, coordination, and ability to get to the heart of any problem increased operational and administrative efficiency and effectiveness.. The impossibility of any situation does not occur. Excellent counselor: Unique ability to reach a troubled person and give fair, honest guidance without equal among peers.

Superior ability and performance. Boundless potential. Exceptionally skilled in all facets of technical specialty. Totally professional and dedicated. Performance underscored by pride, personal involvement, and accomplishment. Awards and accolades include:......

Industrious and creative--an achiever. Likes to get into "nuts and bolts" of problems regardless of complexity or magnitude. Outstanding technical knowledge and managerial ability. Achievements and accomplishments include: ...... Submits smooth, well documented staff work.

Unbound initiative. Extremely conscientious. Actions well planned, organized, and smoothly executed. Team player, fosters cooperation and harmony throughout command. A forceful, dynamic, and compassionate leader, knows how to motivate subordinates. Unlimited potential. (name) is a head and shoulders performer.

Great potential. (name) sustained superior performance has been inspiration to each member of this command. Deep respect and sincere affection received from all hands manifests superlative qualities of leadership and integrity. Fostered unparalleled productivity and esprit de corps in command. Embodiment of pride and professionalism.

Ability to anticipate potential problem areas or external factors which impact on current and future operations has resulted in timely compliance with all .... Distinguished self through the following specific accomplishments:......Instills high-performance, motivation and creativity. Stimulates individual growth and responsibility. In a word, (name) performance, across the board, has been nothing less than outstanding.

Truly outstanding (peer group). Potential for positions of higher authority unlimited. Demonstrates unfailing diligence, job-aggressiveness, and total dedication to excellence. Thoroughly prepared for every assignment.. Personal initiative and leadership skills guarantee exceptional results of all tasks assigned or assumed.

Top shelf organizer, manager, and administrator. Unique ability to assimilate myriad of diverse inputs and produce timely, accurate, and detailed results. Experience, managerial abilities, and administrative talents were of immense significance in command earning ... Accolades include......

Poised and mature (peer group) with matchless thirst for knowledge and increased responsibility. Leadership, example, and skill in expressing views directly responsible for...... Most capable of making independent judgments. Earned my complete trust and confidence,. Strong performer during entire tour. Proven top achiever, demonstrates those specific talents and character traits required for ascent to positions of high responsibility.

Extremely knowledgeable, industrious. Completely resourceful. Performance of all duties singularly outstanding. Personally selected to assume..... Exceptionally fine administrator. Superb ability to write clear, concise, and accurate material. Stands alone in sheer excellence. I have seen none finer.

Continually striving for personal growth. Plans ahead, stays on top of every project or assignment until quality results achieved. Superb watch team leader, takes rapid, effective action without guidance from above. Excellent counselor, particularly adept in solving problems encountered by junior personnel. Unlimited potential for responsibility and challenge. All-around quality (peer group). Without reservation (name) has my highest recommendation for .....Number One (peer group) in my command.

(name) is an industrious, conscientious, and highly motivated (peer group) who exhibits the highest degree of professionalism in accomplishing all tasks. As (billet), (name) has been directly responsible for the outstanding performance of......Contributed personally to this command's mission during critical operations that lead to receiving.....Developed and implemented comprehensive ..... The first of its kind. Forwarded to TYCOM for use as a model.

(name) is an accomplished leader, manager, and organizer who has demonstrated the following personal traits and characteristics: Convincing speaker. Keen judgment. Meticulous administrative skills. Tireless worker. Inspiring leader. Tactful leader of subordinates. Informed and well read. Diplomatic personality. Alert, farsighted manager. Active, physically fit. Backs superiors and command policy.

(name) is a rising star who has implemented many programs within organization which have served to upgrade operational capability and increase morale. Served with distinction in collateral duties as:...... (name) is an informed, concerned individual with gift for getting along with others. Advice is actively sought by juniors and seniors. Bold, imaginative leader, ready for promotion now.

(name) is an efficient and highly knowledgeable (specialty) whose performance, singularly and collectively, has been outstanding. Demonstrated unbound ability and capacity to successfully assume positions of greater authority and jurisdiction. Firm, earnest, exacting, and flexible.(name) provided outstanding operational support to various critical elements of this command. Adaptable, polished, and receptive, the one to see when a job needs completed with dispatch and efficiency.

(name) is a self-starter, confident of abilities and work. Volunteers to tackle any assignment without doubt or hesitation. Completely dedicated to Navy, its role and mission. Works zealously to complete each task as perfectly as possible. Possessed of a sound management background, strong moral fiber of this (peer group) combined with an analytical mind and adaptability to changing situations. (name) should be promoted ahead of contemporaries and assigned to most demanding and challenging billets. Enjoys my complete trust and confidence in any assignment, regardless of difficulty or complexity.

(name) is an absolute top performer in every respect. Outstanding leadership, superb management techniques, and total dedication to duty. Head and shoulders above contemporaries. Unlimited growth potential. Every operational commitment met or exceeded. Organization received numerous expressions of appreciation from various commands for superior support.

Dedication and ability to get job done regardless of circumstances. (name) has my complete confidence to represent the command in any circumstances. Quiet manner, commanding presence. Total consideration for others.. These traits earned the genuine respect of seniors, juniors, and peers alike. Extremely well-rounded individual. In addition to demanding duty schedule, actively engages in a wide range of off-duty activities. Specifically:...... (name) has demonstrated potential for greater responsibilities through uncompromising performance and professionalism.

174

Dedicated to Navy . Unlimited potential. Requires each person to give a full measure of productive work each day. The imagination, intelligence, and business-like manner taken into each assignment virtually assures success. (name) is an extremely intelligent and dynamic leader with limitless potential. Top (peer group) in this command.

Solid, proven leadership and management principles were highlighted by..... Initiative and professionalism above approach: Inspired unequaled loyalty and esprit de corps. (name) is an asset to this command and the United States Navy.

The type of self-starting individual needed by our Navy in order to meet tomorrow's challenges. (name) is a model (peer group). Always adds more to the job than expected, putting it ahead of own interests. Inquisitive, creative, and foresighted. Consistently makes sound management decisions. An energetic personality, positive "can do" attitude, and deep pride in country and the Navy highlight daily performance. Promote now.

TOP PERFORMERS
(5.0-4.0)

PERFORMANCE APPRAISAL
SAMPLE #1

Superior leader, manager, and organizer. Virtually unlimited potential. Continually supports and enforces command goals and policy. Mature, articulate, and dedicated, meets or exceeds all deadlines. Accomplishments include:
-Reenlisted 7 of 8 eligible personnel.
-All personnel in (organization) qualified for advancement.
-Received Letter of Appreciation for outstanding work on, and support of, command 3M duties.
-Qualified OOD (Inport) in 3 months, OOD Underway in 6 months. Less than half average time. Runs taut watch team and enjoys my complete confidence and support.
-Excels in self-directing and self-pacing.
-Attains quality results at any tasking level.
-Uses penetrating and objective analysis in arriving at decisions. -Chaired ad hoc committee on human resource management and development. Excellent results.
-Immaculate personal appearance.
-Cheerful, witty, and friendly, asset to high morale.
-Maintains articulate and up-to-date records.
-Active in community: Vice President PTA; Editor local VFW chapter newsletter; Church leader.

Unequalled ability to obtain maximum results of available material and manpower resources. Unyielding dedication and loyalty. Analytical in thought, reasoned in mind. Humane and compassionate. Works full day on operational matters and then dedicates off-duty hours to catch up on administrative matters. "Head and shoulders" above contemporaries.

(name) is a self-starter and inspirational leader. Seasoned counselor. Demanding yet fair, impressive leader and organizer. Strong moral fiber, respected by subordinates and superiors. Top achiever of boundless potential and ability. (Recommendation for advancement/duty assignment.)

PERFORMANCE APPRAISAL SAMPLE #2

Industrious, meticulous, and accurate, (name) aggressively tackles any job. Unparalleled potential. Intolerant of mediocre performance, yet aware of personal limitations. Unhesitatingly offers constructive criticism when warranted. Subordinates are tactfully led to desired level of performance. Accomplishments and strengths include:

*Chairman of command ... Committee.
*Led department to superb 89.2 grade on annual competitive operational exercises.
*Reviewed and made constructive recommended changes to three Navy warfare/operational publications.
*Maximizes strengths of subordinates.
*Encourages open, two-way communications.
*Positive influence in achieving command goals.
*Promotes working environment conducive to individual creativity.
*Achieves high quality results regardless of tasking level.
*Stimulates pride and professionalism.
*Excels in self and subordinate development.
*Unusually accurate, thorough, and effective in oral and written communications. Drafts smooth correspondence and instructions.

(name) optimizes available manpower and material resources. Firm and fair, an advocate of equal treatment and opportunity. Flawless planning and execution efforts virtually guarantee success of any job. Highly respected throughout chain of command for professional knowledge and personal professionalism. Unbounded potential. (name) is a proven leader, manager, and organizer. Unlimited potential. (Recommendation for advancement/duty assignment.)

PERFORMANCE APPRAISAL SAMPLE #3

(name) most productive and versatile (peer group) at this command. Proven top quality organizer, administrator, and manager. Unlimited potential for increased responsibility and authority. I awarded him a Navy Achievement Medal for sustained superior performance. Possesses great deal of energy, highly industrious, doesn't believe in idle time. Friendly personality, quick wit, establishes and maintains atmosphere of pride and professionalism. Partial listing of accomplishments includes: *Drafted finest organization manual I ever read. 250 Page document was comprehensive, precise, easy to read. Dedicated 750 hours in construction, 500 were off-duty hours. By request, copies given to other commands. *Constructed $150,000 budget that allowed efficient and effective operations, yet employed financial restraint. *Qualified OOD (Inport). Enjoys my complete and confidence and is highly capable of making independent judgement and decision. *Planned and coordinated activation of command's... *Organized and tracked 500-manday maintenance package with unqualified success. *Researched action that updated 10 Naval Warfare Publications. *Personally picked to conduct command ... Classes. *Conducted management workshops explaining requirement for proper recognition for superior performers and swift, humane, and just corrective action for substandard performers. *EDUCATION: Completed 6 college courses during off-duty time with straight A average, and earned an Associate's Degree graduating with 3.74 GPA.

(name) fully enjoys Navy life, is quick to point out career benefits, and will not tolerate open dissent toward Navy or command policies or procedures. "Recruit Poster Quality" image. Poised and mature with thirst for knowledge and desire for challenge. Positive motivator, intelligent, and articulate. (name) is a self-starter whose great personal initiative and leadership skills identify (him/her) as being "head and shoulders" above contemporaries. Runs an orderly and highly productive organization in any environment. Commanding presence, decisive, and determined. (name) has earned my strongest endorsement for immediate advancement and for promotion to Limited Duty Officer. Unlimited potential, of immense value to Navy—promote now.

PERFORMANCE APPRAISAL SAMPLE #4

(name) sets the standards by which excellence is measured. A proven manager and leader of unbounded ability. (his/her) superb working knowledge of systems and equipments has increased the operational excellence and capability of (organization) and was the basis for being awarded a Navy Achievement Medal. Displays the character, initiative, and resourcefulness to accept and accomplish the most demanding tasks. The energetic and conscientious dedication displayed in transforming a work group to a viable operating element within two months of assuming charge set the example—and pace—for the entire (organization). Reestablishing a quality control program that had been idle for some time was among (his/her) first priorities. Within 2 months (he/she) initiated a comprehensive test and control package that resulted in equipment availability percentages second to none. As tedious and demanding as this task was, (he/she) made time to assist in other important areas. (his/her) ideas and suggestions greatly assisted in developing new procedures to improve on existing watch station qualification standards and contributed significantly toward a more effective administrative and operational environment.

(name) is a self-starter. (he/she) took it upon (himself/herself) to take charge of an inexperienced maintenance crew, identify numerous material and wiring deficiencies, and then executed a highly successful repair and upgrade program. That (he/she) has been capable and able to accomplish these and more tasks, individually and collectively successful, attests to (his/her) bold and imaginative leadership and management style. (name) potential is unlimited.

(name) is especially adept in dealing with people. Understands the worth and dignity of each individual and successfully pursues a "follow me" leadership role. (his/her) demeanor, confidence, and spirit of cooperation have been highly commendable in many "crisis management" situations. (name) is a dedicated professional who thrives on new challenges. (name) is a dynamic leader and a superb manager. Ideally suited for top supervisory positions.

PERFORMANCE APPRAISAL SAMPLE #5

(name) is a dedicated, cheerful, and hard-working individual who performs all duties in an accurate and enthusiastic manner. Boundless potential. (his/her) ability to adapt to change and perform in a superior manner became quite evident during periods when (he/she) was called upon to assume several different billet functions. Never wavering, (he/she) accepted all responsibilities and challenges in stride, demonstrating versatility and exceptional managerial skills. Displaying a positive attitude, (he/she) has generated enthusiasm at all levels within the (organization).

(name) dress and grooming are impeccable. Always presents neat and dignified appearance, reflecting obvious pride in self and service. Athletically inclined, an active participant in a variety of command sponsored sporting events. (name) calm and affable manner are a prime asset in the daily coordination of activities. Always contributes full measure to any task and (his/her) willingness to accept added responsibility enhance (his/her) potential for positions of higher authority. Quick to take the lead in coordinating activity and providing necessary guidance and supervision. Completely self-reliant, strives for perfection and sees all projects through to their successful conclusion. Whatever the task or situation, fully exploits the information and tools available to produce the most effective response. Gives fair and equitable treatment to all while ensuring the job at hand is done correctly.

(name) expresses (himself/herself) excellently both in writing and speech. Logical and direct in approach and factual in argument, making points clearly and concisely.

(name) is a consistent top performer within (his/her) peer group, constantly seeking new and more effective methods in performing (organization) duties. Knowledgeable of all methods and procedures within area of responsibility and uses these skills as effective tools and guide lines in meeting all command tasks. (name) individual drive is motivating and refreshing. Believes in the Navy and its purpose, always upholding the highest tradition of the Naval Service. Unbound potential.

(name) is motivated toward a career in the Navy, and his devotion to duty and willingness to perform above and beyond what is normally expected mark him as an excellent candidate for increased and more demanding duties. (Recommendation for advancement/duty assignment.)

PERFORMANCE APPRAISAL SAMPLE # 6

This special evaluation is submitted to recognize and document the all-around superior performance (name) has displayed throughout this abbreviated reporting period. Unlimited potential. An exceptional manager and organizer whose demonstrated expertise as a leader has measurably improved the overall performance and readiness of this command. An individual who commands the fullest respect and support of those with whom (he/she) works. Willing to accept any assignment regardless of scope. An original thinker who has demonstrated the ability to devise and organize operational and administrative procedures that weigh time, personnel, and money while ensuring the most efficient and economic methods are applied to any task. Some of (name) many accomplishments include: -Reorganized the (organization) work schedule. Superb administrative and managerial abilities resulted in slashing 25% of originally scheduled manhours required to (job). The job was completed within timetable without detracting from overall effectiveness. -Developed and implemented a training program that attained remarkable results in minimum time. (his/her) (organization) went from 25% to 87% watch station PQS qualified in 2 months. In one month 3M PQS qualifications jumped from 45% to 100%. -Developed and implemented 25 detailed, accurate, and well written SOPs. Much of this work was accomplished during normal off-duty hours. -Received "OUTSTANDING" at two command zone inspections for the cleanliness and high state of preservation of assigned workspaces. (name) is a self-starter whose work is marked by integrity and initiative. (he/she) is meticulously accurate with a great sense of responsibility for quality of work. A tireless worker, cheerfully devotes numerous extra hours to ensure that all projects and problems are being taken care of and are followed through to a successful conclusion.

(name) accomplishments listed above speak for themselves. A true professional in every sense of the word. The courage of conviction and strong moral character (he/she) exhibits foster high morale, esprit de corps, and a total winning attitude. (Recommendation for advancement/duty assignment).

PERFORMANCE APPRAISAL SAMPLE # 7

(name) sterling performance noted in (his/her) previous evaluation has continued throughout this reporting period. Excellent potential. (he/she) has consistently executed the weighty responsibilities of (billet) with fervor, determination, and overall superb success. Very talented...good sense of organization...a spontaneous propensity to leadership...a reputation for dependable and timely work. Strong and able in all areas, (his/her) most significant quality is the ability to impart (his/her) extensive operational experience and knowledge to subordinates.

Specifically, (name) was responsible for the following list of significant accomplishments: *Streamlined record-keeping procedures which has noticeably eased the administrative workload and allowed primary emphasis on the operational mission. *Revised operational techniques in (area) that led to a decrease in manpower requirements by 15 %. *Updated logging procedures for (area), that ultimately led to one person being available for reassignment to a more operations-oriented billet. *Developed a comprehensive PQS package for (billet). Spent upwards of 50 off-duty hours perfecting this package.

(name) has infused his (organization) with (his/her) enthusiasm and dedication. (his/her) astute management of personnel and equipment assets and close attention to the material condition of assigned work spaces have markedly improved the operation, working conditions, and physical appearance of (organization). (name) has proven a tactful yet strong leader by instilling in each subordinate the same desire to excel as (he/she) displays. The efforts and accomplishments listed above have made a specific and definite contribution to this command. (name) is truly an exceptional (peer group). Ready for increased responsibility now. (name) is a "front runner" within peer group. (Recommendation for advancement/duty assignment.)

PERFORMANCE APPRAISAL SAMPLE # 8

(name) is an outstanding (peer group). Unlimited potential for future growth and increased value to the Navy. Discharges all responsibilities with complete professionalism and tireless dedication. Conscientious, tireless, and persevering. As (billet/job), (he/she) has had to manage around problems not normally present in a strictly operating environment. This did not dull (his/her) enthusiasm or slow productive output. As a result of (his/her) sound leadership techniques and effective management, the ... project was completed well weeks ahead of schedule. Regardless of difficulties encountered, (name) always found a way to turn a potentially damaging problem into a short-term inconvenience. Throughout this demanding period (he/she) always received maximum support from subordinates because of (his/her) ability to generate enthusiasm through "follow me" leadership and direct supervision.

In spite of an already heavy workload, (name) found time to complete other noteworthy projects. They include: *Maintained organization's equipment in an operational, on-line status 98% of the time. Best in recent memory. *Planned and implemented watch station PQS standards for 5 new operating positions. *Reduced financial expenditures by 36% over those of (his/her) predecessor during an equal period.

(name) appearance and personal behavior are on par with (his/her) other exceptional qualities of performance. Records and correspondence are always correct and up to date and are among the best in (organization).

(name) is a proven leader and an accomplished specialist in (his/her) professional field. (organization) outstanding retention and advancement record, extremely low disciplinary rate, and the superior military bearing of (his/her) personnel are just a few examples of the positive indicators signaling (his/her) effectiveness and value to the Navy. (name) is recommended for promotion under the Navy's Warrant Officer Program.

PERFORMANCE APPRAISAL SAMPLE #9

(name) is a top performer. Unlimited potential. Totally professional, poised, mature, and dedicated. Significant achievements include: - Awarded Navy Achievement Medal for ... -Awarded Letter of Commendation from ... for sustained superior performance during (period). -Awarded Letter of Appreciation for off-duty assistance in civic functions.

Self-starter. Can plan, coordinate, direct, and finish job right the first time. Highlights of specific accomplishments include: -Established superb supply system within (organization) that affords complete and accurate stock control management and auditing capabilities. -(organization) Key person in Navy Relief, Combined Federal Campaign, and special Red Cross Drive. 100% participation. -Drafted two command instructions and fifteen SOPs. All excellently researched, documented, and accurate. -Managed and led 15-person "tiger team" in installation of new (equipment) and systems package. Completed three months ahead of schedule and $10,000 under budget.

Neat, trim, and fit. Immaculate "recruit poster" quality appearance. Articulate in speech, polite in manner. Submits timely and accurate paperwork. (name) enjoys loyalty, cooperation, and support of subordinates. Intelligent and dedicated, always volunteers for additional work to help shipmates and increase own knowledge, skill, and worth. A rising star of unlimited potential. Highly qualified and recommended for any demanding and challenging billet up to two pay grades above present rate/rank.

(name) does not believe in idle time or unfinished projects. Manages own time and that of others to best possible advantage. Possesses managerial and organizational expertise rarely observed in contemporaries. Completes large volume of work each day, frequently working extra hours. (Recommendation for advancement/duty assignment.)

PERFORMANCE APPRAISAL SAMPLE # 10

(name) performance, both militarily and professionally, is nothing short of outstanding. Has potential to fill positions of greater trust and responsibility not normally available within the enlisted structure. Displaying a keen interest, (he/she) sets and maintains a high standard of performance for (himself/herself) and subordinates. Continually maintains a high state of operational and material readiness despite antiquated equipment and non-availability of spare parts and material support.

Some of (name) more significant accomplishments include:
(list accomplishments)

Methodical and extremely conscientious, (name) actions are well planned, smoothly executed, and in the best interest of a job well done. In addition to (his/her) primary duties, (he/she) is a qualified ... Operations Watch Officer and is called upon to act in that capacity during personnel shortages. As expected of a leader of his caliber, (his/her) watch team consistently produces quality results while being sensitive to the needs of command. (he she) volunteered to assume responsibility for the command combined federal campaign, and as always, (his/her) enthusiasm infiltrated the command resulting in 97% participation and the highest dollar average per man in recent history. An active member of a Parent Teacher's Association and a coach for a little league team. (Recommendation for advancement/duty assignment.)

PERFORMANCE APPRAISAL SAMPLE # 11

Regardless of complexity or magnitude of the task at hand, (name) can be relied upon to see that it is completed expeditiously and efficiently. (his/her) high level of expertise is particularly exemplified by the in-depth, complete direction (he/she) provided the maintenance shop during overhaul. As a direct result of (his/her) guidance, complete equipment and systems were updated and refurbished to the extent that the level of dependability was equal to that equipment at the original time of installation. Not only a skilled technical specialist, (he/she) is also a dedicated leader whose standards of integrity and military bearing are of the finest quality. (his/her) spaces continually stand out at zone inspections with a sustained grade point average of 96.5%. The outstanding material condition of spaces is totally impressive.

An overview of (name) accomplishments include:
(list accomplishments)

An accomplished counselor, (name) readily shares (his/her) experience with personnel in both military and personal matters and they seek out (his/her) advice with regularity. (he/she) personally encourages every subordinate to set the highest possible goals for themselves and then counsels them on means available to realize those goals, both professional and personal. (name) is highly recommended for the Warrant Officer Program.

PERFORMANCE APPRAISAL SAMPLE # 12

(name) is one of the finest (peer group) in the United States Navy. (his/her) potential is unlimited. In two years of dedicated service to this command (he/she) played a vital role in the achievement of this command's mission and is a cornerstone of technical knowledge, management skill, and military tradition. I awarded (him/her) a Navy Achievement Medal for (his/her) work as (billet). (his/her) vast experience is enhanced by intelligence, sincerity, and an ability to communicate effectively with all levels of command. Many of the improvements (he/she) either initiated or carried out have made lasting marks on operations and administration within the ... Department. (his/her) intense dedication to duty, personal sacrifice, and uncompromising standards of conduct have provided the impetus for the organizational growth and development of the department.

(name) strong leadership, management acumen, technical knowledge, and personal diligence have resulted in the following specific achievements: -Development of systems layout, standard operating procedures, and organizational design for the department. -Efficient procurement and management of operational and administrative assets saved the command ... dollars in sorely needed financial assets. -Brought the standards of military behavior and personal appearance in the department to the highest level through and intensive program of inspections, training, and personal leadership. -Closely involved in the planning and implementation of equipment and manpower changes due to department consolidation.

(Name) is the most highly respected (peer group) in this command. (his/her) total commitment to the Navy, support of seniors, and leadership of those who serve under (him/her) have significantly enhanced readiness, retention, and morale. (he/she) is most strongly recommended for promotion to Limited Duty Officer. I would be pleased to have (him/her) as a member of my wardroom either afloat or ashore. (Recommendation for advancement/duty assignment.)

PERFORMANCE APPRAISAL SAMPLE # 13

(name) sets an exceptional example as a leader and manager. Virtually unlimited potential. (he/she) works a full day in assigned job and then consistently puts in many extra hours assisting in areas outside normal area of responsibility. As a result, (he/she) has attained professional and technical knowledge and competence rarely observed within (his/her) peer group. The ability to obtain quality results in any environment and to relate to all age groups are the cornerstone of (name) success as a leader.

(name) displays a genuine concern for others and always finds time to help those in need of counseling and personal assistance. The emphatic demeanor and timely responsiveness (he/she) is known for has inspired and maintained high morale and team spirit throughout the department.

(name) ability to communicate (his/her) thoughts and commands, both verbally and in writing, are excellent. An exceptional orator. Staff work always timely and correct. Neat, trim and physically fit, (he/she) is a model of military bearing and Navy tradition.

(name) contributions to mission effectiveness include:
*Supervised a pilot program to test the effectiveness and feasibility of two new operational systems. The test was successful, in large measure, to the exceptionally efficient and methodical approach taken by (name).
*Implemented the operational phase of the equipment systems program with unparalleled success.
*Drafted 4 command instructions on systems test and operations. Throughout (name) tenure as (billet), the innovative approach (he/she) displayed in day-to-day operations, as well as special programs, were consistently above the expected norm.

In summary, (name) has consistently performed all duties in an outstanding manner and has exhibited those traits that are highly desirous of a Naval (peer group)—strong leadership abilities; an excellent manager of material and equipment; tact and compassion; and, an innovative and intelligent view of the future. Recommendation for advancement/duty assignment.)

PERFORMANCE APPRAISAL SAMPLE # 14

(name) is an intelligent, energetic manager and organizer. Enjoys fast-paced work environment. "Head and shoulders" above contemporaries with virtually unlimited potential. Quick thinker, makes positive decisions that are easily supported. Completely dependable, performs all tasks with accuracy and dispatch. Professional attitude radiates to subordinates, causing them to respond in kind with full effort and cooperation.

A sampling of (name) accomplishments include:
*Awarded Letter of Appreciation for suggestion on how to reduce equipment operation time when not on-line without detracting from operational capability. Suggestion will save Navy approximately $15,000 a year in reduced spare parts costs.
*Awarded Letter of Appreciation for work as Chairman of Command ... As a direct result of (his/her) foresight, recommendations, and actions, command morale has been enhanced.
*Qualified OOD (Underway).
*Drafted and implemented Department Regulations Manual. The 125 page instruction is complete, correct, and easy to read. *Instituted many procedures that improved and streamlined department operations and administrative effort.
*Active in command recreation activities, and serves as Vice President of local Parent-Teacher Association.

(name) has a knack for getting job done where others fail. Informed on current Navy career programs. Information quickly passed on to supervisors who become highly responsive to needs of subordinates. Established routines that strengthened chain of command, facilitated smoother flow of correspondence, and created highly professional working atmosphere. Always a contributor to group effort. Works easily with seniors and subordinates. Sobriety, punctuality, and strong sense of duty highlight daily performance. Trim, physically fit, always "inspection ready."

(name) overall outstanding performance has contributed significantly to the high level of success achieved by this command. (Recommendation for advancement/duty assignment.)

PERFORMANCE APPRAISAL SAMPLE # 15

Outstanding (peer group). Top notch manager and organizer. Well versed in all facets of technical specialty. Energetic and resourceful, plans ahead. Impressively managed (organization) transition from operating to overhaul environment. Structured organization meeting or exceeding all tasking. Devised highly effective management control system to track and identify delay or deficiency in shipyard or contractor work encompassing ... dollar, ... -manday overhaul package. Subsequently identified and corrected various operating and design problems.

Accomplishments and achievements include:
-Managing ... manday ship's force overhaul and rehab work package. All major work ahead of schedule. -Tracking and providing technical advice and assistance on ... SHIPALTS, including installation of (nr.) new equipments. -Letter of Appreciation from (command) for personal assistance to that command. -Drafted comprehensive ... page organization manual. Implemented and proving highly successful. -Revised billet and training structure to better meet post-overhaul operational commitments. -Excellent staff and paperwork—well researched, timely, and accurate. -Ambitious career counseling and training program: 100% assigned personnel promoted from last two Navy-wide advancement examinations; 73% reenlistment record, first in the command; and, 100% completed off-duty college or self-study courses. -Fit, trim, and erect in carriage.

(name) is a self-starter with desire for challenge. Has great deal of energy, doesn't believe in idle time. Firm, fair unbiased leader. Demands high standards of performance from self and subordinates. Effectively capitalizes on subordinate strengths and improves weaknesses. Enjoys fast-paced work environment. Should be selectively detailed to demanding and responsible billets. Highly talented, a front runner. (Recommendation for advancement/duty assignment.)

PERFORMANCE APPRAISAL SAMPLE # 16

(name) excels wherever assigned. An invaluable manager and counselor, and a source of knowledge and inspiration in every area of responsibility. Has capacity for higher responsibility. Early in this reporting period (he/she) was called upon to head a revitalized department training program. The response was immediate and decisive. Without waiting for guidance, (he/she) formed ad hoc groups to tackle the element problems (he/she) had observed. Each group was informed of what was ultimately expected, but allowed to approach their individual problem area as they saw fit, so long as the final result met desired goals. Within six weeks, an appropriate training site was secured, a short- and long-range curriculum was finalized, instructors had been trained, and the entire training program was off the ground five weeks ahead of schedule. In the first four months, (number) personnel completed the course, almost double the number expected.

Based on the strong managerial and leadership traits (name) displayed in (his/her) first major undertaking, (he/she) was subsequently assigned duties as ... Again, (he/she) proved (himself/herself) up to the challenge. Administrative records were quickly brought in line with organizational policy; operating procedures were established and fed back into the training cycle; and, a new chain-of-command organization structure was devised and implemented with good success.

(name) tact, coordination, and the ability to get to the heart of any problem have increased the operational and administrative efficiency and effectiveness of the department. The impossibility of any situation does not occur to (him/her). (he/she) is an excellent counselor with a unique ability to reach a troubled person and give fair, honest guidance. Without equal among peers.

(name) is dedicated to the Navy and has unlimited potential. (he/she) looks out for people, yet requires each to give a full measure of productive work each day. The imagination, intelligence, and business-like manner (he/she) takes into each assignment virtually assures success. (Recommendation for advancement/duty assignment.)

PERFORMANCE APPRAISAL SAMPLE # 17

(name) is an extremely intelligent and dynamic leader with limitless potential. (he/she) is the top (peer group) at this command.

When (name) was assigned to (his/her) present billet, the department was faced with austere manning, antiquated operating procedures, and a core of untrained and unproven front-line supervisors. Never wavering, (he/she) quickly and accurately assessed the situation and immediately set out to generate solutions. By working with other divisions (he/she) was able to obtain administrative assistance to update operating procedures. Front-line supervisors attended up-to-date training sessions. (name) personally conducted organizational and managerial classes attended by middle-manager cadre. Solid, proven leadership and management principles were highlighted and used as a foundation on which to build. The idea quickly caught on, key personnel began seeing the organization as a whole and their specific part in the operation. Suggestions started to flow up the chain of command from all levels. Many ideas proved effective almost immediately; some became effective after minor alteration; and, the suggestions without merit were quickly identified and discarded without undue delay. Within three months (name) had structured an organization that was dynamic in nature and allowed for self-evaluation and internal correction. All deadlines began being met; morale improved dramatically; and, the total workload placed on each individual actually decreased as a result of people knowing what their job was, and what time-consuming, duplicating efforts could be jettisoned. Throughout this hectic time (name) displayed compassion and concern, and inspired unequalled loyalty and esprit de corps.

Other achievements and accomplishments include:
(list)

(name) is an asset to this command and the United States Navy. (Recommendation for advancement/duty assignment.)

PERFORMANCE APPRAISAL SAMPLE # 18

(name) performance continues to be underscored by pride, self-improvement, and accomplishment. Excellent potential. Awarded Navy Achievement Medal for superior performance at (his/her) previous command. Overall performance and dedication to duty are no less evident at this command. Initially assigned the primary duties of (job), (he/she) found time to assume other, equally demanding tasks. Filling in as ... (he/she) organized the monumental task of constructing a set of viable files and records following an extended period of inattention. In the area of training, (he/she) personally planned and scheduled the assignment of 15 personnel to 22 various schools. Made 3 no-cost TAD trips to various locations, ensuring necessary training was received and that NEC billets were filled within authorized limits. (he/she) volunteered to assume the increased and diverse duties of (job) when the person filling that billet was unexpectedly transferred. In this capacity (he/she) managed the successful efforts to meet all operational tasking. The job was particularly demanding and time-consuming with the department only 75% manned.

Working with others in a unified and cohesive manner is a particularly strong asset of (name). (he/she) has the ability to immediately establish and maintain excellent rapport with subordinates on all levels. Much of this is due to the fair, open, and unbiased manner (he/she) has in dealing with them. Person know that they will be given an equal opportunity, commensurate with capabilities, to work in any job or assignment, and that all will be given the opportunity to learn.

Eager to stay abreast of the latest changes in management, technology, and operations, (he/she) is currently enrolled in two courses at ...University, attending night classes. Recently completed three Navy training schools and two correspondence courses.

(name) is an achiever possessed with imagination and initiative. (Recommendation for advancement/duty assignment.)

193

PERFORMANCE APPRAISAL SAMPLE # 19

Superior ability and performance. Boundless potential. Exceptionally skilled in all facets of technical specialty. Totally professional and dedicated. Performance underscored by pride, personal involvement, and accomplishment.

(name) awards and accolades include:
-Navy Achievement Medal for superior performance as Project Manager of ...
-Navy Expeditionary Medal (period time).
-Message of Appreciation from TYCOM for professional assistance in ... Exercise as (job).
-Letter of Appreciation for community involvement in ...

Industrious and creative—an achiever. Likes to get into "nuts and bolts" of problems regardless of complexity or magnitude. Outstanding technical knowledge and managerial ability. Achievements and accomplishments: - Identified equipment placement and workflow design discrepancies in ... operating spaces during major equipment reconfiguration project. - Managing highly accurate progress flow charts and reference files on more than 75 command and contractor work packages. All ship's work progressing ahead of schedule and all contractor work on track due, in large measure, to (name) personal initiative, drive, and coordination efforts. -Instrumental in revising department billet structure to eliminate administrative inefficiency and increase operational readiness. - Educational interests: Completed three off-duty college courses through ... University pursuing ... Degree; and, completed six Navy correspondence courses. -Able and highly capable administrator, submits smooth, well documented staff work.

(name) has unbound initiative and is extremely conscientious. Actions well planned, organized, and smoothly executed. Team player, fosters cooperation and harmony throughout command. A forceful, dynamic, and compassionate leader, knows how to motivate subordinates. Unlimited potential. (name) is a head and shoulders performer. (Recommendation for advancement/duty assignment.)

PERFORMANCE APPRAISAL SAMPLE # 20

Unlimited potential. (name) sustained superior performance has been an inspiration to each member of this command. (he/she) is the embodiment of pride and professionalism. These concepts are, and have always been, (his/her) benchmark as an advocate of tradition, loyalty, and a strong Naval Service. Outspoken support of the chain of command, firm enforcement of military standards, and equitable treatment of each subordinate has optimized morale and promoted effective mission accomplishment within the command.

(name) is never too busy to listen to a personal problem and is never reluctant to respond with positive action. Ability to anticipate potential problem has resulted in timely compliance with all administrative and operational requirements.

Distinguished accomplishments include:
a. Served with distinction as Chairman of the Command ...
b. Played a key role in preparation for a command inspection. The command received high marks in all graded areas due, in large part, to (name) active involvement.
c. Brought all administrative files up to date and participated actively in reviewing and updating command instructions.
d. Developed and implemented a personnel placement document, the first of its kind at this command. This resulted in a more effective assignment of personnel assets.
e. Developed performance standards for 5 administrative positions. The quality of these written standards was such that they have been used as models for other commands in the local area.

(name) unparalleled ability to manage money, material, and personnel place (him/her) number one in peer group at this command, if not the Navy. To highlight abilities, (he/she): -Builds on understanding and encourages feedback from subordinates. -Instills high-performance motivation and creativity. -Stimulates individual growth and responsibility. In a word, (name) performance, across the board, has been nothing less than OUTSTANDING. (Recommendation for advancement/duty assignment.)

PERFORMANCE APPRAISAL SAMPLE # 21

Truly outstanding (peer group). Potential for positions of higher authority unlimited. Demonstrates unfailing diligence, job-aggressiveness, and total dedication to excellence. Thoroughly prepared for every assignment. A true self-starter. Personal initiative and leadership skills guarantee exceptional results of all tasks assigned or assumed.

Top shelf organizer, manager, and administrator. Unique ability to assimilate myriad of diverse inputs and produce timely, accurate, and detailed results. Developed innovative management system to track manhours and work progress of all (organization) operations and management maintenance efforts. Experience, managerial abilities, and administrative talents were of immense significance in command earning ... Excellence ("E") Award, and grade of "outstanding" during Command Inspection. Constructed itemized $100,000 FY Budget which reflected most efficient and effective use of available funds.

Drawing on extensive administrative talents, (name) dedicated over 500 man hours of off-duty time constructing the most thorough, comprehensive, and precise Command Training Program package I have ever read. Accolades routinely received from senior attendees. Poised and mature (peer group) with matchless thirst for knowledge and increased responsibility. Leadership, example, and skill in expressing views directly responsible for others seeking higher education. Always quick to point out career benefits. Directly responsible for persuading top performers to apply for officer and special enlisted education programs. Erect in posture, trim in carriage. Qualified as OOD (Inport), earned my complete trust and confidence, most capable of making independent judgements and decisions required to run highly effective watch team.

A strong performer during entire tour. A proven top achiever, demonstrates those specific talents and character traits required for ascent to positions of high responsibility. (Recommendation for advancement/duty assignment.)

PERFORMANCE APPRAISAL SAMPLE # 22

(name) is extremely knowledgeable, industrious, and completely resourceful (peer group). Performance of all duties singularly outstanding. Personally selected to assume ... duties of a 75-man division for six months. Selected because of demonstrated superior management and leadership abilities. Division quickly and efficiently reorganized to meet increased operational tasking.

Exceptionally fine administrator. Superb ability to write clear, concise, and accurate material. All administrative matters submitted on time in smooth, ready for signature form. Originated incomparable division record in general administrative matters; training; and, equipment management. Devoted literally months of intense off-duty effort and produced quality package that stands alone in sheer excellence. I have seen none finer.

Continually striving for personal growth. Completed three (undergraduate/graduate) courses, three Navy and one civilian correspondence course. (name) plans ahead, stays on top of every project or assignment until quality results achieved. Superb watch team leader, takes rapid, effective action without guidance from above. Excellent counselor, particularly adept in solving problems encountered by junior personnel. Unlimited potential for responsibility and challenge. All-around quality (peer group). Without reservation (name) has my highest recommendation for early advancement to (grade).

Other accomplishments include:
(list)

(name) is the Number One (peer group) in my command. (Recommendation for advancement/duty assignment.)

PERFORMANCE APPRAISAL SAMPLE # 23

(name) is an industrious, conscientious, and highly motivated (peer group) who exhibits the highest degree of professionalism. As (billet), (name) was directly responsible for the outstanding performance of (his/her) undermanned (organization) as evidenced by the following specific accomplishments: -Contributed personally to this command's mission during critical operations that lead to receiving... Unit Commendation. - Achieved equipment and systems reliability of 96.8%, despite heavy, taxing operations. -Designed and completed major upgrade of obsolete wiring. Task completed in half allowed time without any loss of operational capability. -Developed and implemented comprehensive Personnel Qualification Standards Program for ... First of its kind. Forwarded to TYCOM for use as a model.

(name) is an accomplished leader, manager, and organizer who has demonstrated the following personal traits and characteristics: *Convincing speaker.   *Keen judgement.
*Tireless worker.   *Inspiring leader.
*Informed and well read.   *Diplomatic personality.
*Alert, farsighted manager.   *Active, physically fit.
*Tactful leader of subordinates.
*Meticulous administrative skills.
*Backs superiors and command policy.

(name) is a self-starter who has implemented many programs within (his/her) organization which have served to upgrade operational capability and increase morale. (he/she) served with distinction in collateral duties as: NJP Investigating Officer; HRM Instructor; Member Command Training Team; and OOD. (name) is an informed, concerned individual with a gift for getting along with others. (his/her) advice is actively sought by juniors and seniors. Aware of need for effective communications, (he/she) successfully elicits continued high performance and morale from subordinates. (name) is a bold, imaginative leader, ready for promotion now. (Recommendation for advancement/duty assignment.)

PERFORMANCE APPRAISAL SAMPLE # 24

(name) is an efficient and highly knowledgeable (specialty) whose performance, singularly and collectively, has been outstanding. Demonstrated unbound ability and capacity to successfully assume positions of greater authority and jurisdiction. Firm, earnest, exacting, and flexible. Ensures highest degree of operational and administrative support while maintaining extraordinarily high morale. Shortly after assuming present position, (name) identified many equipment deficiencies and took corrective action as follows:

a. Identified and had 95 ... equipment deficiencies corrected within first two months, resulting in increased availability and reliability of equipment.

b. Obtained ... equipment that allows for real-time information and instantaneous reporting of operational evolutions.

c. Updated antiquated maintenance SOPs and procedures that reduced paperwork by 25%.

d. Measurably improved habitability of assigned work and living spaces.

e. Received "excellent" or "outstanding" at all weekly zone material inspections.

(name) has provided outstanding operational support as well as continued superior administrative skills to various critical elements of this command. Adaptable, polished, and receptive, the person to see when a job needs completed with dispatch and efficiency.

(name) is a self-starter, confident of abilities and work. Volunteers to tackle any assignment without doubt or hesitation. Completely dedicated to the Navy, its role and mission. Works zealously to complete each task as perfectly as possible. Possessed of a sound management background, the strong moral fiber of this (peer group) combined with an analytical mind and adaptability to changing situations makes (him/her) highly effective in any situation. (name) should be promoted ahead of contemporaries and assigned to most demanding and challenging billets. (name) enjoys my complete trust and confidence in any assignment, regardless of difficulty or complexity. (Recommendation for advancement/duty assignment.)

PERFORMANCE APPRAISAL SAMPLE # 25

(name) is an absolute top performer in every respect. (his/her) outstanding leadership, superb management techniques, and total dedication to duty place (him/her) head and shoulders above contemporaries. Unlimited growth potential. (his/her) organization has received numerous expressions of appreciation from various commands for superior support. Selectively reassigned to the billet of ...because of overall superior performance. (his/her) dedication and ability to get the job done regardless of circumstances were immediately evidenced. Within first month received personal Letter of Appreciation from (organization) for outstanding support and cooperation. Performs many collateral duties with the same thoroughness and professionalism as primary duty. One of the top OOD watchstanders in my command. (he/she) has my complete confidence to represent the command in any circumstances. Quiet manner and commanding presence. Displays total consideration for others in all endeavors, whether professional or personal. These traits have earned (him/her) the genuine respect of seniors, juniors, and peers alike.

(name) is an extremely well-rounded individual. In addition to a demanding duty schedule, (he/she) actively engages in a wide range of off-duty activities. Specifically, (he/she): Completed a two-week ... School, one week of which was leave time; actively participated in church and social activities, donating upwards of 100 off-duty hours working on community improvement projects; and, was the motivating force in organizing and managing various intramural athletic programs. (name) has demonstrated (his/her) potential for greater responsibilities through uncompromising performance and professionalism. The type of self-starting individual needed by our Navy in order to meet tomorrow's challenges.

(name) is a model (peer group). Always adds more to the job than expected, putting it ahead of personal interests. (he/she) is inquisitive, creative, and foresighted. Consistently makes sound management decisions. An energetic personality, positive "can do" attitude, and deep pride in his country and the Navy highlight daily performance. Promote now. (Recommendation for advancement/duty assignment.)

CHAPTER 7

AVERAGE PERFORMERS
(3.0)

AVERAGE PERFORMERS
(3.0)

WORD BANK

ABILITY	ABLE	ACCEPTABLE
ACCURATE	ADAPTABLE	ADEQUATE
AGREEABLE	ALLOWABLE	AMPLE
APPROPRIATE	ATTENTIVE	AVERAGE
BENEFICIAL	BENEFIT	CAPABLE
CAREFUL	CAUTIOUS	COMMON
COMMONPLACE	COMPATIBLE	COMPETENT
CONFIDENT	CONFORMS	CONSTRUCTIVE
CONTRIBUTES	CONVENTIONAL	CORRECT
CORRECTLY	CREDIBLE	DECENT
DEDICATED	DELIBERATE	DEPENDABLE
DESIRABLE	DESIRED	DETERMINED
DILIGENT	EAGER	EARNEST
EFFECTIVE	EFFICIENT	ENERGETIC
ENHANCES	ENOUGH	ERRORLESS
EVEN	EVERYDAY	FAIR
FAITHFUL	FAVORABLE	FORMULATED
GENEROUS	GOOD	HELPFUL
HOPEFUL	INFORMED	KNOWLEDGEABLE
MEANINGFUL	MEDIOCRE	MEDIUM
METHODICAL	MIDDLE	MIDDLE-OF-THE-ROAD
MIDDLING	MILD	MINDFUL
MODERATE	MODEST	NEAT
NORMAL	ORDERLY	ORDINARY
PASSABLE	PERSEVERING	PERSISTENT
PLAIN	PLEASANT	PLEASING
POSITIVE	PRACTICAL	PRODUCTIVE
PROFICIENT	PROMISING	PROMPT
PRUDENT	PUNCTUAL	QUALIFIED
QUALITY	REASONABLE	REGULAR

RELIABLE	RESPECT	RESPECTABLE
RESPONSIBLE	RUN-OF-THE-MILL	SATISFACTORY
SATISFY	SATISFYING	SENSIBLE
SIMPLE	SKILL	SKILLED
SO-SO	STABLE	STEADY
STEADY-GOING	SUCCESS	SUCCESSFUL
SUFFICIENT	SUITABLE	TALENTED
THOROUGH	THOUGHTFUL	TIDY
TIMELY	TRUE	TYPICAL
UPBEAT	USABLE	USUAL
VALUABLE	VALUED	WORTHY

BULLETS

(3.0)

faces challenges
inspires others
on-time performance

...helped update
...noteworthy performance
...team effort

keen judgment
tireless worker
pleasant surprise

...hard work
...cooperative in ...
...dedicated professional

faithfully performs ...
popular appeal
fully enjoys ...

...sensitive to ...
...always busy
...ambitious goals

behavior always ...
overcomes obstacles
dedicated to ...

...gained respect
...well meaning
...credit to ...

able to ...
created professional ...
painstaking efforts

...knowledgeable in/of ...
...high achiever
...looks after ...

capacity for ...
tireless individual
drafted new ...

...average in ...
...beneficial to ...
...worked hard

clear thinking
active in ...
never wavered

...efforts gained ...
...team player
...human understanding

normally completes ...
contributed to ...
performance continues ...

...poised & ...
...above expectations
...energetic organizer

streamlined operation
committed to ...
no errors

...helped further ...
...easy demeanor
...take-charge person

noteworthy accomplishments
diverse background ...
total support

...acceptable conduct
...motivates others
...high principles

accurate in/at ...
energetic person
meaningful contribution

decisive action
within standards
solid performance

asset to ...
personal diligence
launched new ...

helpful in
anticipates problems
encourages trust

organized new ...
polished manner
coordinated successful

responsible for ...
ample knowledge
little supervision

average proficiency
affable manner
timely response

accomplished counselor
benefit to command
mild mannered

a model ...
compassionate leader
fair share

sizable contribution
achieved goal(s)
guards against ...

sheer willpower
always willing ...
practical application

...correctly completes...
...strictly enforces
...positive contribution

...skillfully performed
...fair minded
...work benefits ...

...fosters camaraderie
...extremely conscientious
...somewhat effective

...proficient in/at ...
...talented & ...
...high energy

...self confident
...dependable work
...ignores obstacles

...capable of ...
...patient training
...efforts helped ...

...builds on ...
...effective in/at ...
...impetus for ...

...successfully completed ...
...skillful in/at ...
...boosted the ...

...prepared for ...
...people oriented
...dedicated leader/supervisor

...earned respect
...improved conditions
...competent work

...eager to ...
...skillful ability
...meticulous in ...

205

contributions are ...
productive & ...
always punctual

completes all ...
open minded
undying determination

improved on ...
created new ...
error free ...

supports all ...
highly skilled
confident & ...

versatile individual
minimum errors
unified various

versatile & ...
increased standards
desired results

satisfactorily completed ...
unceasing devotion
constructed new ...

valuable addition
achieves high ...
proponent of ...

constructive outlook
enthusiastic about ...
seasoned in ...

good contribution
tactful in/at ...
proven leader

studious nature
researched new ..
energetic, self-starter

...work sufficiently ...
...decent work
...basic needs

...positive action
...good at ...
...sincere affection

...efforts succeeded
...developed new ...
...managed successful ...

...developed comprehensive
...good progress
...successful in/as ...

...accomplished in/at ...
...established new ...
...congenial personality

...progressed to ...
...good opportunity ...
...very helpful

...enterprising individual
...highly accomplished
...amicable personality

...morale booster
...energetic personality
...initiated new ...

...achieved success
...highly successful
...individual needs

...promptly completes ...
...content with ...
...watchful for ...

...beneficiary of ...
...infused ... with ...
...complies with ...

worthy of ...
able to complete ...
positive, prompt action

deep respect for ...
confident of abilities
fully understands ... systems

work sufficiently good...
considerate of others
delivers ... on time

tries hard to ...
accurate & proficient
directly responsible for ...

full knowledge of ...
demanding, yet fair
commendable job in/as ...

prompt work habits
credible work habits
solves everyday problems

developed way to ...
positive, constructive outlook
made improvement in/to ...

constantly aware of ...
hardworking with limitless ...
always supports command ...

desired results in ...
has no problems ...
identified & corrected ...

thorough knowledge of/in ...
positive attitude infectious
eliminated admin inefficiency

achieved goal of ...
in timely fashion
developed performance standards

...deliberate work habits
...fair & unbiased
...good understanding of ...

...promotes high morale
...solid, dependable leadership
...energetic & helpful

...skillful ability to ...
...broad experience as/in ...
...made progress in/on ...

...delegates authority effectively
...credible knowledge of/in ...
...gained skills to ...

...relentless, energetic drive
...positive influence to/on ...
...satisfactory progress in/on ...

...showing steady progress
...diplomatic approach to ...
...encourages subordinates to ..

...thorough work habits
...competent in performing ...
...adapts quickly to ...

...bolsters morale by ...
...has advantage of ...
...genuine concern for ...

...friendly & cordial
...motivated, enjoys challenge
...works diligently to ...

...concerned & involved
...efforts resulted in ...
...encourages others to ...

...goes around obstacles
...educated others in ...
...always willing to ...

technically competent in/on ...
made contribution by/to ...
improved quality of ...

benefit to organization
very productive in/at ...
logical & foresighted

earned respect of ...
increased efficiency of ...
thoughtful, concerned supervisor

enhanced operation of ...
satisfactory, dependable leadership
thoughtful member of ...

long, hard work
builds team spirit
adequate leadership qualities

progress in ... satisfactory
determination led to ..
gets job done

.smart military appearance
.industrious & versatile
.keen appreciation of ...

.solid work habits
.promotes good will
.makes personal contribution

.pleasing, outgoing personality
.brought pride to ...
.innovative view toward ...

.discharges responsibilities with ...
.knows how to ...
.always in compliance ...

.follow-me leader who ...
.keen knowledge of
.developed & implemented

...suitable progress in/on ...
...goes forward despite ...
...constantly searching for ...

...keen ability in/to ...
...gets involved in ...
...positive asset to ...

...found better way to ...
...makes positive decisions
...satisfactory, dependable work

...caring & concerned
...added life to ...
...developed method to ...

...conscious effort to ...
...motivated & involved
...good use of ...

...industrious & studious
...experienced & talented
...fosters good camaraderie

...creates positive ... climate
...poised & mature
...distinct benefit to ...

...good uniforms & ...
...considerable talent for ...
...logical & direct

...engenders trust & ...
...works closely with ...
...treats others fairly

...credible ability to ...
...takes initiative in/at ...
...gets results from ...

...effective at teaching ...
...loyal & devoted
...played key role

enhanced operational effectiveness
possesses skills to ...
contributed personally to ...

good ability to ...
gives freely to ...
acute awareness of ...

work benefits all ...
especially effective at ...
cooperative, friendly spirit

industrious & willing
actively participates in ...
lives up to ...

good military bearing
take charge person
noteworthy contribution to ...

with little supervision ...
effectively delegates responsibility
personally involved in ...

on-time performance
highly successful in ...
supportive of command ...

implemented procedure that ...
actions spur results
takes direction when/if ...

agreeable military appearance
supports efforts to ...
inquisitive & creative

experienced & dedicated
particularly effective at ...
good problem-solving abilities

efficient operation of ...
assists others in ...
personal involvement stimulates ...

...motivator within team
...suitable knowledge in/on ..
...enjoys close rapport

...improved conditions of ...
...fit perfectly in ...
...successful in enforcing ...

...played crucial role
...always responds with ...
...enjoys working in/with ...

...moved quickly to ...
...effective use of ...
...completed ... with dispatch

...important part of ...
...successful approach to ...
...helps shipmates learn ...

...firm, fair leader/supervisor
...lends reassuring hand
...especially adept in/at ...

...innovative & resourceful
...good talent for ...
...willingness to serve

...completed large scale ...
...more than expected
...high degree of ...

...particularly adept in/at ...
...takes pride in ...
...helps others when ...

...opened way for ...
...fair, even-handed leader
...nice job of ...

...leads team by/with ...
...exerted influence to ...
...highly accomplished at ...

performance meets standards
competent knowledge of/in ...
sufficient leadership abilities

completes demanding tasks
subordinates tactfully led
instituted procedures that ...

faithful, reliable work
tactful & courteous
leads by example

exercises mature judgment
quality results in/as ...
orderly completion of ...

practical application of ...
highly accomplished in/as ...
quickly & accurately ...

established system to ...
tackles jobs with ...
leads highly competent ...

favorable results in/as ...
achieves more than ...
swift resolution of ...

highly competent in ...
person of great ...
highly effective in/at ...

leads others to ...
team player, always ...
willingly accepts work

sound in judgment
average ability to ...
proficient at job

alert for new ...
highly proficient in/as ...
adopted successful policy

...efficient solution to ...
...organized & tracked ...
...made ... look easy

...has skill to ...
...persistent, steady workload
...helps others to ...

...never wavered in ...
...achieved success in ...
...prudent use of ...

...supports goals of ...
...achieves desired results
...talented & effective

...composed under stress
...streamlined operation of ...
...prudent work on/in ...

...works hard at/to ...
...interacts well with ...
...proven quality leadership

...neat & correct
...exceeded requirements of ...
...attention to detail

...integral part of ...
...achieves success when ...
...quick to adapt

...productive member of ...
...concern for others
...uncompromising standards of

...excellent attitude toward(s) ...
...quality work in/on ...
...well versed in ...

...sound, mature judgment
...responsible for completing ...
...fine example of ...

.natural talent for ...
.typical progress on/in ...
.proved to be ...

.reacts positively to ...
.step ahead of ...
.moderate work habits

.set tempo of ...
.aids others in/by ...
.timely response to ...

.skillful developing subordinates
.built solid foundation
.timely compliance with ...

.satisfied requirements of/for ...
.requisite skills to ...
decent appearance & ...

meets or exceeds ...
readily shares experiences
very effective in ...

steady progress in ...
conforms to standards
makes sound decisions

timely & correct
very good at ...
reliable member of ...

grasps essentials of ...
demonstrated initiative in/at ...
ability to do ...

devotion to duty
meets all commitments
good, steady-going performance

received high marks
earned high praise
always punctual with ...

...always ready to ...
...understands ... better than .
...understands value of ...

...used sound judgment
...took lead in ...
...great ability to ...

...decent ability to ...
...seeks added responsibility
...requires limited supervision

...calm, affable manner
...meets standards in ...
...ability to ... deserves ...

...varying degrees of ...
...steady, dependable in ...
...decisive in action

...natural aptitude for ...
...dependable & conscientious
...guiding light for ...

...requires little supervision
...built organization that ...
...devised method to ...

...counted on to ...
...secured loyalty of ...
...stepped up & ...

...real problem solver
...totally fair & ...
...capable & dedicated

...dignity & poise
...stays up-to-date on ...
...courteous & cooperative

...duties skillfully executed
...uses initiative to ...
...dependable, timely work

valued member of ...
respected member of ...
very sharp appearance

stays ahead of ...
cordial & respectful to ...
accepts hard jobs with ...

always positive, can do attitude
enforces unified team action
works in harmony with ...

friendly & cooperative spirit
tactfully directs efforts to ...
worth & dignity of others

never at loss when ...
creative in problem solving
good measure of success

dependable & thorough in ...
cheerful, witty & friendly
always willing to help others

takes time to teach others
led to advancement of ...
goes out of way to ...

constructive in area of ...
instills in each subordinate ...
makes good use of ...

ability to motivate others
positive outlook & attitude
attends to each detail

fit, trim in posture
persistent in ability to ...
places high values on ...

asset to high morale
full effort & cooperation
wins subordinate trust by ...

...timely completion of ..
...average knowledge of/in ...
...proficient in leading ...

...warm, helpful manner
...steady, solid progress in
...logical & direct in action

...competent in all aspects of ..
...played key role in ...
...demonstrated initiative in/at .

...effective at motivating others
...average ability & talent
...displays good ability to ...

...takes prompt action on/in ...
...alert & responsive to ...
...doesn't believe in idle time

...found better way to ...
...meets all requirements of ...
...inspires trust & confidence

...can be counted on to ...
...conforms to standards of ...
...friendly & fair towards all ...

...regularly meets all tasking
...follows through on all tasks
...timely & accurate results

...contributes to team effort
...energetic in carrying out ...
...informed & up to date

...leads & directs team with ...
...impartial, just & ethical ...
...always follows through on ...

...determined to do best
...does good job of ...
...resourceful in use of ...

earnest belief principles of ...   ..promotes letter & spirit of ...
competent in any situation   ...with dispatch & efficiency ...
gives full measure to ...   ...respected for ability to ...

quick to lend helping hand   ...energetic at problem solving
well thought out ideas   ...knows how to motivate
fully up to date in/on ...   ...faces challenges head on

great deal of energy   ...interested in every facet of ..
has skill teaching others   ...quality of work meets ...
skillful manager of time   ...productive in area of ...

willingly helps others to ...   ...qualified in all areas of ...
made short work of ...   ...work correct & efficient
job in/as ... worthy of ..   ...on pace to complete ...

enhanced morale by improving ...
applies corrective counseling, received in positive manner
steady & reliable, compiled impressive ... record

daily performance highlighted by ...
earned genuine respect of ...
ability to develop correct & logical use of assigned resources

discipline enforced on fair, consistent basis
takes positive, correct action when ...
correct & cooperative work habits

effective balance between needs of service & needs of individual
cultivates harmony & esprit de corps
prompt in completing ... qualifications

eager, willing & able complete most difficult tasking
demeanor quickly gains support of juniors
informed leader/supervisor who genuinely cares about others

completed ... requirements on schedule
steady, reasonable amount of work
completed ... requirements in timely fashion

logical & direct in approach to difficult tasking
ability to devise ... procedures that get job done correctly
good person to call on if/when ...

takes personal & professional interest in each sailor
accomplishes work within required limits
properly divides tasks & allocates responsibility

competent & capable, leads by doing & showing
discharges responsibilities with ...
supplies effective remedies to unforeseen problems

applies practical solutions to ...
cooperative, gets along well with others
pleasant personality blends well in any work group

takes maximum advantage of ...
insists on fair & equal treatment to all service members
completes ... tasks without direct supervision

aggressive in job accomplishment
agreeable personality beneficial to good ...
level-headed & logical approach to leadership

provided organizational design for ...
clearly demonstrated capacity for directing others
good counselor, ability to ...

pleasant personality helps others to ...
working knowledge in/on/of ... continues to improve
energetic leader & organizer

personalized approach when dealing with subordinates
supportive of command's equal opportunity program & policies
supports command mission & objectives

acceptable appearance & behavior
does not hesitate to provide assistance to juniors
constructive imagination necessary for ...

does not require supervision to accomplish daily tasks
especially adept at fitting people to jobs & training them quickly
suitable progress in ... qualifications

adequate progress on PQS qualifications
ideally suited to work with today's young, inquisitive sailors
applies self in highly resourceful manner

requires supervision only on most difficult tasking
provides meaningful work assignment to each individual
personally planned & executed

sufficient knowledge of ... to ...
frank, sincere & fair in all interpersonal relationships
informed leader with genuine concern for well being of juniors

directly supports & assists ...
established & strictly enforced highly effective ...
successfully stepped into new job of ...

imaginative use of on-board assets
takes crash projects in full stride
directs energy correctly in attacking all tasks

good amount of drive & persistence
lends helping hand when/if ...
ample knowledge & ability to ...

poised & confident supervisor/leader
meets standards of performance in/on ...
enthusiasm for ... paid off

work in/on/as ... credible with good results
requires only occasional supervision
dependable work without direct supervision

continuing source of new, workable ideas
steady, cautious progress in/on ...
above average ability to/in ...

directs others without dulling initiative
adequate knowledge of (rating/specialty)
person to see when job needs to be completed on time

supports command objectives by ...
directs others with firm but fair hand
cooperative & dependable in/at ...

takes initiative in seeking additional responsibilities
established new & effective ...
allows juniors latitude for growth & creativity

satisfactory working knowledge of/in ...
positive approach to equal opportunity
approaches each task with enthusiasm

impartial leader/supervisor with ability to ...
forceful without being overbearing
direct involvement in training & readiness led to ...

confident of abilities, takes action when necessary
assertive yet considerate in supervising juniors
remains calm when faced with ...

takes rapid, effective action without guidance
places high priority on human goals
gets juniors personally involved in team efforts

always busy, yet patient & understanding with subordinates
can do attitude infectious on others
ensures upward mobility of juniors

works well on own, requiring little assistance
leaves no loose ends of job for others
adds more to job than expected

friendly personality instrumental in gaining confidence of juniors
takes sincere interest in improving subordinate performance
genuine interest in welfare & morale of others

contributes full measure to ...
raises subordinate self-esteem by ...
dependable, reliable work habits

goals & objectives met without supervision
always meets requirements of tasks at hand
learns easily observing others

individual productivity sufficient to ...
completes all tasks with zeal
attains quality results in/as ...

rapid, thorough & highly accurate in admin & staff work
instills pride in accomplishment among others
desirable outcome when required to ...

takes special interest in developing juniors
leads with force & confidence, gets quality results
gained respect of juniors & peers

establishes challenging, attainable goals
thoughtful & considerate of others, promotes good morale
satisfied requirements of/for ...

ability to organize own time & that of others
guides & directs juniors with understanding & tact
capacity for independent learning

ensures unified, team effort
achieved moderate success in/by ...
readily tackles any assignment

industrious & motivated, completed(s) ...
industrious completion of assigned tasks
reinforces good behavior, corrects substandard behavior

evaluates facts before acting
plans ahead with good foresight
ability to recognize potential of subordinates

.good-natured attitude generates positive ...
.always has time for juniors despite heavy workload
.sound logic used to arrive at valid conclusions

.takes time to inform shipmates about ...
.guidance to subordinates clear & comprehensive
.positive results with no organizational friction

.work in ... without serious error
.achieves desired results in all areas
.persistent & conscientious in tackling any task

.leadership policies prudent & implemented impartially
.completes all work successfully & on time
.ensures team cohesiveness by ...

.tactful, dedicated leader/supervisor
.enjoys loyalty of subordinates
.stays with job until completed

does not accept substandard performance
accomplishes fair amount of work
works on morale & understanding between ...

enhances relationships between ...
counseling techniques accepted in positive manner
tactful, positive manner quickly gains support of juniors

steady progress made in/on ...
efficient organizer with good sense of ...
strong sense of dedication wins support of subordinates

courage to stand on principal
actively sought by juniors to help with personal problems
style of leadership improves proficiency & morale

punctuality & strong sense of duty highlight daily performance
does not sacrifice quality for quantity
enjoys respect & understanding of subordinates

demands high standards from/of ...
works methodically & carefully
effective at getting subordinates to ...

stimulates individual growth & responsibility
creates environment for subordinates to seek Navy career
deep concern for well being of others

attentive to any & all responsibilities
strong sense of responsibility for equal treatment ...
enhances effectiveness of others by ...

dedicated & hard-working, successfully completed ...
efficient organizer with strong sense of duty
demeanor promotes trust & efficiency

attends to welfare & well being of ...
effective in most any situation
correctly balances schedule & workload according to priorities

submits timely & accurate ...
provides subordinates with positive guidance
efficient procurement & use of ...

beneficial to good morale & ...
appealing personality allows ...
builds on understanding of diverse groups by ...

works independent of supervision & gets job done correctly
steadily gaining technical knowledge in ...
enhanced operational effectiveness

accepts responsibility & challenge in stride
never too busy to guide & lead others
maintains composure under pressure

sharp appearance evidenced daily
thoroughly prepared for every assignment
smart, neat & dignified appearance

maintains fair & positive attitude toward ...
understands needs & capabilities of each subordinate
timely results working in/with ...

receptive to new information on/in ...
encourages feedback from subordinates
maintains good work organization & discipline

respected by subordinates for work in ...
strictly enforces safety rules & regulations
never reluctant to pitch in & help others

puts duty & responsibility ahead of personal interests
stays sharply focused on task at hand
encourages participation of juniors when ...

successfully integrates mission requirements with individual needs
maintains good order & discipline
never loses sight of responsibilities as leader & supervisor

maintains positive control & minimizes internal friction
realizes people are Navy's most important resource
very quick & thorough in performance of job

virtually no errors in/when ...
timely completion of primary & collateral duties
successfully pursues follow me leadership style

encourages respect for Navy tradition
volunteered to assume additional responsibilities as ...
totally reliable in execution of all responsibilities

strengthens feeling of belonging into each junior
makes personal contribution to ...
encourages self-development of juniors & peers

elicits positive & productive response from juniors
ability to communicate sincerely with others results in ...
subordinates put forth best effort

consistently successful in obtaining willing cooperation of others
arouses interest in others by ...
believes each individual is important

ability to create enthusiasm for any given task
deals with juniors competently & impartially
efficient & effective work habits

constructive contributions
affable manner wins support in ...
takes advantage of slack periods to ...

displays concern & compassion
enjoys discussing rewards & adventures of Navy life
works quickly & efficiently, yielding best possible work

ample quality & quantity work...handles crisis management situations
instills self-confidence in subordinates
carries out ... with determination

ensures safe working environment
able to complete independent work without supervision
diligent, dependable supervisor/leader

performs all duties without prompting
full effort & support of subordinates
leadership achieves desired results

good working relationship with subordinates
interactions with others always ...
adaptable to changing situations

work efficiently planned & correctly completed
even temperament & steadying influence on ...
capitalized on subordinate strengths, improves weaknesses

completes ample amount of work
job accomplishment always number 1 priority
honest, sincere with unquestionable integrity

developed operating procedures for ...
attacks all responsibilities with equal success
leader who understands & uses delegation

cheerful personality, others willingly follow
ensures each individual treated with equality & fairness
able to do job with little direct supervision

sound ideas, innovative suggestions
possesses good working knowledge of/in ...
instills sense of personal responsibility for quality of work

practices preventive rather than remedial leadership
good working relationship among ...
assisted in development of ...

knowledgeable & proficient in/at ...
astute on-scene leadership/supervision led to ...
ensures job done correctly first time

handles subordinates firmly & positively
plans ahead, anticipates upcoming requirements
completes assigned work on schedule

achieves good success when/if ...
skillful working knowledge of/in ...
excels in self & subordinate development

loyal, energetic & conscientious leader/supervisor
able to perform all job functions
sincere & persuasive manner encourages subordinates to

quality work in any environment
good working knowledge of/in
highly competent manager & administrator

helpful to subordinates outside work hours by ...
performance regularly meets requirements
knack for passing own knowledge & experience to others

exerts personal influence with tact
skilled in technical aspects of ...
actions & manners always reflect favorably on Navy

uses ... knowledge to good benefit of command
fair & unbiased in relationships with ...
well versed in field of ...

sensitive to needs of others
conduct conforms to standards
solves most new technical problems with ease

produces results quickly & efficiently
orderly mind, knows how to ...
meticulous in manner & attentive to detail

organization functions smoothly & effectively
energetic & earnest work habits
sets & achieves realistic goals

gets steady, solid results
helps individuals develop professionally
works zealously to complete each task

concerned with well-being of subordinates
able to work independent of supervision
skilled in maintaining good order & discipline

keen interest in work, completes ...
well-being of others major ...
not satisfied with average performance

juniors work to earn a personal well done
good talent for directing & counseling juniors
favorable results at/when ...

conducts career opportunity briefings with subordinates
juniors always respond with full effort
actions well planned & executed

sets & maintains high standards of/in ...
orderly & productive in/at ...
gets to heart of difficult problems

plans work schedule wisely
able to work without supervision completing ...
uses authority to accomplish task in firm, fair manner

energetic & dedicated, leads by example
good practical application of ... skills
strict leader without generating resentment

helps others develop professionally
well-rounded knowledge of Navy's latest career programs
key person to see when/if ...

quick to offer positive advice to subordinates
made noticeable improvement in/to ...
solid working knowledge of ...

neat, highly acceptable appearance in uniform & civilian attire
fair, open manner wins support of others
professional attitude radiates to subordinates

strengthens morale by cultivating sense of belonging
confident of abilities, leads with compassion
openly encourages & expects professional development

seizes every opportunity to ...
understands practical applications of ...
willingly accepts leadership roles

progressing in ... qualifications without prompting
upstanding & respectful, good leader
never too busy to take time to teach & guide subordinates

progressing well on advancement qualifications
explains advantages of successful Navy career
fair & equal in treatment of ...

solves technical problems with limited assistance
prepared for & handles emergencies in full stride
knowledge of job continues to be ...

diligent in carrying out duties
ensures juniors develop at rapid pace
works well under pressure

grasps pertinent details quickly
firm grasp & use of effective leadership principles
just & fair in treatment of ...

motivates personnel with positive involvement
seeks some additional tasking
unafraid of accepting new & added duties

energetic & proficient at completing ... work
helpful in helping others ...
performs all duties with ease & confidence

upward mobility of juniors always major concern & goal
work does not require correction
achieves meaningful results as ...

skillful in demanding & receiving ...
knowledge of ... sufficient to complete assigned tasks
completes tasks correctly & timely

solves technical problems in desired manner
produces highly accurate work
mission oriented, team player

quick to offer juniors pat on the back when appropriate
well versed in all aspects of ...
able to win support for ...

fair & exacting, leads by example
job proficiency improved in area(s) of ...
good troubleshooting skills working in/on ...

neat & orderly in completing ...
made good progress qualifying in/for ...
good shipmate, helps others in/by/to ...

sound reasoning & wise decision-making facilities
keeps superiors & subordinates aware of changing situations
good practical working knowledge of/in ...

high state of morale due to ...
actions well planned, smoothly executed
favorable quality of work

active enforcement of human equality
straight forward in direction & action
motivates others instead of driving them

adaptable to changing job requirements, while completing ...
secures complete cooperation & support of juniors
unbiased in dealings with others

solicits juniors for new ideas
understands technical aspects of ...
goal oriented with strong sense of duty

plans ahead, stays on top of job
high level of drive & energy
quick to take lead in/when ...

smooth relationship between ...
extremely low discipline rate
most tasks completed on time & correct

puts forth favorable effort
good sense of organization
satisfies all requirements of ...

uncompromising standards of ...
keeps subordinates well informed of Navy's career programs
obvious pride in self & service

actively encourages individual growth & development
high sense of personal responsibility for quality of work
stable, productive member of ...

gives earnest, sincere effort
employs proper safety precautions in ...
uses available resources with good results

maintains atmosphere of pride & can do spirit
obvious willingness to serve with pride in any assignment
promoted good morale by ...

good results in all assigned tasks
never too busy to help others
actively solicits additional tasks & duties

satisfactory progress in/on ...
understanding manner secures subordinate loyalty
promotes harmony & fosters high morale

radiates complete trust & confidence
offers sound advice to junior sailors on career programs
real leader/supervisor with knack for getting job done

sincere counseling techniques secures trust & loyalty
employs proper techniques in ...
runs efficient & productive organization

skilled at developing subordinates
good representative of command in ...
timely, accurate & detailed work in/as ...

offers sound professional advice
uses subordinates to best possible advantage
work complete, thorough & highly accurate

good rapport with subordinates
needs supervision only if/when ...
needs supervision only in unfamiliar areas

stays focused on job at hand
records & correspondence always ...
gives good account of self

acts correctly without waiting for guidance
met ... requirements on time
work complete & on time

encourages development of subordinates
gives juniors unified purpose & sense of direction
recognizes potential of subordinates & provides necessary guidance

stimulates pride & professionalism
talented & knowledgeable in/on ...
sincere, honest, concerned leader
offers sound, constructive advice to subordinates

CHAPTER 8

WORD PICTURE PERSONALITY

UNFAVORABLE

WORD PICTURE PERSONALITY

JOB APPLICATION

The list of adjectives below express the emotional quality—the product of many factors—which manifests itself in the way an individual attacks and carries through on problems.

UNFAVORABLE

erratic	careless	casual
indifferent	indolent	intermittent
lazy	negligent	perfunctory
procrastinating	slow	sluggish
tactless	uncooperative	vacillating
unresourceful		

PERSONAL CHARACTER

The following list of adjectives express the inward traits of an individual and can only be learned after long and close association.

UNFAVORABLE

arbitrary	audacious	biased
bigoted	confused	dependent
disloyal	dominant	dominating
domineering	fickle	flaccid
hypercritical	idealistic	intolerant
irresolute	magnanimous	narrow-minded
negative	opinionated	prejudiced
selfish	superficial	timid
unfriendly	unstable	unsteady
weak	vindictive	

MENTAL OR EMOTIONAL TRAITS

The adjectives listed below express the outward qualities of an individua which generally denote possession of inward mental or emotional traits.

UNFAVORABLE

antagonistic	belligerent	complaining
conceited	evasive	excitable
fault-finding	gullible	hypercritical
ill-tempered	impetuous	impulsive
indifferent	indulgent	insipid
irritable	irritating	morose
naïve	pessimistic	pugnacious
restless	resentful	spiritless
submission	supercilious	

KNOWLEDGE

The following adjectives express a degree of subject matter an individua may possess, but NOT necessarily the ability to use the information.

UNFAVORABLE

crass	dabber	dense
half-scholar	ignorant	shallow
smatterer	thick	unconversant
unerudite	uninformed	unscholarly
unlearned	unlettered	

MANNER
The following adjectives express outward qualities of manner.

UNFAVORABLE

affected	aloof	blunt
boisterous	brusque	caustic
crude	curt	disdainful
dogmatic	frigid	inattentive
inconsiderate	indifferent	intolerant
loquacious	loud	moody
obsequious	obtrusive	offensive
taciturn	unresponsible	unresponsive

INTELLECTUAL EQUIPMENT
The below lists of adjectives express a type of, and ability to use intellectual equipment.

UNFAVORABLE

average	dull	formalist
impractical	inane	inept
mediocre	medium	obtuse
ordinary	perspicacious	second-rate
stupid	theoretical	undistinguished
unimaginative	unwise	

MENTAL FACULTY & CAPACITY

The following adjectives express intellect, intelligence, or in this case, lack thereof.

UNFAVORABLE

absurd	dense	dull
foolish	ignorant	inept
insensible	insignificant	irrational
obtuse	ridiculous	meaningless
senile	senseless	shallow
short-sighted	simple	superficial
trifling	unaware	uninformative
unintelligent	unlearned	

PRESENCE OR IMPRESSION

The adjectives listed below express the mental impression that an individual's outward qualities produce on others.

UNFAVORABLE

colorless	eccentric	floppish
odd	pompous	severe
slovenly	unattractive	undignified
undistinguished unimpressive		untidy

JOB RESULTS

The following adjectives express the degree, kind, or type of results obtained by an individual.

UNFAVORABLE

adequate	below-par	commonplace
contradictory	defective	fair
faulty	inaccurate	ineffectual
inefficient	moderate	ordinary
passable	poor	presentable
questionable	second-rate	tolerable
undistinguished	unsatisfactory	worthless

CHAPTER 9

BELOW AVERAGE PERFORMERS
(2.0-1.0)

BELOW AVERAGE PERFORMERS
(2.0-1.0)

WORD BANK

ABNORMAL	ABRUPT	ABUSED
ABUSIVE	ADVERSE	AIMLESS
ALOOF	AMBIGUOUS	ANEMIC
ANGUISH	ANIMOSITY	APPALLING
APPAULED	ARGUMENTATIVE	ARROGANT
AVOIDED	AVOIDS	AWFUL
AWKWARD	BAD	BADLY
BAFFLED	BEHIND	BELOW-PAR
BERATED	BERATES	BITTER
BLATANT	BLEAK	BLUNDER
BORDERLINE	BOTCH	BOTCHED
BOTTLENECK	BRASH	BURDEN
BURDENED	BURDENSOME	BURNOUT
CARELESS	CASUALTY	CHAOS
CIRCUMVENTED	COLLAPSED	CONCEALED
CONFRONTATIONAL	CONFUSE	CONFUSED
CRUDE	CRUMBLED	CUT-RATE
DAMAGED	DECEIVED	DECEPTION
DECEPTIVE	DECIMATED	DECLINE
DECLINING	DECREASE	DECREASING
DEFECT	DEFECTIVE	DEFICIENT
DEGENERATED	DEGRADED	DEMISE
DEMORALIZED	DENIED	DEPLETED
DEPLORABLE	DEPRESSING	DERELICT
DESPAIR	DESPERATE	DESPERATION
DESTROYED	DESTRUCTIVE	DETERIORATED
DETERIORATING	DETRIMENT	DEVASTATING
DEVIATES	DEVIOUS	DIFFICULT
DIGRESS	DIMINISHED	DISAGREEABLE
DISAPPOINT	DISAPPOINTED	DISAPPOINTING

DISASTER	DISCREDITED	DISGRACE
DISGRACEFUL	DISINCLINED	DISMAL
DISPARITY	DISREGARD	DISRUPTED
DISSERVICE	DISTASTEFUL	DISTRACTION
DISTRAUGHT	DISTRUSTS	DISTURBING
DO-NOTHING	DOUBT	DOWNFALL
DOWNSIDE	DOWNSLIDE	DOWNTURN
DREADFUL	DUBIOUS	DWINDLED
DWINDLING	DYSFUNCTIONAL	EMPTY
ENCUMBER	ERODED	ERODES
ERR	ERRANT	ERRATIC
ERRONEOUS	ERROR	EVADES
EVASIVE	EXCESSIVE	EXPLOITED
FABRICATED	FADING	FAIL
FAILING	FAILURE	FALLACY
FALLIBLE	FALSE	FALTERED
FALTERING	FALTERS	FAULTY
FIZZLED	FLAWED	FLIP-FLOPPED
FLOP	FLOUNDERED	FOOT-DRAGGING
FORGETFUL	FORGETS	FRUITLESS
FUTILE	GRIDLOCK	GULLIBLE
HAMPERS	HAPHAZARD	HARM
HARMFUL	HARSH	HAZARD
HEAVY-HANDED	HELPLESS	HESITATED
HINDERED	HOPELESS	HOSTILE
HOSTILITY	HURTS	IGNORES
ILL-GOTTEN	ILL-INFORMED	ILL-PREPARED
ILL-SUITED	ILLUSIVE	IMPATIENT
IMPEDE	IMPEDED	IMPERFECT
IMPROPER	IMPULSIVE	INABILITY
INACCURATE	INADEQUATE	INAUSPICIOUS
INCOMPETENT	INCOMPLETE	INCONSISTENT
INCORRECT	INDECISION	INDECISIVE

INDIFFERENT	INDISCRETION	INEFFECTUAL
INEFFICIENT	INEPT	INEXPERIENCE
INEXPERIENCED	INFERIOR	INSECURE
INSENSITIVE	INSIGNIFICANT	INSTABILITY
INSUFFICIENT	INTIMIDATED	INTOLERABLE
JEOPARDIZED	KNIT-PICK	LACKING
LACKLUSTER	LACKS	LAPSE
LIABILITY	LIMITED	LITTLE
LOST	LOW	LOW-GRADE
LOWLY	MANIPULATES	MEAGER
MEANINGLESS	MEDIOCRE	MINIMAL
MINIMUM	MINISCULE	MISBEHAVIOR
MISCALCULATED	MISERABLE	MISFIT
MISGIVINGS	MISGUIDED	MISHAP
MISLED	MISMATCH	MISMATCHED
MISSED	MISUSE	MISUSED
MUNDANE	NEGATIVE	NEGLECT
NEGLECTED	NEGLECTFUL	NEGLIGENCE
NEGLIGENT	NIGHTMARE	OBSTRUCTED
OFFENSIVE	OPPOSED	OUTDATED
OVERCONFIDENT	OVERLOOKED	OVERRATED
PAINFUL	PAINSTAKING	PANIC
PANICKED	PITFALL	PLUMMETED
POOR	PROCRASTINATED	QUESTIONABLE
QUIT	QUITS	RECKLESS
REGRET	REMISS	REPREHENSIBLE
REPRIMANDED	RUINED	RUTHLESS
SARCASTIC	SECOND-RATE	SELF-DESTRUCTIVE
SELF-DOUBT	SETBACK	SHALLOW
SHAMBLES	SHORTCOMING	SIMPLE
SLACK	SLACKER	SLOWDOWN
SLUGGISH	SLUMP	SLUMPING
SMALL	SPARSE	SQUANDERED
STAGNANT	STAGNATION	STALE

STIFLED	STONEWALLED	STOPPED
STRUGGLES	STUBBORN	STUMBLED
SUBSTANDARD	SUBVERTED	SUPERFICIAL
TARNISHED	TEMPERAMENTAL	TERRIBLE
TRAGEDY	TRAGIC	TRIVIALIZES
TROUBLE	TUMBLED	TURMOIL
UNACCEPTABLE	UNACCOMPLISHED	UNAWARE
UNCERTAIN	UNCERTAINTY	UNCHECKED
UNCLEAR	UNCONCERNED	UNCOOPERATIVE
UNDERMINED	UNDISCIPLINED	UNDISTINGUISHED
UNEQUAL	UNEVEN	UNEXCEPTIONAL
UNFAIR	UNFAMILIAR	UNFAVORABLE
UNFIT	UNFITTING	UNFOCUSED
UNFOUNDED	UNIMPRESSIVE	UNNECESSARY
UNPREDICTABLE	UNPREPARED	UNPRODUCTIVE
UNPROVEN	UNRAVELED	UNRELIABLE
UNSAFE	UNSATISFACTORY	UNSETTLING
UNSKILLED	UNSKILLFUL	UNSTABLE
UNSUCCESSFUL	UNSUITABLE	UNSURE
UNWANTED	UNWELCOMED	UNYIELDING
USELESS	VACILLATING	VIOLATED
VIOLATES	VIOLATION	VULNERABLE
WANTING	WASTE	WASTED
WEAK	WEAKENED	WEAKNESS
WEARY	WITHOUT	WORSE
WORSENED	WORST	WORTHLESS
WRONG	WRONGFUL	

BELOW AVERAGE PERFORMERS
(2.0-1.0)

BULLETS

shaky grounds
continued unabated
lagged behind

grave error
collapsed under ...
holds back

limited in ...
bothered by ...
cosmetic effort(s)

shaky ground
raised doubts
corroded the ...

incompetent in/on ...
hit bottom
limited foresight

tainted reputation
decision-making problem(s)
miserable showing

sad consequences
incapable of ...
courted disaster

painfully clear
obstructs routine ...
consumed with ...

severely restricts ...
largely untrained
could not ...

...undercut standards
...failed policy/policies
...less appealing

...turned down
...infectious pessimism
...plagued by ...

...indifferent to ...
...dismal record
...declining confidence

...decline in ...
...unacceptable actions
...inclined towards ...

...vast void
...lackluster performance
...inherently flawed

...interfered with ...
...complete collapse
...playing catch-up

...mood swings
...buck passer
...refused to ...

...slacked off
...all-time low
...faltered badly

...went overboard
...rocky ride
...bleak outlook

marginal performance
neglected duties
gradual decline

unduly tested
counter productive
sharp decline

dark days
far from ...
serious problem(s)

sharp decrease
painfully obvious
strays from ...

troubled reputation
negative influence
going nowhere

futile effort(s)
unfit for ...
shirks responsibility

fear of ...
openly criticized
growing impatience

conspicuously absent
bad timing
tragic results

slow in/to ...
uninterested in ...
cannot learn

feeble attempt
reluctant to ...
easily distracted

unsuccessful in/at ...
serious setback
doubts abounded

...protracted decline
...slip shod
...tragic circumstances

...little success
...damaging consequences
...offensive nature

...callused disregard
...cannot be ...
...uneven temperament

...late completing
...rejected by ...
...bad idea

...overwhelmed by ...
...morale plummeted
...leadership crisis

...abrasive personality
...confronts authority
...weak technical ...

...disturbing results
...long decline
...suffered from ...

...fumbled through
...painfully obvious
...not dependable

...drastic decline
...weak performance
...agonizingly slow

...serious repercussions
...lost opportunities
...dim prospect(s)

...major setback
...outright flop
...substantially below

.fell apart
.loose cannon
.afraid of ...

.troubled history
.slow to ...
.negative impact

.failed completely
.serious trouble
.unnecessary waste

lost battle
generally unreliable
slow worker

badly misjudged
adverse effect
not forthcoming

shoddy work
weak link
downward slide

unparalleled decline
barely acceptable
eventually managed to ...

seriously jeopardized
overly methodical
short on ...

ill advised
hampered by ...
caught off-guard

over extended
weak in ...
unprecedented decrease

major flaw
elementary approach
prone to ...

...conduct unbecoming ...
...rock bottom
...effectively crippled

...blames others
...guilty of ...
...performance plummeted

...can't do ...
...remiss in ...
...drained resources

...diminished enthusiasm
...fell sharply
...extensive damage

...persistent problem(s)
...broke faith
...major problem

...careless in/about ...
...friction between ...
...trouble maker

...lost control
...personal failure
...repeatedly ignored ...

...accomplishes little
...few skills
...wicked temper

...needs reform
...sluggish performance
...downward spiral

...abuse of ...
...fumbled away ...
...lost composure

...substandard knowledge
...morally bankrupt
...diminishing returns

brought disfavor
seriously lacking
downward trend

ill prepared
impeded progress
socially awkward

major conflict
unskilled in ...
severe drawback

becomes rattled
embarrassing failure
lost ground

repressive atmosphere
wastes time
morally lacking

harsh reality
frustratingly slow
overly cautious

struggled to ...
abrupt halt
broke down

impending disaster
completely unprepared
disturbing evidence

problems with ...
wasted time/talent
lost confidence

terrible waste
struggled with/for ...
reputation suffered

ceased to function
mounting evidence
desperate effort

...fruitless efforts
...ignored advice
...caught short

...even worse
...unprepared to/for ...
...causes friction

...dire consequences
...made excuses
...personal setback

...ill-suited for ...
...shortcomings include ...
...anti-social behavior

...severe problem(s)
...caustic personality
...unsound policies

...impediment to ...
...somewhat disappointing
...dragged down

...embroiled in ...
...dire straight
...low quality

...severe strain
...behind schedule
...not functioning

...emotional decline
...soft on ...
...desperate for ...

...near panic
...over reached
...has difficulty ...

...ineffective as ...
...empty attempts
...narrow vision

ineffective when …	…sorely lacking
bitter disappointment	…lack of …
in jeopardy	…disappointing effort
hot headed	…virtually helpless
severe shortage	…wishful thinking
growing discomfort	…completely ruined
numerous problems	…inept in/at …
stunning blow	…desperate act
without dedication	…second rate
gross misuse	…rapid decrease
painful process	…suffers from …
rocky start	…totally unprepared
shrunk from …	…little effort
strong-arm tactics	…obsessed with …
suffered through	…crumbled under
messed up	…neglected to …
futile effort(s)	…argumentative toward
backed down	…not compatible
undue tension	…self-destructive behavior
abnormally slow	…tough time
melancholy approach	…reality gap
painful setback	…recurring problem(s)
grave mistake	…lagged in …
weakened by …	…serious crisis
obstacle to …	…bad choices
shaky start	…low expectations
constant difficulties	…mediocre results
failed to …	…unwilling to …
serious damage	…little hope
bad experience	…empty handed
preoccupied with …	…breaks rules
inconsistent with …	…hastily executed
violent reaction	…overly careful

challenges understanding
so-so performance
threat to ...

distracted by ...
entire unacceptable
unanswered questions

questionable values
oblivious to ...
inexperienced in ...

did nothing
gross negligence
breakdown in ...

mixed bag
hasty decision
painful lesson

isolated from ...
departed from ...
poor showing

completely collapsed
below expectations
lackluster in ...

wasted time
technically weak
inadequately equipped

dissatisfied with ...
uses people
missed opportunities

disregard for ...
unable to ...
disrespectful to/towards ...

sagging performance
built-in bias
insecure in ...

...detrimental to ...
...resists changes
...poor rapport

...below average ...
...checkered performance
...stunned by ...

...lip service
...worst ever
...threatened by ...

...violated trust
...squeezed out
...inaction caused ...

...collapse of ...
...erosion of ...
...riddled with ...

...squandered opportunities
...overly ambitious
...disappointing results

...empty words
...unaware of ...
...personally insecure

...stern warning
...raised concerns
...very bad ...

...unacceptable work
...too timid
...hindered by ...

...never did/could ...
...lacks direction
...borderline carelessness

...deficient in ...
...poor ability
...costly mistake

rough edges	...heavy handed
vulnerable to ...	...insignificant contribution
dead last	...worst possible ...
costly error	...insufficient progress
tore down	...minimum effort
moral despair	...zero improvement
botched attempt	...poorly coordinated
sank to ...	...inadequate ... skills
haunted by ...	...questionable decision
very disappointed	...misuse of ...
growing concern	...stepped aside
radical change(s)	...hollow promises
disaster struck	...under achiever
discontented with ...	...irregularities abounded
negligent in ...	...declining results
lingering problems	...complete failure
besieged by ...	...overly aggressive
vulnerable to ...	...derelict in ...
strains of ...	...tarnished record
undependable in ...	...inconsistent performance
mixed results	...poorly executed
wasted opportunities	...difficult time
breach of ...	...disinterested in ...
complains about ...	...warning signal(s)
never achieved ...	...below par
over zealous	...continuing struggle
dashed hopes	...limited ability
ignores efforts to ...	...negative influence on ...
lacking in confidence	...violates standards of ...
totally inefficient in/on ...	...lost sight of ...
great difficulty in ...	...haphazard work habits
neglected duties	...obstructs efforts to ...
bad to worse	...less than impressive

filled with disappointment
waited too long
inherently reluctant to ...

worst possible outcome
came up short
takes away from ...

dimmed the spirits
inefficient use of ...
of little consequences

problems spread to ...
little if any ...
lost control of ...

dampened the spirits
grave threat to ...
ill equipped to ...

lacking in cooperativeness
hit-&-miss work habits
little impact on ...

difficult to understand
poor ability to ...
extremely limited in ...

opposes attempts to
disagreeable attitude causes ...
technically weak in ...

over stepped bounds
placed drag on ...
fails to contribute

negligent in maintaining ...
weakened fabric of ...
limited knowledge of ...

dug a hole
harsh treatment of ...
lost touch with ...

...neglects work for/to ...
...a real mess
...waste time in/when ...

...lacks mental dexterity
...lost willingness to ...
...weak and ineffective

...little effect on ...
...hurt reliability of ...
...total lack of ...

...work suffers from ...
...not prepared for ...
...cast doubt on ...

...futile effort of/to ...
...lost all enthusiasm
...failed to realize

...weak in enforcing ...
...takes undue risks
...negligent in helping ...

...crushed spirits of ...
...failed to take ...
...less than stellar

...got into trouble
...less than desired
...had bad time ...

...dangerously close to ...
...ill-suited to lead ...
...little improvement despite

...exhibits no desire .
...blemish on record
...unfair dealing with ...

...cast shadow on ...
...irresponsible attitude toward
...pessimistic outlook hinders .

weighed down with/by ...
suffered from neglect
not mission oriented

ordinary jobs appear ...
dead set against ...
efforts in vain

permanent stain on ...
far too little
jeopardized operation of ...

fell into disrepair
negligent use of/in ...
lightening rod for ...

dislike of ... causes ...
shirks duties of ...
has great difficulty ...

difficult at best
abrasive personality irritates ...
unreliable performance in/as...

suffered major setback
not inclined to ..
little interest in ...

long history of ...
made mess of ...
dismal performance record

out of element
demonstrated bias toward ...
substandard performance as/in ...

chose to ignore ...
emerging pattern of ...
sorrowful performance in/as ...

sorry showing in/as ...
shook foundation of ...
well short of ...

...abnormal behavior toward ..
...lack of ambition
...crossed the line

...broke spirit of ...
...impatient dealing with ...
...haphazard approach to ...

...out of control
...unimpressive behavior in ...
...lack of ... hinders ...

...out of touch
...major turn downward
...severe and on-going ...

...causes problems when ...
...exercise in futility
...lackluster performance in/as

...passes the buck
...less than successful
...major shortcoming in ...

...no contribution to ...
...work routinely defective
...did not qualify

...sorry showing in/as ...
...fell into disarray
...paid the price

...hit or miss
...increasing signs of ...
...unacceptable behavior in ...

...lacks ability to ...
...not effective at/in ...
...not able to ...

...avoids ... when possible
...ducked the issue(s)
...sorrowful performance in/as

.needless use of ...
.substandard knowledge of/in ..
.improper use of ...

.could not handle ...
.unable to plan
.dismal record as/in ...

.riddled with mistakes
.problem-solving abilities lacks ...
.superficial efforts to ...

.needless loss of ...
.less than acceptable ...
not skilled in ...

loses sight of ...
flagrant violation of ...
had difficult time ...

disregards welfare of ...
close to failure
subordinates do not ...

diverted much needed ...
needs more experience
room for improvement

serious lacking in ...
accepts less than ...
derelict in duty

paid little attention
own worst enemy
state of denial

eventually managed to ...
bad work habits
accomplished virtually nothing

lacks necessary ... to ...
slow in reacting
failed to impress

...mistake led to ...
...long way from ...
...erratic performance in/on/as

...state of confusion
...fell far short
...has no initiative

...derailed efforts to ...
...not concerned with ...
...without interest in ...

...short attention span
...in a rut
...small step forward

...resisted attempts to ...
...short of expectations
...lacks confidence to ...

...everything went wrong
...noted weakness in ...
...unable to maintain ...

...inadequate enforcement of ..
...fell deep into ...
...flat record of ...

...without a clue
...lacks enthusiasm to ...
...not capable of ...

...superficial performance in/as
...inadequate skills in ...
...did little to/for ...

...cooked the books
...served only to ...
...did not follow ...

...not competent in ...
...routinely deviates from ...
...inclined toward stubbornness

low-grade performance in ...
went too far
did not deliver

unable to correctly ...
rarely completes tasking ...
not ready for ...

acted with haste
barely able to ...
slow, plodding work

continued loss of ...
doesn't care about
lack of enthusiasm

hinders morale by ...
does not understand ...
low point in ...

short-sightedness resulted in ...
contributed to bad ...
did not complete ...

all but failed
sloppy work in/as ...
turned back on ...

hampered operation of ...
simply gave up
lack of confidence

very short memory
still not enough
destroyed much of ...

lost ability to ...
tug of war
slipped from grasp

last person to ...
folds under pressure
lack of direction

...does not support ...
...proficiency in ... not ...
...stood idly by

...continued failure to ...
...folded under pressure
...doomed to failure

...despite best efforts
...lapse of judgment
...had hard time ...

...at odds with ...
...firestorm of controversy
...small amount of ...

...unable to comprehend ...
...inadequate progress in/on
...developed cold feet

...failed to adequately ...
...unable to complete ...
...high and dry

...loss of confidence
...basic disregard for ...
...failed to achieve ...

...behind learning curve
...allows juniors to ...
...despite repeated attempts

...unusually slow in ...
...upset delicate balance
...beginning to fail

...heavy-handed leadership
...virtually no progress ...
...did little to ...

...symbolic gesture only
...frequently forgets to ...

overly slow & cautious
goals & objectives not met
erratic quality of work

lack of initiative caused ...
slow to produce results
added insult to injury

does not take time to ...
behind others in ability to ...
low marks in ... due to ...

out of step with ...
failed in attempt to ...
lost sense of direction

well below average in ...
off on a tangent
gave little thought to ...

failed to adhere to ...
ignored all efforts to ...
below average ability to ...

hard to understand
sorely lacking in ability to ...
lack of ability to ...

ignores every effort to ...
did not contribute to ...
hinders smooth flow of ...

impatient dealing with others
lacks direction and focus
too many errors in ...

ignored repeated efforts to ..
did not do homework
struggled in face of ...

fell by the wayside
negligent in duties of ...
failed to keep pace

...nothing to show for ...
...total lack of focus
...avoids working with others

...barely kept up with
...cannot be relied upon to ...
...not up to the challenge

...got caught up in ...
...came to a halt
...took turn for the worse

...exhibits no desire to ...
...does not respond to ...
...not sound in judgment

...in your face attitude
...slow to react to ...
...below par progress in/on ..

...hopeless in ability to ...
...not ready to face ...
...total lack of initiative

...wide range of problems
...out of tune with ...
...ground to a halt

...ineffective & inefficient in ..
...below average in area of ..
...slow to make progress in ..

...out of tune with ...
...won't get involved in ...
...from bad to worse

...helpless when it comes to
...juniors reluctant to follow ..
...fails to set realistic goals

...mediocre work at best
...only person not able to ...
...difficult to deal with

too little, too late
shook the foundation of ...
interferes with efforts to ...

heading in wrong direction
made more difficult by ...
does not fit in as member of ...

only person not able to ...
refused to budge on ...
inept when it comes to ...

shot down efforts to ...
tactless in area of ...
out of touch with reality

unable to get motivated
lax & lazy attitude
severely lacking in judgment

rubs people wrong way
failed to take action on/when ...
flagrant violation of ...by ...

not attentive to detail in ...
turn for the worse
does not get the job done

...relies on others for ...
...got off on wrong foot
...fails in timely completion of

...last person in ... to ...
...overly slow & cautious
...ran out of gas

...not able to perform ...
...fell out of favor
...failed to meet simplest ...

...does not look for work
...too easily influenced by ...
...well behind qualifying in/as

...failed to timely complete ...
...relies too heavily on ...
...reluctant to take lead

...well behind peer group in ..
...out of touch with reality
...dismissed out of hand

...sank to new low
...remiss in attending to ...
...lost

rarely completes tasking on schedule
unacceptable attitude harms team effort
has difficulty adapting to changes

mediocre results outside specialty
needs constant and close supervision
put good face on otherwise ...

lacks proper problem-solving skills to ...
unable or unwilling to perform even simplest ...
lack of ability to communicate effectively adversely impacts ...

great difficulty motivating juniors
abrasive personality irritates others.
bad record-keeping caused/led to ...

acceptance of unsafe working conditions resulted in ...
reluctant to pitch in & help shipmates
cannot capably direct efforts of others due to ...

accepts substandard performance from juniors
unreliable, does not make effort to ...
doesn't work well with others

more than adequate counseling failed to ...
has trouble complying with standards of ...
completes assigned work only when ...

negligent in duties as supervisor/leader
lackluster performance of (organization) due to ...
unsatisfactory knowledge in/of ...

accepts suggestions of subordinates without proper evaluation of facts
        presented.
exhibits no desire to become proficient in management details.
relies too heavily on others for/to ...

does not instruct others in ...
good work only when closely supervised
uncertain when it comes to ...

perfectionist to an extreme
cannot function as a member of ...
across the board decrease

mishandles minor incidents leading to ...
low quality work prevents assisting others
needs constant guidance to ...

declining morale due to ...
hinders smooth operation of ...
unable to assist others due to ...

has difficulty adapting to changes in policy or work conditions.
unimpressive leadership abilities
avoids any task or responsibility not directly associated with primary
        duties.

reluctant to make decisions in matters within scope of responsibility.
inferior work routinely needs ...
lackluster attitude in preparing for ...

insignificant progress in/on ...
mediocre performance at best
needs regular supervision to meet minimum standards of ...

reluctant to accept responsibility
has difficulty trouble-shooting ...
performance continues to decline

is a perfectionist to an extreme.
uncooperative helping shipmates in/to ...
failed to take proper course of action

.unable to distinguish between ...
.makes more mistakes than ...
.lack of knowledge in/on ... results in ...

.does not help subordinates develop
.assumes responsibility only when necessary
.relies too heavily on others to give guidance and
        direction to subordinates.

.impatient dealing with subordinates
.reluctant to make decisions
.jeopardized team unity by ...

.overly methodical & slow
.has little interest outside specialty field.
.inability to work with others detracts from ...

job proficiency below par due to ...
late for work on too many occasions
performance declined to point of ...
lack of persistence causes

knowledge of ... less than ...
careless work habits caused ...
uncooperative in efforts to ...

almost worthless in ... because of ...
evades work to maximum extent possible
inexperienced and disinterested in administrative details.

places little reliance on others
unresponsive to repeated attempts to ...
manipulates others for own ends

despite repeated counseling, failed to ...
overly methodical, slow to produce results.
reluctant to exert authority when needed

needs much more experience
lacks necessary persistence and conscientiousness to
        properly apply technical skills.
overly berates subordinates when they fail to ...

low quality work prevents ...
major shortcoming in ability to ...
knowledge in/on ...continues to be ...

inclined to retain all responsibility and not give subordinates
        a chance to grow professionally.
unable to function properly in/as ...
needs immediate improvement in/to ...

errors in judgment led to ...
places undue burden on others because of ...
reluctant to assume new duties

fails to promote team unity & effort
has difficulty expressing views and opinions in writing (or orally)
lack of tact hinders ability to ...

tasks routinely not completed on time
despite repeated instruction, cannot ...
unimpressive knowledge in/of ...

impatient in dealing with subordinates.
close supervision routinely required when ...
efforts to ... have been unsuccessful

overly forgetful when it comes to ...
collapsed under the weight of ...
plain bad performance in/as ...

below average progress in/on ...
much too fault-finding with subordinates
reluctant to accept responsibility.

lacks communication skills to effectively ...
teaching methods not consistent with ...
unable to provide desired unity in/of ...

lackluster performance in/as ...
best suited for routine jobs adequately covered by instructions
inactivity best description of ...

overly berates ... when they fail to ...
possesses limited knowledge of/in ...
undecided in time-sensitive situations

sometimes takes more time than expected in performing
        independent tasks, being diverted by any number
        of personal interests.
.lacks patience to train others
.fails to work for unified effort

.without technical competence in ...
.does not have spark of leadership required to ...
.lacking in cooperativeness & teamwork

.negligent in performance as/on ...
.unable to work without close supervision
.leadership capacity is limited and less than desired.

.of limited use in area(s) of ...
.prefers easy, simple tasks, reluctant to ...
.slow progress in ... despite ...

little desire to become proficient in ...
below average supervisory/leadership traits
inclined toward stubbornness, usually ...

needs constant supervision to ...
detrimental to team work & morale
work below par compared to peers

unimaginative and stodgy, best suited for routine jobs that
    are adequately covered by detailed instructions.
frequently reluctant to assume responsibility

disagreeable personality makes it hard to lead others
substandard knowledge in/on/of ...
preoccupation with minor details frequently impairs
    soundness of judgement.

no attention to administrative details
of limited use at best in ...
inclined to overly berate subordinates when they fail to live
    up to expectations.

unable to solve simple problems on/in ...
teamwork suffers because/due to ...
requires routine guidance in ...

preoccupied with minor details
little interest outside specialty
without technical expertise in ...

berates others on petty matters
simply does not get job done satisfactorily
unable to solve simplified problems in/of ...

numerous errors in judgment led to ...
produces only mediocre results outside area of specialty.
limited success qualifying in/for ...

puts work off as long as possible
no desire to help or train others
disruptive to good order & discipline

quality of work suffers when/if ...
response not sufficient to ...
leadership capacity limited by ...

too forceful & overbearing to others
not interested in professional development of ...
superficial performance in/as ...

fails to take prompt action when ...
will not work as effective member of ...
problem-solving abilities lacking in ...

no measurable improvement in/on ...
lacking in cooperativeness and teamwork.
ran out of time...off on a tangent

routinely diverted from duties for personal matters
should be selectively detailed and assigned to office and clerical duties
not well suited to lead today's sailors

does not contribute to team effort
produces quality work only when closely supervised.
less than satisfactory performance as/in ...

unsatisfactory results when supervising/leading ...
limited success motivating others
fails to keep subordinates up to date on ...

leadership sorely lacking in ...
takes more time than expected to ...
unskilled & uninterested in ...

well behind in ... qualifications
satisfactory results only when ...
not interested in qualifying in/for ...

requires close supervision when working in (...) positions.
retains all responsibility, subordinates unable to grow
too many shortcomings in ...

work frequently rejected because ...
produces good work only when closely observed and supervised.
less knowledge than peers in ...

lackluster performance entire reporting period
does not complete most jobs on schedule
unwelcomed behavior exhibited by ...

less than desired results in ...
virtually worthless when it comes to ...
requires close supervision when/to ...

not technically competent in/on ...
work frequently needs to be redone
progress in/on ...continues to be ...

disruptive to team efforts because of ...
abusive to others, hinders ...
very low quality of work on/when ...

limited knowledge of rating/specialty prevents ...
very weak knowledge of/in ...
violated Navy instructions on ...

does not achieve standards in/of ...
requires constant (routine) guidance in determining what is
        major and what is minor in importance.
virtually nothing to show for ...

does not carry through on ...
work routinely suffers when/if ...
not productive in area(s) of ...

little desire to become proficient in/as ...
work suffers from lack of ...

PARAGRAPHS

(name) is conscientious, honest, and thorough. However, somewhat lacking in cooperativeness and in dealing with those who do not have (his/her) technical proficiency. Somewhat of a perfectionist with an inclination toward stubbornness, at times irritates those with whom (he/she) works. Reluctant to accept responsibility unless specifically assigned. Positive in handling of subordinates, but inclined to overly berate them when they fail to meet (his/her) perfectionist standards.

(name) is a highly qualified specialist in chosen field. However, (he/she) has little interest outside specialty area and avoids, to the maximum extent possible, any task or responsibility not connected therein. On occasions when forced to undertake duties outside (his/her) specialized field, produces only mediocre results. Both inexperienced and disinterested in administrative details, and has no desire to become proficient therein. Recommended for duty in assignments where specialty will take (his/her) time and is not recommended for duty where (he/she) must lead any number of people or manage large quantities of equipment.

(name) is sincere and thorough, though somewhat unimaginative and stodgy, (name) is best suited for routine jobs which are adequately covered by detailed instructions. Highly accurate and methodical in all that (he/she) does, a slow worker, but makes up for this by willingly working long hours. Has difficulty expressing personal views, and preoccupation with minor details frequently impairs the soundness of (his/her) judgement. (name) requires constant guidance in determining that which is major and that which is minor. Tactful and considerate of subordinates, but places little reliance on them, and is inclined to retain all responsibility. Leadership capacity is limited and less than that desirable of a person of (his/her) rate. (name) should be selectively detailed and assigned to office and clerical billets.

(name) has the manual dexterity and intellectual capacity to be an expert in field of ... However, (he/she) sometimes lacks the necessary persistence and conscientiousness to apply skills. When assigned an independent task, (he/she) sometimes takes more time than expected, being diverted by any number of personal interests. Properly supervised, (name) produces good work, especially when working in technical areas. When required, (he/she) has proven adaptable to changes in working conditions and policy. During the early part of this reporting period, (name) failed to meet physical fitness standards, however, after being placed on a controlled program, (he/she) has recently reached requirements.

(name) is an intense individual whose paramount interest is in the efficiency of (his/her) organization. Personal loyalty, however, sometimes causes (him/her) to execute instructions implicitly, without perceiving that conditions may have altered the situation. Quiet, modest, and unassuming. Unselfish, generous, and idealistic to a fault. (name) enthusiastic interest in (his/her) organization often cause him to accept the suggestions of subordinates without proper evaluation of all pertinent facts.. (name) requires close supervision when working in a management position, but when closely observed and guided (he/she) produces excellent results.

(name) is an industrious and willing worker, extremely accurate in all that (he/she) does, placing great emphasis on details. However, (he/she) is sometimes reluctant to make decisions in major matters within scope of responsibility and relies on others for guidance and direction in those matters that represent departure from normal routine. Operating within a system of prescribed procedures with standardized and definitely specified methods and means, and spelled out functions and responsibilities, (name) secures positive and highly acceptable results. In the performance of duties under such conditions, (he/she) effectively controls and directs workers for whom responsible, and insures that they produce desired results.

(name) is an excellent manager and organizer who is willing to accept any assignment no matter how difficult; nevertheless, (he/she) leans to heavily on subordinates and is too easily influenced by them, accepting their suggestions and recommendations with little or no analysis or consideration. An excellent conversationalist with a ready answer. (name) talks with force and finality though, on occasion, answers when analyzed, turn out to be "just words." (he/she) has a good sense of organization and an excellent administrative ability. However, leniency in the management of subordinates and the uncritical manner in which (he/she) accepts their work tends to reduce (his/her) effective value. This matter has been discussed with (him/her), but (he/she) seems to be inherently reluctant to question or challenge the veracity and soundness of judgement of subordinates.

(name) is conscientious, honest, and thorough. However, somewhat lacking in cooperativeness and is impatient in dealing with those who do not have own technical proficiency.

Difficulty expressing own views, and preoccupation with minor details frequently impairs soundness of judgment.

Somewhat of a perfectionist with an inclination toward stubbornness, at times irritates others. Reluctant to accept responsibility unless specifically assigned.

Requires constant guidance in determining that which is major and that which is minor in importance.

(name) is an excellent manager and organizer who is willing to accept any assignment no matter how difficult. Nevertheless, leans to heavily on subordinates and is too easily influenced by them, accepting their suggestions and recommendations with little or no analysis or consideration.

Positive in handling subordinates, but inclined to overly berate them when they fail to meet own perfectionist standards.

Both inexperienced and disinterested in administrative details, and has no desire to become proficient therein. Recommended for duty in assignments where specialty will occupy time. Not recommended for duty where leadership skills are required.

(name) is sincere and thorough, though somewhat unimaginative and stodgy. Best suited for routine jobs which are adequately covered by detailed instructions.

Highly accurate and methodical, although a slow worker. Makes up for this by willingly working long hours.

259

(name) is an industrious and willing worker. Extremely accurate in all tasking, sometimes placing too much emphasis on details.

(name) highly qualified specialist in field. However, has little interest outside specialty and avoids, to the maximum extent possible, any task or responsibility not connected therein. On occasions, when forced to undertake duties outside specialized field, produces only mediocre results.

Tactful and considerate of subordinates, but places little reliance on them, and is inclined to retain all responsibility personally.

Leadership capacity limited and less than desirable of a person of (paygrade). Should be selectively detailed and assigned to office and clerical billets.

(name) has manual dexterity and intellectual capacity to be an expert in (specialty field). However, sometimes lacks the necessary persistence and conscientiousness to apply skills. When assigned independent tasks sometimes takes more time than expected, being diverted by any number of personal interests.

Properly supervised, (name) produces good work, especially when working in technical areas. When required, can adapt to changes in working conditions and policy.

(name) is an intense individual whose paramount interest is organizational efficiency. Own loyalty, however, sometimes results in execution of instructions implicitly without regard to changing circumstances.

Quiet, modest, and unassuming. Unselfish, generous, and idealistic to a fault. Inclined to accept suggestions of subordinates without proper evaluation of facts.

Requires close supervision when working in a management position, but when closely observed and guided can produces good results.

Inherently reluctant to question or challenge the veracity and soundness of judgment of subordinates.

Sometimes reluctant to make decisions in major matters within scope of responsibility. Relies on others for guidance and direction in those matters that represent departure from normal routine.

Operating within a system of prescribed procedures with standardized and specified methods can secure positive and acceptable results.

Has a ready-made answer for everything, whether or not factual.

Lenient in management of subordinates and the uncritical manner in which work is accepted reduces effective value. This matter has been discussed with member.

CHAPTER 10

BRAG SHEET

BRAG SHEET

This short chapter is possibly the most important chapter in this writing guide for you personally.

A comment was made earlier in this book to the effect that "If you don't know how to write a performance appraisal, you don't know how to read one—your own included." Unfortunately, most people being evaluated don't learn the real difference between a good, strong write-up and one that "sounds" good until it is too late in their career to do much good. Because of rank, position, or education, many "khakis" falsely believe that they are automatically good performance appraisal writers. As a result of this false assumption, they hurt themselves and the good performers who work for them. A "sounds good" narrative is as much your fault as it is the person who writes it—you let him or her do it to you. A good write-up must have some substance, some job accomplishment specifics.

Regardless of how you end up with a "low," say-nothing narrative, if you are a good performer it is your fault and you are the one who is going to be "passed over" at selection time.

Everyone has an opportunity to submit information they would like to have considered when performance appraisal time comes around. For example, if you submitted an input that contained the following facts, your superiors would be hard-pressed to not use the information in your narrative.
-Qualified DC PQS in 2 months, one-third the normal time.
-Completed 3 correspondence courses.
-Qualified OOD (Inport) in 3 weeks, 4 months ahead of schedule.
-Initiated watch station PQS standards for 4 work groups totaling 25 people. Standards were approved and implemented.
-Worked 75 off-duty hours drafting and finalizing a Division Organization Manual.
-Assigned personnel received "OUTSTANDING" at 3 department and 2 command personnel inspections.

The list could go on and on. The point is THERE IS A LIST. Commit yourself to maintaining a "brag sheet" file throughout a reporting period. If you don't come up with two or three items a week to place in the file, you are not trying-or you are not doing your job. When it is time to provide an input to your performance appraisal, break out everything you have, compile it and then decide what you want to use.

Keep in mind, your superiors probably don't have the time to record all of the accomplishments of everyone who works for them. As a top performer, they would be happy to include any important information you submit. Plus, providing this information makes a superior's job of constructing a narrative much easier. The more information you have in your brag file the better. Include dates, hours worked, and any other information needed to give specific accomplishments and tasks.

The following items are offered to get you started. Add to it items particular or unique to your job or billet. These items could be appropriate to you individually, or to your work group.
1. Reenlistment (numbers/percentages).
2. Advancement (numbers/percentages).
3. PQS (military/professional) completed.
4. Correspondence courses.
5. Off-duty education.
6. Inspection results:
   -zone...material...security...command...
   safety...administrative...personnel....
   berthing/barracks...type training...
   3M...retention team...
7. Graded exercises.
8. Financial budget (save $).
9. Organization manning allowance/onboard/ onboard percent.
10. Average work-week hours.
11. Accomplishments/Distinctions received by department/ command (and what you did to help).
12. Organization correspondence forwarded correct/ timely.
13. What your organization did to help meet command objectives and commitments.
14. Special/Additional assistance given others (individuals or organizations).
15. New programs you had a hand in starting.
16. Improvements to spaces/working conditions.
17. Directives, SOPs, instructions originated/up-dated.
18. Command and community involvement.
19. Collateral duties (volunteer for many): Navy Relief Key Person, CFC Key Person, Welfare & Recreation... This list is almost endless. Volunteer for several. Many require only a few hours a month/year, and the rewards are well worth the effort.

20. Major evolutions participated in.
21. Extra hours worked.
22. Extra projects worked on (outside normal area of responsibility or outside normal working hours).

A good way to meet this challenge would be to go over a long list of possible "achievements," pick out the ones you like best, and go and do them—and then make additions to your brag file. Again, it's your write-up; it's your future...Leave no stone unturned.

CHAPTER 11

COUNSELING

CONDUCTING FITREP & EVAL COUNSELING SESSIONS

TYPICAL 2-WAY CONVERSATION
Before conducting a counseling session it is important to realize how difficult a simple 2-way conversation can become. Keep the below information in mind when attempting to communicate your thoughts to someone. When sending an important message, elicit some kind of response or feedback from the listener to ensure the message was received and correctly understood.

STEP 1 - SPEAKER'S THOUGHTS
(WHAT SPEAKER WANTS TO SAY)

STEP 2 - SPEAKER SENDS MESSAGE (TALKS)
* (See Note 1 Below)

STEP 3 - SPEAKER'S VISUAL ELEMENT ADDED TO
MESSAGE (GESTURES, FACIAL EXPRESSIONS,
VOICE TONE & INTENSITY, ETC.)

STEP 4 - LISTENER'S RECEPTION OF MESSAGE (HEARS)
** (See Note 2 Below)

STEP 5 - LISTENER'S UNDERSTANDING
(WHAT LISTENER HEARD & SAW)

STEP 6 - LISTENER'S THOUGHTS

STEP 7 - LISTENER SENDS MESSAGE RESPONSE (TALKS)
* (See Note 1 Below)]

STEP 8 - LISTENER'S VISUAL ELEMENT ADDED TO MESSAGE
(GESTURES, FACIAL EXPRESSIONS, VOICE
TONE & INTENSITY, ETC.)

STEP 9 - ORIGINAL SPEAKER'S RECEPTION OF RESPONSE
(HEARS) ** (See Note 2 Below)

STEP 10 - ORIGINAL SPEAKER'S UNDERSTANDING
(WHAT SPEAKER HEARD & SAW)

The most potent part of this 2-way exchange of information is the VISUAL element, not the spoken word.

* NOTE 1:
Incorporated into a speaker's message is that speaker's:
- personality type (including talking direct/indirect & autocratic, diplomatic, etc.)
- past experiences
- education
- understanding of subject matter
- phraseology of subject matter
- emotional involvement & state of mind
- how to correctly convey message to particular listener

** NOTE 2:
Incorporated into a listener's reception of the message is that listener's:
- personality type
- past experiences
- education
- understanding of subject matter
- emotional involvement & state of mind
- perception of the speaker
- attention or inattention to speaker

Research has shown that at the end of a day at work the average person has correctly retained only about 25 percent of the verbal input received. The other 75 percent was misunderstood or forgotten.

ACTIVE LISTENER

One of the most important skills that anyone can have, especially a counselor, is to be a good listener. Being a good listener means to be an ACTIVE LISTENER. Being an active listener means keeping the mind focused on the person speaking. Focus your attention on the speaker and only on the speaker. That is more difficult than you might think. The average person talks at the rate of about 150 words a minute. The brain can "listen" at the rate of about 450 words a minute. This means that the brain has a lot of idle time even when listening to someone talk. If you are not an active listener your mind can jump to other matters. If you start thinking about a response to another person when that person is still talking, you are not actively listening. If your mind drifts off to other matters, you are not actively listening. If you interrupt a person who is speaking, you are not actively listening.

COUNSELING

BEFORE COUNSELING BEGINS

Before counseling someone about their performance, take a few minutes to prepare yourself and your surroundings.

People are more comfortable & relaxed in a familiar environment. These conditions afford you the luxury of feeling more confident & in control of a conversation. If possible, arrange counseling sessions in your own office and at your own desk.

SETTING
- In private, 1-on-1 talk
- Comfortable temperature
- No outside noise distractions
- No interruptions

SEATING ARRANGEMENTS

- SITTING ON OPPOSITE SIDES OF DESK:
    MORE COMBATIVE, SUBORDINATE FEELS **LESS AT EASE**

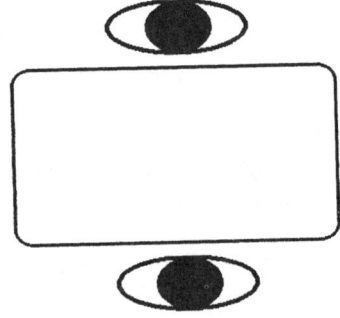

DESK/TABLE

- CORNER-TO-CORNER SEATING:
      LESS COMBATIVE, SUBORDINATE FEELS **MORE AT EASE**.

- DO write down all performance areas you want to discuss.
- DO mentally go over WHAT information you are going to cover.
- DO mentally go over HOW you are going to present the
    information.
- DO think of what the person to be counseled might say in response
    to the information you present and formulate your response.

DURING COUNSELING
One way to start a counseling session might be to read aloud the job description of the individual being counseled. Then, take it from there. All too often a person thinks he/she is doing a good job while the superior may have other thoughts. When possible, start with the positive aspects of the individual. Give the person a "well done" where deserved. This will help to put the individual at ease and reduce the chances of getting started on a negative note.

Remember, one of the most important things you can do for a subordinate is to state your goals and objectives, and your expectations of him/her.

- DO NOT conduct an I TALK, YOU LISTEN counseling session.
- DO NOT raise your voice during counseling.
- DO NOT become threatening during counseling.
- DO NOT allow a confrontation to surface.
- DO NOT be ambiguous about the information you present.

271

DO be friendly, cheerful & upbeat.

DO make frequent eye contact.

Do keep the entire counseling session on a POSITIVE note. This means don't say things like, "Your performance in area of ... was less than expected." Instead, say something like, "Can you think of any area(s) where you might improve yourself." Or, "Maybe you can become more effective if ..."

DO try to reduce tension & increase trust & understanding.

DO express your confidence in the individual.

DO present the most important information direct & simple.

DO get the person being counseled to state what improvements or changes that he/she will attempt to make.

DO elicit & listen to feedback.

DO try to understand what the other person is saying.

DO set goals, objectives & commitments.

DO determine, if there is a problem, if additional training is needed.

DO remember the main theme of the counseling session is to motivate and challenge the individual.

DO keep meeting focused on main subject(s).

DO remember the person being counseled needs to become involved in the counseling process.

DO remember that leadership is something you do WITH people, not TO people.

DO remember that leadership is a function of relationships.

DO remember, usually the more involved a person is in a task or project, the more motivated that person will become.

ENDING COUNSELING SESSION

- DO end counseling session with high enthusiasm on both sides.
- DO end counseling session by restating highlights of the meeting and all proposed actions. And, put the proposed actions in writing.
- DO get a commitment from the individual on proposed action(s).
- DO end session on a positive note.
- DO follow up on goals, objectives & commitments.
- DO NOT promise improved marks based on ASSUMED improvement

CHAPTER 12

E-7, E-8, E-9

SELECTION BOARDS

E-7, E-8, E-9 SELECTION BOARDS

PRECEPTS

Each selection board is given general guidance or instructions in the form of "precepts" by SECNAV, CNO, NMPC, and other Navy offices as appropriate. Standard precepts routinely include the following:

*Quotas for each rating are established by CHNAVPERS.

*Candidates compete only with other candidates in their particular rating.

*Age and number of times competing for advancement are not considered.

*Being overweight will not stop a candidate from being selected for advancement; however, commands are required to withhold advancement until percent of body fat requirement is met.

*Pre-determined, specific career patterns and duty rotation are not established by selection boards. However, duty assignment experience and variation are considered.

*Each candidate must be fully qualified for advancement before he/she can be selected.

*Each candidate's record must reflect that he/she is capable of performing the duties of the next higher pay grade.

GENERAL INFORMATION

The voting membership of a selection board consists of a president (Captain) and officer and enlisted board members. Prior to looking at a single record the board determines what subjects (evaluations, duty assignment, education, etc.) will receive advancement "points." Next the board determines the maximum amount of points that can be earned in each subject area. While one board may have a maximum point value of, say 750, another may max out at 1200. Regardless of the maximum value set by any given board, the weight factor percent on any subject remains relatively constant. That is, the board with 750 possible point could be expected to give approximately 400 points for evaluations (marks and narrative), or about 53% of the total points available. The board with 1200 possible points would probably give approximately 600 points for evaluations (marks and narrative), or about 50% of the total points available.

It can be noted at this point that evaluations are always the heaviest single-weighted area. The Work Sheet Sample in this chapter lists generally accepted percentage values for individual areas or traits. When subject areas and point or weight factor values have been agreed upon by the general board membership, a Work Sheet (or scoring form) listing subjects and point value parameters is constructed. The board is then broken down into small individual groups, with each group setting at a separate table. Each "table" consists of at least one officer and one or more master chief petty officer personnel in one professional area. A Boatswain Mate sits at a BM table, a Hospital Corpsman sits at the HM table, etc. If a particular rating is not represented by a master chief, that rating is screened by a table that has a closely related rating member.

Next, a board member takes a candidate's folder (consisting of a microfiche record, selection board brief sheet, and any correspondence received before or during the board's deliberation period), screens it, and transfers points "earned" to the selection board work sheet (or scoring form). A second board member then screens the same record and, using a separate work sheet, transfers points from the folder/record to the work sheet. If the two work sheets are consistent in total points awarded, the results stand. If there is any significant difference, the record is screened at least one more time. Table members go through each record in this fashion.

"Slating" is accomplished by arranging candidates from top to bottom by numerical point totals. Quotas then determine who is above and who is below the "pass" line. As a general practice, the records of candidates whose point totals are just above or just below the "pass" line are re-screened to assure point total accuracy.

Board members at the table must then agree on each candidate they are recommending for advancement. Next, table members become "sponsors" and "sell" each individual to the board's general membership via an oral brief, noting why a particular candidate is deserving of selection. The entire board votes on each candidate selection recommendation—majority rule.

Following initial voting action, the board then determines whether or not it is in conformance with special guidance precepts handed down by Navy officials.

WORK SHEET REVIEW

When reviewing the Work Sheet material on the following pages, keep the below information in mind.

Percentages are used on the Sample Work Sheet instead of actual point values. To equate what percentages mean in relation to point values, assume that 10 points equals 1%; therefore, 1000 points equals 100%.

When reviewing the work sheet, your first impression might be that the areas which award only 1 or 2 percentage points are not subject areas of strong concern. All areas deserve consideration and attention. Selection boards are looking for the "best qualified" candidates. In any given subject area some candidates are going to receive at least some of the points available. If you receive ZERO points in only 3 or 4 "minor" areas, that collective total of points "lost" is going to be very hard to make up in other areas. It is a good assumption that the candidates selected are going to earn points in virtually every subject area, and they are going to score high in the heavily weighted areas. It is a fact that usually there are only a few points (perhaps less than 1 percentage point) separating the last name on the "selectee" list and the first name on the "non-selectee" list. No subject area can be conceded by a "front runner."

To see how your record would hold up in front of a selection board, go through it and award yourself points in each subject area. Grade yourself honestly and you can see where you need additional work. Think of all the people in your pay grade going up for advancement, give the person you rate highest in each graded area maximum points and then award yourself points based on that "ideal" maximum. Some weak areas can probably be improved upon by next evaluation period. Others may require careful planning (duty station variation and the like).

Areas/Traits listed under one particular heading in the following Work Sheet may appear under a different heading on another selection board work sheet. (For example, "Command/Community Involvement" is listed under the heading of "Potential." On another work sheet that area maybe listed under a separate heading. In either case "Command/Community Involvement" will be worth about the same. Point values remain somewhat constant, regardless of what subject area a graded trait falls under.

E-7 AND E-8/9 SELECTION BOARD

WORK SHEET OVERVIEW (SAMPLE)

MAXIMUM PERCENT		CANDIDATE'S POINT TOTAL
1. EVALUATION PERFORMANCE	(31%)	
a. Overall Evaluation Marks	20%	_____
b. Peer Group Standing	6	_____
c. Leadership/Supervision Marks	5	_____
2. EVALUATION NARRATIVE (25%)		
a. Narrative Agrees with Marks	10	_____
b. Job Accomplishment	3	_____
c. Accept Challenge/Responsibility	3	_____
d. Managerial Ability	3	_____
e. Supervisory Ability	3	_____
f. Administrative Ability	3	_____
3. CAREER HISTORY (16%)		
a. Range/Variety Duty Stations	5	_____
b. Range/Variety Jobs Held	4	_____
c. Sea/Arduous Duty Performance	4	_____
d. Special Qualifications	2	_____
e. Special Assignments	1	_____
4. POTENTIAL (16%)		
a. Early/Late Starter in Paygrade	3	_____
b. Initiative	3	_____
c. Performance Consistency	3	_____
d. Volunteer Extra Work/Projects	2	_____
e. Future Duty Recommendations	2	_____
f. Advancement Recommendations	1	_____
g. Problem Areas	1	_____
h. Command/Community Involvement	1	_____
5. PERSONAL AWARDS (6%)	6	_____
6. EDUCATION (6%)	6	_____
TOTAL **100%**		
ADVANCEMENT EXAM (E-7 ONLY)	4%	
(4% taken from areas 1 through 6)		

WORK SHEET BREAKDOWN

(SAMPLE)

1. EVALUATION PERFORMANCE
a. OVERALL EVALUATION MARKS (200 points)
Breakdown Scale
5.00   200 Points
4.98   195
4.96   190
4.94   185
4.92   180
4.90   175
etc
4.80   150
4.70   125
4.60   100

b. **PEER GROUP STANDING**   (60 points)
Top Ranking Points (1 area only)
-Consistently Ranked Top/Nr. 1   50 Points
-Usually Ranked Top/Nr. 1   40
-Sometimes Ranked Top/Nr. 1   30
-Rarely Ranked Top/Nr. 1   20
-Once Ranked Top/Nr. 1   10
-Never Ranked Top/Nr. 1   0

Number Ranked Against
-Many   10
-None   0

Evaluations received for the most recent 5-year period.

c. **LEADERSHIP/SUPERVISION MARKS** (50 points)
Scale breakdown as noted for "OVERALL MARKS" above.

2. EVALUATION NARRATIVE

a. NARRATIVE AGREES WITH MARKS (100 points)
This area is a hedge against inflated marks. If very high marks are not justified in the narrative, a low number of points will be received in this

area. Conversely, average marks and a good, meaningful narrative will receive extra points.

b. JOB ACCOMPLISHMENT(30 points)
What was accomplished? How was it accomplished? Was accomplishment more/less than norm?

c. ACCEPT CHALLENGE & RESPONSIBILITY (30 points)
Volunteer/Ask for additional assignments. Was accomplishment more/less than norm?

d. MANAGERIAL ABILITY (30 points)
Demonstrated managerial skills, including areas of material, finance, time resources, and ability to plan and organize activities of others.

e. SUPERVISORY ABILITY (30 points)
How many people were supervised? Under what conditions? What were the results?

f. ADMINISTRATIVE ABILITY (30 points)
Administrative area is a mixture of:
-Administration: Paperwork, files, records, etc.
-Administrator: Includes managerial fringe areas.

3. CAREER HISTORY

a. RANGE/VARIETY DUTY STATIONS (50 points)
The more varied command assignments, and therefore the more varied command missions, the more points. A geographical spread is also helpful.

b. RANGE/VARIETY JOBS HELD (40 points)
The more varied jobs/duties the better.

c. SEA/ARDUOUS DUTY PERFORMANCE (40 points)
Sea duty includes duty stations that are considered sea duty for rotational purposes. What was performance at sea/arduous duty assignments?

d. SPECIAL QUALIFICATION (20 points)
Points awarded for special qualifications: OOD, ESWS, SS, Diver, Instructor, etc..

e. SPECIAL ASSIGNMENTS (10 points)
Includes duty assignments in following areas: Independent, isolated, embassy, instructor, recruiter, recruit company commander, etc..

4. POTENTIAL

a. EARLY/LATE STARTER IN PAYGRADE (30 points)
A comparison between performance when first entering a higher paygrade and later performance. (Which is to say: "Does it take time to "grow" into a higher position/pay grade?")

b. INITIATIVE (30 points)
Recognizing work that needs to be accomplished, and taking the lead in getting it accomplished without waiting for direction. This can include both command and community activity.

c. PERFORMANCE CONSISTENCY (30 points)
Sustained superior performance--all "peaks" and "valleys."

d. VOLUNTEER EXTRA WORK/PROJECTS (20 points)
Ask for more jobs/work, and perform well in those assignments. Work extra hours. Evaluation narrative should read "volunteered" versus "assigned."

e. FUTURE DUTY RECOMMENDATIONS (20 points)
Recommendation to fill special billets and billets of increasing responsibility and complexity: Instructor duty, Command Master Chief, and the like.

f. ADVANCEMENT RECOMMENDATION (10 points)
Recommendation for advancement in all evaluations. Strong
recommendation? Recommendation for Warrant Officer/LDO?

g. PROBLEM AREAS (10 points)
Personal/Performance problems noted in an evaluation and not
subsequently listed as being corrected/resolved...Or, no problems.

h. COMMAND/COMMUNITY INVOLVEMENT (10 points)
Serve on command boards/committees, be a Navy Relief Key person, etc.
Join community activities/projects. And, do more than just attend
meetings; get involved and accomplish something.

5. PERSONAL AWARDS

AWARDS (Examples)	Points Each
Navy Cross	20
Navy Commendation Medal	7
Navy Achievement Medal	5
Good Conduct Medal	3
*Letter of Commendation	2
*Letter of Appreciation	1

*Letters must be signed by approved senior officer ranks.

Unit awards (PUC, NUC, MUC, etc.) do not count.

6. EDUCATION

NAVY SCHOOLS: Points earned from schools vary depending of length,
course content, type school, etc. Includes career counselor, instructor
training, and job related schools. (Maximum 10 points)

NAVY CORRESPONDENCE COURSES: Both the number and the
frequency with which completed are considered, looking for "sustained
superior performance." (Maximum 10 points)

CIVILIAN EDUCATION:	Points (Maximum 40)
Each college course	1
1 Year College	10
AA Degree (2 years)	20
BA/BS Degree (4 years)	30
Masters Degree	40

7. ADVANCEMENT EXAMINATION (E-7 only) (40 points)

Not all E-7 selection boards award points in this area. When they do, the highest test passers earn maximum and low test passers earn progressively less.

E-7, E-8, E-9 SELECTION BOARD

YOUR SERVICE RECORD

Does your service record reflect an accurate picture of you for the selection board? How the selection board views your record determines whether or not you will be advanced.

You should request a free copy of your microfiche record 3-6 months prior to selection board convening date. Include in the letter your full name, rate, social security number, and the complete address of where the record is to be sent. Don't forget to sign your full name. Telephone requests are not honored since your signature is required to have your record released. Allow 4-6 weeks for delivery.

If, after reviewing your record, you find errors or omissions, you may request the proper corrections. The record entry correction packet should contain all filmable documents that are missing from the master record.

To ensure that important information omitted from your record or any other pertinent information is presented before the board, a selection board packet should be sent directly to the appropriate board via certified or registered mail.

CHAPTER 13

LDO/CWO PROMOTION

CWO - LDO ENDORSEMENT

WRITE-UP
As you read through the sample endorsements you may notice that many of them read somewhat alike. Selection boards have evolved to their present state over time. Proven methods of selection slowly give way to change, little by little. As a result, change from one year to the next is barely noticeable. So, too, proven ways of positively influencing selection boards change little from year to year.

Recent CWO/LDO selection boards have been consistent in their search for candidates who possess "proven" specific traits and characteristics. A good CWO/LDO endorsement write-up should encompass, either directly or indirectly, as many of the following areas as possible.

POTENTIAL	-For continued growth and value.
TECHNICAL	
COMPETENCE -	More so for CWO candidates.
EDUCATION	-A minimum of 60 semester hours college or AA Degree is practically a MUST for LDO. College for CWO is not mandatory, but is definitely helpful. In either case, the more the better.
DUTY/	-Wide range/variety. Much arduous/sea
EXPERIENCE	duty.
LEADERSHIP	-Proven leadership in variety of jobs/ positions.
PAST SUCCESS	-Brief highlight in write-up.
SUSTAINED	-Brief highlight in write-up. Your
PERFORMANCE	record should speak for itself in this area.

INITIATIVE   MOTIVATION   ORGANIZER   MANAGER

The above areas are directly related to well rounded "professionals." Selection boards are also looking for "well rounded" persons with high personal character and varied interests outside a strictly professional environment. While jogging, hobbies, and the like can be covered in your personal write-up, the command endorsement should convey the "whole person" in such areas as:

INTEGRITY, RELIABILITY, MORAL STANDARDS, FINANCIAL/FAMILY STABILITY, and SOCIAL INVOLVEMENT and ACCEPTANCE (i.e. being a member of a PTA shows social involvement; however, being president, secretary, etc. shows social acceptance). Selection boards realize that when they promote someone to the officer ranks, that officer can stay around for years with only average performance. The board would obviously hesitate when asked to promote someone of "questionable" character.

LOCAL INTERVIEW BOARD

Some years ago an officer candidate was required to go before a Local Interview Board. Sometime in the mid-1970's this requirement went away. So the Interview Board requirement comes and goes. If there is a Board, candidates must do their best to favorably impress board members.

The questions board members ask are as varied and diverse as the members who sit on the board. There is no standard question list, each member is free to venture into any area he or she may choose. The variety of questions might range from, "If you saw a close friend of yours taking drugs, what would you do?" to, "What do you think about the United States' policy on (whatever)?" Local interview board members, for the most part, want your thoughts, ideas, and opinions on subjects. They are not looking for cut-and-dry "right" or "wrong" answers.

INTERVIEW BOARD HINTS

-Be straightforward, honest, and sincere.

-Don't talk too fast (or too slow).

-Don't talk with your hands (don't wave them around).

-Sit still, do not squirm around.

-Eye-to-eye contact. Use eye-to-eye contact when talking to board members. Don't look at only one individual. You are talking to the entire board. Share your eye contact with all members.

-Appearance. Must be above reproach from haircut to shoes.

-World events. Be prepared to discuss world events (watch the news on TV and read the newspaper) know at least what's behind the headlines.

CWO - LDO ENDORSEMENT
SAMPLE #1

1. Forwarded, strongly recommending approval.

2. (name) superior management and leadership abilities place (him/her) head and shoulders above (his/her) contemporaries. (his/her) work habits and "follow me" style of leadership have won the respect and admiration of (his/her) division, department, and the command. (name) exceptional administrative abilities have been sought for a variety of department and command projects, all with equally outstanding results. A cheerful, creative and industrious individual, (he/she) is, in every sense of the word, an "achiever."

3. (name) filled a division officer's billet in (his/her) first ... months at this command. During that time the command received numerous letters and messages of appreciation and commendation as a direct result of (his/her) efforts. Originators included: ..., ..., ..., and ... These achievements were especially noteworthy considering (his/her) division was continually understaffed by 20-25 percent of allowance. As a result of these and other accomplishments, I recently transferred (name) to a division where (he/she) relieved a LTJG as division officer. Within a month of (his/her) reassignment this command received a letter from ... expressing specific appreciation to (name) for (his/her) invaluable assistance in the indoctrination and training of their prospective (billet/job).

4. (name) honesty and integrity, coupled with (his/her) outstanding operational and technical competence, generates immediate confidence in (his/her) abilities by all with whom (he/she) comes in contact. (name) thoughtfulness, concern and compassion for all Navy members further enhance (his/her) strong supervisory abilities. (he/she) believes in the proper training and professional development of all subordinates is a matter of personal concern and prime importance, and (he/she) has adeptly integrated this feeling into daily division operations.

5. (name) ability to plan, coordinate and supervise the activities of others is second to none. (he/she) is a "head and shoulders" performer in the (peer group) ranks and I have every confidence in (his/her) ability to perform equally well as a (WO/LDO).

6. (name) is a proven leader who displays the technical knowledge, managerial ability, and constructive thinking required to perform exceptionally well as a (WO/LDO). (he/she) is ready for promotion now. I would be especially pleased to have (him/her) as a member of my wardroom now or in the future.

CWO - LDO ENDORSEMENT
SAMPLE #2

1. Forwarded, recommending approval.

2. (name) consistently performs in an enthusiastic and outstanding manner. Evaluations from previous commands indicate that (he/she) has continually maintained this excellent record throughout (his/her) Naval career. (name) possesses the ability to foresee and prepare for future needs as well as to act on present requirements. Utilizing (his/her) positive attitude and professional expertise, (he/she) engenders confidence in (his/her) subordinates, co-workers, and seniors. (name) outstanding military bearing is complimented by (his/her) no-nonsense approach to duties, constant awareness of responsibilities, and (his/her) personal appearance which is always impeccable.

3. (name) performance, not only as a leader, but in the wide and varied technical billets held, coupled with (his/her) extensive schooling and on-the-job training, demonstrates (his/her) potential for outstanding performance as a (WO/LDO) in the ... specialty field. (he/she) has demonstrated the attributes of determination, loyalty to the Navy, a mature sense of responsibility, and a pride of (his/her) work which exemplify the most desirable traits of an officer.

4. (name) has consistently displayed a truly superlative performance in any assignment. (his/her) career pattern reflects strong and steady growth in every endeavor as evidenced by the numerous Letters of Appreciation and Commendation (he/she) has received for outstanding performance. At this command (he/she) has performed in three challenging, demanding billets requiring exemplary leadership and a thorough working knowledge of (his/her) rate. In (name) initial assignment as a ..., (he/she) performed in such a superior manner that (he/she) was selected for transfer to the ... Division to fill a Master Chief Petty Officer billet. In this much more demanding billet (he/she) was given a broad charter to improve operational readiness and the level of support provided to ... departments. (name) initiative and skill in devising new operating procedures dramatically improved the division's readiness and earned (him/her) the respect and admiration of the entire command.

5. (name) is a top performer in the enlisted ranks and (he/she) has the potential to be a top performer in the officer ranks. (name) is highly recommended for promotion to (WO/LDO).

CWO - LDO ENDORSEMENT
SAMPLE #3

1.   Forwarded, strongly recommending approval.

2.   (name) is an outstanding performer in every respect. I have complete confidence, not only in (his/her) proven managerial and administrative abilities, but also in (his/her) maturity, discretion, and personal judgement. (he/she) is already performing at a level that I would expect from a (WO/LDO).   (he/she) is a stand out (peer group)—a strong, positive leader, and an expert in (his/her) technical field.

3.   (name) career as a ... has been broad and varied. (he/she) supervised watch sections at ... and ... (he/she) has been Leading..., Department 3M Coordinator, Career Counselor, and Training Officer, and (he/she) is a qualified Inport OOD. (his/her) record confirms that (his/her) performance in these and other assignments has been an appreciable "cut above" the typical "good" performer. (he/she) is extremely well prepared to make the transition to (WO/LDO) in the ... community.

4.   (name) has demonstrated a strong desire to improve (himself/herself) personally and professionally. (he/she) recently completed requirements for an Associate of Arts Degree and is continuing (his/her) education, working toward a Bachelor's Degree. (he/she) maintains a stable family life and is committed to, and deeply involved in, a variety of civic and community affairs and projects. (he/she) is always in the thick of the action.

5.   (name) career shows strong self-motivation and an attitude toward the Navy that exemplifies the concept of "pride and professionalism."   A proven leader who always obtains results surpassing command objectives and possessing a genuine desire for commissioned service, (name) is an outstanding candidate for selection as a (WO/LDO).   I most strongly recommend (name) for immediate promotion to commissioned officer status.

CWO - LDO ENDORSEMENT
SAMPLE #4

1.   Forwarded, most strongly recommending approval.

2.   (name) is a "hard charger" who is an exceptionally talented and well qualified candidate for commissioning as a (WO/LDO). (he/she) is a forceful, dynamic leader who knows how to motivate subordinates and get outstanding results. (he/she) is the best (peer group) in my command and I frequently seek (his/her) assistance to take on special projects, both operational and administrative in nature. Without fail, (he/she) has responded enthusiastically, with positive results, and ahead of schedule.

3.   (name) is eminently qualified and prepared to accept the greater responsibilities and trust of a (WO/LDO). (his/her) career has been varied and (he/she) has held a number of increasingly more demanding billets and positions. The hallmark of all (his/her) past assignments is exemplary performance. (name) has an intense desire to excel in all endeavors. (he/she) is an outstanding candidate for (WO/LDO) in the ... Category.

4.   (name) academic ability is best reflected in (his/her) completion of ... hours of college work, during off-duty hours, with an overall grade average of ... The many correspondence courses (he/she) has completed range from ... to ... (name) consistently places at or near the top in all service schools. And, (he/she) has the ability to improve the performance of those around (him/her).

5.   (name) has a cheerful, sincere, and professional attitude. (he/she) is always polite and courteous to seniors, and is demanding, considerate, and imaginative in (his/her) leadership of subordinates. (name) believes in the Navy, is highly motivated toward a Naval career, and is an outstanding example for junior personnel to look to for guidance and assistance.

6.   (name) manifests the attributes most desired in an officer candidate. (he/she) is intelligent, versatile, highly motivated, and continually exemplifies the highest possible standards of professionalism and performance. (he/she) is eminently qualified in all respects for advancement to commissioned officer status.

7.   The Navy needs men of (name) ability and potential in responsible positions. I would actively seek to have (him/her) assigned as a member of my wardroom, either afloat or ashore. I recommend him for promotion to (WO/LDO) in the strongest terms possible.

CWO - LDO ENDORSEMENT
SAMPLE #5

1. Forwarded, highly recommending approval.

2. (name) is an outstanding candidate for the Navy's (WO/LDO) Program. (he/she) is an energetic and methodical individual with the proven ability to excel in any assignment. (his/her) unique ability to immediately establish, and maintain, a close rapport and harmonious working relationship with today's young, inquisitive sailor led to (his/her) assignment as (organization) Career Counselor. In this capacity, (he/she) made significant improvements to the organizational structure and record keeping practices that ultimately led to improved effectiveness and an increase in first term reenlistments by 25%. (name) has been particularly effective in maintaining close liaison with the local Personnel Support Detachment to ensure that responsive support is provided and that all command requirements in the personnel area are met. (he/she) has the maturity to maintain the fine balance between mission requirements and concern for the individual, which is particularly difficult to define in administrative matters. As a result, (he/she) is exceptionally effective in dealing with subordinates, peers, and superiors.

3. (name) performance is second to none. (he/she) can be depended upon to accomplish any task presented and on several occasions sacrificed (his/her) off-duty time to insure that a job was completed with utmost accuracy. As a supervisor and leader (his/her) professional and military competence is continually tested and has never been found lacking. (name) steady and uncompromising approach toward good leadership leaves no doubt in the minds of (his/her) subordinates as to what is expected of them and makes following (his/her) lead an easy choice.

4. (name) academic achievements are truly impressive. Despite the disruptions of transfers (he/she) has aggressively availed (himself/herself) of the opportunity to study and complete classroom and correspondence courses in order to earn a college degree. (he/she) recently completed all requirements for an Associates Degree and is expected to earn a BA Degree within the next year.

5. (name) is a complete professional and an outstanding example of the dedicated careerist needed in today's Navy. (he/she) is most strongly recommended for the (WO/LDO) Program. I would be particularly pleased to have (him/her) as a member of my wardroom.

CWO - LDO ENDORSEMENT
SAMPLE #6

1. Forwarded, highly recommending approval.

2. (name) expertise in the ... field has ranged from being an operator in ..., to a supervisor's job in ..., through a management position in a systems analysis and testing organization aboard a major combatant. (his/her) technical expertise, leadership, and management abilities far exceed those normally expected of a (peer group). These attributes, coupled with (his/her) rapid advancement through the enlisted ranks, are indicative of (his/her) desire and ability to accept positions of much greater responsibility. (he/she) is an outstanding candidate for selection to (WO/LDO) status in (his/her) first preference designator of ...

3. (name) is a top-notch leader, using an excellent blend of tact and direct supervision to elicit the maximum effort of subordinates. (his/her) correct appearance, military bearing, and flawless conduct project obvious pride in the service of the Navy and (his/her) country.

4. (name) has a goal of obtaining a BS Degree in Business Management. (he/she) has completed numerous courses leading toward attainment of this goal and is presently attending night classes with the University of ... (his/her) military schooling and Navy correspondence courses show extensive training not only for (his/her) rating, but in management as well.

5. (name) is a staunch supporter of the Navy and its career programs and (he/she) has been observed on frequent occasions discussing career reenlistment options with junior personnel throughout the command. (he/she) recently completed off-duty correspondence courses in the area of Navy Counselor to broaden (his/her) knowledge of, and gain insight into, these vitally important and rapidly changing subjects.

6. In my ... years of Naval Service, I have not seen a more qualified candidate for (WO/LDO). I would be particularly pleased to have (name) as a member of my wardroom, both ashore and afloat.

CWO - LDO ENDORSEMENT
SAMPLE #7

1. Forwarded, strongly recommending approval.

2. (name) demonstrates extraordinary professional ability, in depth technical knowledge, and uncommon perceptiveness in advancing the morale and welfare needs of (his/her) people while at the same time meeting all command goals and objectives. In recommending (name) for (WO/LDO), I am thoroughly convinced that (he/she) exemplifies those qualities and traits that merit (his/her) selection.

3. (name) is an exceptionally talented and well-qualified candidate who has consistently displayed superlative performance in a wide range of duties. (his/her) career pattern reflects a steady growth in both technical and management skills, and (he/she) is the recipient of numerous Letters of Appreciation and Commendation for outstanding performance.

4. (name) ability to adapt to any assignment and (his/her) strong motivation toward self improvement indicate the potential for outstanding performance in diverse occupational fields within the officer corps. (his/her) self assurance, professional approach, and confident attitude make (him/her) an outstanding candidate for selection to (WO/LDO).

5. (name) academic ability is very impressive. (his/her) successful completion of a variety of military schools and correspondence courses attest to (his/her) desire to improve (himself/herself) personally and professionally. Additionally, (his/her) selection of correspondence courses has been geared toward more fully preparing himself for advancement to commissioned officer.

6. (name) is fully qualified in all respects and will perform extremely well as a (WO/LDO) in the ... Category. (he/she) possesses the technical ability, administrative talent, mental acuity, and self-confidence to carry out all duties to which (he/she) may be assigned.

7. (name) is highly qualified for appointment to the (WO/LDO) Program, and (he/she) is strongly recommended for selection.

CWO - LDO ENDORSEMENT
SAMPLE #8

1. Forwarded, highly recommending approval.

2. (name) is an excellent candidate for (WO/LDO). The ability (he/she possesses to organize and make correct decisions is outstanding (his/her) professional knowledge, technical competence and attention to detail is impressive. (name) supervisory ability, demonstrated by (his/her rapport with subordinates and work accomplishment, is excellent.

3. (name) is thoughtful, concerned, and compassionate in (his/her dealings with subordinates. In (his/her) position as supervisor, teacher and counselor (he/she) displays the concerned compassion and professionalism of a model (peer group). (name) is actively involved in this command's retention team effort, and to enhance (his/her effectiveness (he/she) requested and attended Career Counselor School In addition to conducting group and one-on-one counseling sessions (he/she) has been active in setting up and conducting command-wide workshops that have received praise from all officers at this command.

4. A thorough review of (name) record substantiates the fact that (his/her performance of excellence has continued throughout (his/her) Nava career. As revealed through personal letters of commendation and appreciation, it is quite apparent that (he/she) has continually devoted (himself/herself) to the Navy.

5. (name) academic ability and progress are outstanding. (he/she) has completed ... semester hours of college credit at the University of ... with a grade point average of ... and has consistently graduated in the upper hal of (his/her) class at service schools.

6. (name) is highly motivated toward a career in the Navy and fo selection to commissioned status. In view of (his/her) continued display of loyalty, dedication, and reliability, (name) is considered an excellen candidate for appointment to (WO/LDO).

CWO - LDO ENDORSEMENT

SAMPLE #9

1. Forwarded, most strongly recommending approval.

2. (name) is intelligent, energetic, and innovative. Throughout (his/her) career (he/she) has consistently excelled in (his/her) rating and in a leadership capacity. (his/her) comprehensive technical knowledge, initiative, and superb leadership was aptly displayed during this command's (mission). (name) enthusiastic approach toward setting and achieving mission goals, and (his/her) natural flair for counseling significantly enhanced the performance of the (organization) department. Through (his/her) leadership, patience, and uniquely personalized instructional technique, many less than receptive personnel have been successfully motivated and inspired to work to the highest level of their ability. (his/her) unparalleled proficiency in (his/her) technical specialty and in ... operations place (him/her) at the absolute forefront of ...

3. (name) strong technical background is the result of a long and diverse series of operational assignments. (his/her) experience base is broad and encompasses a wide range of professional specialties. Recognized as the resident authority in the area of PMS, PQS, and damage control, (name) is consistently sought out for technical advice. (his/her) achievements in the technical aspects of (his/her) rate are amply documented in (his/her) enlisted performance evaluation and testify to the thorough knowledge of (his/her) rate.

4. A concerned and humane individual, (name) affable personality and willingness to assist others in any capacity instills high morale and a strong sense of esprit de corps in those around (him/her). Through personal industry and the effective use of correct management techniques (he/she) has shown that (he/she) can judiciously utilize personnel and material resources.

5. Dedicated to professional growth and personal self-development, (name) has methodically accumulated a record of academic accomplishments of unequalled magnitude. (he/she) has earned a Bachelor of Science Degree from the University of ..., and has completed ... Navy correspondence courses and ... service schools.

6. A proven performer of strong personal integrity and superb leadership and technical ability, (name) enjoys my absolute confidence that (he/she) will be an exceptional (WO/LDO). I would actively seek to have (him/her) assigned as a member of my wardroom, either ashore or afloat.

298

CWO - LDO ENDORSEMENT
SAMPLE #10

1. Forwarded, highly recommending approval.

2. (name) professional knowledge and technical competence is truly outstanding. (he/she) has fully demonstrated the strong leadership, exceptional management ability, and meticulous administrative skills that will enable (him/her) to discharge, in a superior manner, the broader duties and greater responsibilities of a (WO/LDO).

3. (name) professional performance has been consistently superior. (he/she) is currently serving as (billet) for the ... Department and has performed numerous division officer functions in this capacity. In all assignments, (name) has consistently performed (his/her) duties with skill, eagerness, ingenuity, and imagination, and has been extremely effective in guiding assigned personnel in the performance of their duties. (his/her) personal contributions to command readiness and to mission effectiveness are well documented. (he/she) received a Navy Achievement Medal from ... for professional work and technical competence (he/she) displayed during (period). I personally awarded him a Letter of Commendation for (his/her) active and successful participation in ...

4. Evaluations received in well-rounded duty assignments are evidence of (name) sustained superior performance and a strong desire to excel. (his/her) qualities of self-confidence, excellent physical condition, and commanding presence give (him/her) an unusual talent for the control of personnel. (name) maintains an impeccable personal appearance and commands similarly high standards from subordinates, creating a deep respect for Navy tradition and regulations. (he/she) displays an understanding and an informed sense of judgement in (his/her) dealings with others, regardless of sex, race, or creed.

5. (name) has repeatedly demonstrated that (he/she) possesses those unique qualities of leadership and technical knowledge that identify (him/her) as truly outstanding, and totally committed to excellence. (name) is highly recommended for selection to the (WO/LDO) Program.

CWO - LDO ENDORSEMENT
(SAMPLE #11

1. Forwarded, strongly recommending approval.

2. (name) has thoroughly exhibited the potential to excel in the capacity of a (CWO/LDO). (he/she) is extremely dedicated and strongly motivated toward advancement within the United States Navy. Having clearly demonstrated consistent outstanding performance and potential in managerial and technical competence, (name) was personally selected to lead this command's ... program. (his/her) personal in-depth knowledge and submitted resolutions to potential problems have been instrumental factors in the noticeable improvements to that program. During a Command Inspection conducted by TYCOM, the program was judged as the finest inspected in more than ... years.

3. A meticulous administrator, (name) totally controlled all administrative matters in the department. Confronted with an error rate of 7% in the (area), (he/she) exercised strong supervisory control and promptly decreased the error rate to an impressive 2.1% within two months. This "take charge" administrative and leadership attitude does not end with (his/her) technical undertakings. (name) assumed the responsibility of coordinating the command's zone inspection program and produced equally impressive results. Additionally, these valuable traits and (his/her) superb managerial skills were instrumental in my appointing (him/her) to serve as Command ..., a demanding billet which (he/she) continues to serve in with unequalled distinction.

4. (name) is a well-rounded person of many interests. (he/she) continually takes positive steps to improve (his/her) knowledge and understanding of (his/her) technical field and in the world around (him/her). (name) has completed eleven Navy schools and twenty-three correspondence courses. To date (he/she) has completed forty-eight semester hours of credit with the University of ..., and expects to earn an Associate Degree in the near future.

5. (name) exceptional technical knowledge, superb managerial abilities, and strong, positive leadership acquired through a series of challenging and diverse duty assignments combine in such a balanced manner as to stand (him/her) head and shoulders above (his/her) peers. No better candidate could be found for this program than this eager, mature, and dedicated Navy (man/woman). (name) is an ideal candidate for the (WO/LDO) Program.

CWO - LDO ENDORSEMENT
SAMPLE #12

1. Forwarded, highly recommending approval.

2. (name) is a superb (WO/LDO) applicant in all respects. (his/her) military bearing, appearance, discipline, and moral character are of the highest order. (he/she) aggressively pursues difficult challenges and is tireless in (his/her) efforts to excel. Through successive tours on board ..., ..., and ..., (name) has experienced total diversity within (his/her) professional specialty of ... This experience combined with (his/her) extensive schooling provide and extraordinary high degree of technical knowledge.

3. (name) organizational and managerial skills place (him/her) head and shoulders above (his/her) contemporaries. (he/she) is an exceptionally talented and versatile individual who has consistently achieved superior results in progressively more challenging assignments. Extraordinary professional ability, in depth technical knowledge, and uncommon perceptiveness in advancing the morale and welfare of subordinates highlight (name) daily performance and demonstrate unlimited growth potential. (his/her) desire and motivation to aspire to commissioned rank is refreshing. (he/she) is immediately capable of being promoted to (WO/LDO), and (he/she) has the spiritual force and moral fiber so necessary of a Naval leader. I am thoroughly convinced that (name) exemplifies those qualities and traits which merit (his/her) selection.

4. (name) has proven (himself/herself) an excellent student in all Navy and civilian educational institutions. This education has provided (him/her) with diversified knowledge essential for an expanding Naval career.

5. The leadership and supervisory abilities (name) has demonstrated, coupled with (his/her) forthright confident manner, ensure (his/her) success in the officer community. (he/she) is extremely capable of accepting, and carrying out, the expanded responsibilities and increased trust associated with a (WO/LDO).

6. Throughout (his/her) career, (name) has gained the prerequisite experience to excel as a (WO/LDO). The extraordinary manner in which (he/she) has managed (his/her) (organization) throughout (his/her) tour aboard provides vivid insight to an unlimited potential as a/an (WO/LDO). These strong traits coupled with (his/her) natural leadership abilities make (name) the best (specialty group) candidate for (WO/LDO) in the Navy.

CWO - LDO ENDORSEMENT
SAMPLE #13

1. Forwarded, highly recommending approval.

2. (name) sets the standards in both military and professional performance. (he/she) stands head and shoulders above (his/her) contemporaries in all respects. (his/her) enthusiastic attitude, loyal dedication to the Naval service, and impressive accomplishments truly merit increased responsibility now.

3. (name) has firmly established (himself/herself) as an outstanding leader whose performance and personal characteristics make (him/her) the epitome of what is desired in a Naval leader. Exceptional technical competence and moral leadership highlight (name) daily performance. (he/she) possesses the extra initiative, personal magnetism, moral fiber, and patriotism that will make (him/her) a welcome addition to the officer corps of the United States Navy.

4. (name) has been a source of major administrative and operational contributions throughout (his/her) tour at this command. (his/her) innovative ideas in ... resulted in considerable savings of manhours for (his/her) department. (he/she) volunteered to conduct an extensive survey and assessment of ... system reliability. Following this survey (he/she) instituted a number of changes, including: updated ...; closer liaison between ... and ... personnel; and, a revitalized and updated quality control testing acceptance program. To implement these sweeping changes, (he/she) followed-up with highly effective, expertly written, operating instructions and procedures, and a viable training program to ensure correct implementation. As a result of these extensive reform efforts, within six months ... system reliability increased from ... to ... percent.

5. As a military supervisor, (name) thrives on good personnel relationships through two-way communications with subordinates and is effective in imparting to them the importance of this human element in the overall mission of the command. (name) deep and abiding personal concern for the welfare of others is not limited to work hours. (he/she) involves (himself/herself) in as many community affairs as time permits and is an active and productive member of ... and ... (name) is a sober, responsible person who maintains a highly stable family life.

6. (name) is a natural choice for selection to the (WO/LDO) Program and (he/she) has my highest recommendation.

CWO - LDO ENDORSEMENT
SAMPLE #14

1.   Forwarded, most strongly recommending approval.

2.   (name) qualifications for the (WO/LDO) Program are without equal. While sustaining an extraordinary high level of performance, (he/she) has consistently demonstrates those qualities required in a (WO/LDO); exceptional technical knowledge, superb managerial capability, and strong, positive leadership. (his/her) superior administrative abilities are known and respected throughout this command. As a leader, (name) successfully couples a strong positive drive for excellence with a sincere concern for the welfare of each member of (his/her) organization.

3.   (name) record is truly impressive. (his/her) career has followed a pattern of steady growth in technical skills and leadership. Since reporting aboard (he/she) has filled increasingly demanding billets with unparalleled success. A self-starter who thrives on challenge, (he/she) performed flawlessly while simultaneously filling eight primary and collateral duties, including ...

4.   (name) need to improve (himself/herself) personally and professionally is manifested in (his/her) intense desire to pursue both on and off duty educational goals. (he/she) has attended a variety of military and civilian educational institutions with consistently high academic performance. Working many extra hours at this command has not diminished this desire. (he/she) has found time to complete five off-duty college courses, in a variety of technical and management subjects, while maintaining a grade point average of ...

5.   (name) personal appearance, military bearing, and personal behavior are commendable. (his/her) sense of humor, mental alertness, and ability to express (himself/herself) both orally and in writing is excellent. (name) is a sound manager with the proven ability to successfully supervise the functions and activities of others while maintaining, or surpassing, all command objectives.

6.   It is without reservation or condition that I recommend (name) for (WO/LDO). I would particularly be pleased to have (him/her) as a member of my wardroom, either ashore or afloat.

CWO - LDO ENDORSEMENT
SAMPLE #15

1. Forwarded, strongly recommending approval.

2. (name) is the most dynamic (peer group) that I have ever observed. (his/her) technical qualifications are absolutely first rate, and (his/her) experience qualifies (him/her) superbly to be a (WO/LDO) technical manager. Even more important, (he/she) is a "military professional" in the fullest sense of the term. (name) is a strong, positive leader who will be a credit to the officer corps. Without hesitation, I rank (him/her) number one of the four enlisted personnel in my command applying for the (WO/LDO) Program.

3. (name) seeks responsibility and is always ready to carry more than (his/her) share of the work load. Although quiet by nature, (he/she) enthusiastically and diligently pursues opportunities to enhance (his/her) career. (he/she) possesses the experience, leadership abilities, motivation, attitude, and loyalty required of a Naval Officer.

4. In (his/her) assignment as ..., (name) consistently performed the duties with skill, eagerness, ingenuity, and was extremely effective in guiding assigned personnel in the performance of their duties. (his/her) exceptional leadership skills and managerial abilities enabled (him/her) to train and develop a highly capable and productive team of professionals. Under (his/her) tutelage and direction (his/her) shop became a model of excellence. Through (his/her) guidance non-productive maintenance was all but eliminated, resulting in substantial monetary savings to the command.

5. After only a short association with (name), it will become readily apparent that (he/she) is unswerving in (his/her) loyalty to the Navy and is steadfastly determined to accomplish any task in an outstanding manner. (he/she) maintains a stable family life, possesses high morals, and is intricately involved in numerous community activities.

6. (name) entire career shows strong self-motivation and a particularly desirable attitude towards the Navy. A proven manager who obtains results equal to or surpassing command objectives, (he/she) is an outstanding candidate for commissioned status as a (WO/LDO).

7. (name) has my strongest possible recommendation for immediate commission as a (WO/LDO).

CWO - LDO ENDORSEMENT
SAMPLE #16

1. Forwarded, highly recommending approval.

2. (name) is an exceptionally talented and well-qualified candidate who has consistently displayed superlative performance in a wide range of duties. (his/her) career pattern reflects steady growth in both technical and management skills. While serving at this command, (he/she) has performed three challenging and demanding billets requiring thorough knowledge of (his/her) rate and exemplary leadership. As (job/billet), (his/her) responsibilities encompassed all aspects of ... (he/she) provided the expertise to maintain a consistent, smooth flowing operation, and ensured errorless (subject). (name) demonstrated maturity and outstanding knowledge of (his/her) technical specialty as Department (job/billet). In (his/her) third job of Department (job/billet), (he/she) was effective in reducing the error rate of ... system from ... to ... percent within the past year, thereby improving the operation of the ... Department and the creditability of this command.

3. (name) off-duty educational achievements are praiseworthy. (he/she)has successfully completed a variety of college level examination tests and night school classes, accumulating a total of ... semester hours of college credit. (he/she) is presently within ... hours of earning a BS in ... through the University of ... (he/she) has earned a place on the Dean's List for academic excellence during each of the last two years.

4. (name) entire career shows strong self-motivation and a positive attitude toward the Navy. A proven manager who obtains results surpassing command objectives, (he/she) is an outstanding candidate for (WO/LDO).

5. (name) is the caliber of Navy professional sought by the (WO/LDO) Program. (his/her) untiring dedication to the completion of tasks and the initiative shown in improving conditions within (organization) and this command have earned my respect and complete confidence in (his/her) abilities. (name) is unconditionally prepared and I strongly recommend him for selection as a (WO/LDO). I would be particularly pleased to have (him/her) as a member of my wardroom.

CWO - LDO ENDORSEMENT
SAMPLE #17

1. Forwarded, highly recommending approval.

2. (name) possesses a well-rounded knowledge of (his/her) rate, both afloat and ashore. (his/her) attention to detail, foresight in planning, and organizational ability are superior in all respects and are demonstrated daily by (his/her) skillful direction of (his/her) work center. (name) counseling expertise, and the meticulous record keeping displayed in the performance of both (his/her) primary and collateral duties, are unequalled. A diverse background as ... operator, ... operator and supervisor, and training petty officer at such major commands as ... and ... have most certainly prepared (him/her) for the increased responsibility (he/she) seeks. This impressive experience coupled with the "can-do" attitude (he/she) consistently demonstrates is ready testimony to (name) potential ability to excel as an ... category (WO/LDO).

3. (name) unique ability to relate to personnel of varied age groups and backgrounds is enhanced by (his/her) use of candor, tact, and diplomacy when dealing with them on a personal basis. This, plus the wisdom that comes with years of experience, makes (him/her) an extremely effective counselor. (name) promotion of fair and equal treatment is openly evident to juniors, peers, and seniors alike. Each person is given assignments commensurate with ability and all are afforded the opportunity to advance.

4. (name) possesses the leadership qualities and the administrative, organizational, and professional abilities to perform extremely well as an officer. (he/she) is considered an outstanding candidate for commissioning as a ... category (WO/LDO).

5. (name) is highly recommended for promotion to (WO/LDO). I would seek (his/her) services as an officer now or in the future.

CWO - LDO ENDORSEMENT
SAMPLE #18

1. Forwarded, highly recommending approval.

2. (name) has been an outstanding (peer group) at this command. (he/she) is a self assured individual who can be relied upon to complete any task. (his/her) management ability was first evidenced when (he/she) was assigned the billet of ..., a demanding job normally held by (pay grade). (name) performed exceptionally well in this assignment. (he/she) regarded these new duties as presenting an opportunity to further (his/her) growth in the Navy, typifying the enthusiasm and attitude demonstrated throughout (his/her) tour at this command.

3. (name) proven supervisory ability, organization aptitude and constant daily awareness of operational requirements are above reproach. (his/her) knowledge of logistics, material, and personnel, and the ability to comprehend task requirements are indicative of (his/her) readiness for increased responsibility as an officer.

4. Human values are extremely important to (name). Accordingly, (he/she) is a model promoter of fair play and equal treatment. (his/her) tactful, but firm, manner of associating with subordinates and peers clearly indicate that (he/she) is a "people person" with the ability to meet all operational tasking. (name) ensures that each job is completed correctly and on time, and that all subordinates are given an equal opportunity to contribute. (his/her) written reports are clear, concise, and require virtually no editing before being forwarded to superiors.

5. (name) ability to perform in an academic setting can easily be seen by (his/her) impressive record of accomplishment in Navy schools and through correspondence courses and off-duty education with ... College. Possessed of keen and disciplined mind, (his/her) study selections show the desire to expand and grow in both professional and military matters, as well as in human behavior studies and administrative skills.

6. (name) flawless military demeanor and conduct are in keeping with (his/her) other superior traits. (he/she) possesses all of the attributes most desired of an officer candidate. (name) is highly recommended for promotion to (WO/LDO).

CWO - LDO ENDORSEMENT
SAMPLE #19

1. Forwarded, highly recommending approval.

2. (name) has performed all military and professional duties in a manner second to none. (he/she) has demonstrated the ability to build and maintain an excellent working organization that has gained the cooperation and support of juniors and seniors alike. (name) is an ardent achiever who welcomes responsibilities and completes each assignment to the best of (his/her) considerable ability. No task is too menial or arduous.

3. (name) is an exceptionally talented and versatile (peer group) who has consistently achieved superior results in progressively more challenging assignments. While serving as (job), (he/she) displayed both exceptional management skill and thorough technical knowledge. As a result of actions (he/she) implemented, operators were afforded a more flexible working environment which improved the responsiveness of (his/her) area of responsibility. Concurrently, (his/her) emphasis on training and organizational procedures improved operating efficiency to the point the ... percent manning posture impacted little on overall division effectiveness. Through careful attention to sound management principles, (he/she) brought about a ... percent reduction in the division budget, accruing a ... dollar savings to the command. In recognition of (his/her) outstanding performance, (name) was subsequently appointed as (job), a billet normally assigned to a (pay grade). In this job, (he/she) is again demonstrating a strong performance in operational, fiscal, and personnel management.

4. (name) total dedication to the Naval service, coupled with well-developed professional, leadership, and management skills make (him/her) an excellent choice for selection as a Naval officer. (his/her) professional capability and dynamic approach to (his/her) job impart a sense of pride, motivation, and initiative in all those with whom (he/she) is associated.

5. (name) is more than ready to assume the increased leadership role of a Naval officer. (he/she) is an ideal candidate and is highly recommended for (WO/LDO).

CWO - LDO ENDORSEMENT
SAMPLE #20

1. Forwarded, highly recommending approval.

2. (name) is a highly qualified (WO/LDO) candidate. (he/she) continually demonstrates exceptional resourcefulness and professionalism as (job/billet). (he/she) exhibits superb managerial skills and high personal initiative in a relentless pursuit of perfection in meeting all daily commitments. (name) is a model supervisor. (his/her) tactful and sincere manner in dealing with subordinates secures their loyalty and inspires them to strive to reach the highest possible level of achievement. (he/she) is poised, confident, and composed at all times. In carrying out (his/her) duties as ..., (he/she) applied past experience and training to make significant improvements in ... procedures and equipment operation. As a result, the ... Division regularly meets or exceeds established standards for ... Concurrently, (he/she) devised and implemented improved procedures and instituted enhanced operator training in systems/equipment and quality control which have measurably improved division operations.

3. (name) continually strives to increase (his/her) knowledge and flexibility. (his/her) off duty study includes managerial and professionally oriented courses. In (his/her) area of technical expertise, (he/she) continually seeks additional responsibility and is ready to give advise and guidance to subordinates when the need arises. (name) speaking and writing ability is far above that normally expected of personnel of (his/her) pay grade. (his/her) correspondence drafts and reports require virtually no editing prior to forwarding to higher authority.

4. In summary, (name) has successfully accepted the challenging and demanding responsibilities of leadership and management in today's Navy. (his/her) performance established new standards of professional and military achievement for (his/her) contemporaries. When considering (his/her) rapid advancement to (rate), it is apparent that (his/her) accomplishments were a testimony to (his/her) creativeness, adaptability, charisma, and overall superior performance. (he/she) is highly motivated and eminently qualified for commission as a United States Naval officer. It is with pride and confidence that I recommend (name) for appointment to (WO/LDO).

CWO - LDO ENDORSEMENT
SAMPLE #21

1. Forwarded, strongly recommending approval.

2. (name) is a sterling example of a fine (peer group), demonstrating outstanding potential for additional responsibility. (he/she) is strongly recommended for this program, and I would be most pleased to have (him/her) serve in my command as a (WO/LDO).

3. (name) is eminently qualified for the (WO/LDO) Program. (he/she) is a dedicated professional who thrives on new challenges. An extraordinary supervisor, (he/she) is highly competent in any endeavor. (he/she) invariably improves all facets of (his/her) area of responsibility and considers efficiency in all jobs to be a matter of routine. (his/her) performance is consistently outstanding as (job) and (he/she) attains brilliant performance from subordinates. (name) supervisory skills are extraordinary. Despite a constant personnel turnover inherent in division operations, (he/she) maintains a smooth-running unit which exceeds all production quotas without sacrificing quality. (name) charismatic personality has greatly enhanced not only (his/her) team's morale, but also that of the entire division.

4. (name) intense desire for self improvement is evidenced in (his/her) steady pursuit of a college degree, accumulating ... semester hours of college credit while working towards an Associate Degree in ...(his/her) advanced education enables (him/her) to easily interpret official directives, technical instructions, and publications. More importantly, (he/she) applies the knowledge gained from past experience in a most practical and highly productive manner.

5. I consider (name) to be one of the finest (peer group) in my command. (he/she) is a superb candidate and is fully capable of handling the increased responsibilities of a (WO/LDO). (he/she) is a highly responsible and loyal career person who is dedicated to contributing (his/her) best to service and country. (name) is eminently qualified and I strongly recommend (him/her) for commission as a (WO/LDO).